RELIGION IN CHINA & ITS MODERN FATE

THE MENAHEM STERN

JERUSALEM LECTURES

BRANDEIS UNIVERSITY PRESS

HISTORICAL SOCIETY OF ISRAEL

RELIGION IN CHINA & ITS MODERN FATE

PAUL R. KATZ

BRANDEIS UNIVERSITY PRESS Waltham, Massachusetts

BRANDEIS UNIVERSITY PRESS / HISTORICAL SOCIETY OF ISRAEL
An imprint of University Press of New England
www.upne.com

Manufactured in the United States of America
Designed by Richard Hendel
Typeset in Arnhem and Transat by Tseng Information Systems, Inc.

University Press of New England is a member of the Green Press Initiative. The paper used in this book meets their minimum requirement for recycled paper.

ISBN 978-61168-542-8 (cloth: alk. paper)
ISBN 978-61168-543-5 (pbk.: alk. paper)
ISBN 978-61168-544-2 (ebook)

Library of Congress Cataloging-in-Publication Data
available upon request.

5 4 3 2 1

CONTENTS

FOREWORD

Meir Shahar

In May 2013 I was invited to a conference on Chinese Esoteric Buddhism, which was jointly organized by the Shaanxi Normal University and the Longhua 龍華 Monastery in Shaoxing County, Zhejiang Province. Recently established, the Longhua Monastery enjoys the generous patronage of lay disciples. It is an enormous establishment, covering several acres of developed land. The temple's striking monuments include a lotus-shaped pedestal which, rising to a height of several hundred feet, can be seen from miles away. The conference took place within the elegantly spacious halls of the monastery, which commands a spectacular view of the Kuaiji mountain range.

I traveled to the Longhua Monastery from Israel, having boarded a night flight from Tel Aviv to Beijing, followed by an excruciating wait for my connecting flight, which was delayed by no less than six hours. By the time I landed in Hangzhou, I was wondering how on earth I would be able to reach the mountain monastery, in pitch darkness, under pouring rain. To my happy surprise, when I emerged from the terminal I saw a friendly-looking person waving a sign with my name on it. I assumed that the welcoming face belonged to a taxi driver who had been hired by the conference organizers, but I quickly realized my mistake. As I eased myself into the leather-covered seat of my driver's luxury sedan, it transpired that he was no paid chauffeur, but rather an affluent businessman who had come to receive me as an act of charity. The manager of a textile factory by day, my new friend dedicated his evenings to the service of the Longhua temple, of which he was an ardent devotee. In this instance he acquired Buddhist merit by transporting the monastery's Jewish guest to his sacred destination.

The episode might serve as an illustration of sometimes-surprising facets of the Chinese religious revival. Following a tumultuous century of civil war and foreign invasion, of cultural revolution and economic reform, religion is alive and kicking in contemporary China, albeit in forms that are sometimes very different from those familiar in the past. This radical transformation of the Chinese religious experience is the subject of Paul Katz's masterly study. *Religion in China and Its Modern Fate* surveys the demise of traditional religious institutions and their replacement with new modes of religious expression in the face of cataclysmic changes. Few human societies have undergone as rapid and as thorough a transformation as China did in the course of its twentieth-century history. The impact of its modern transition on the religious sphere is the topic of this book.

Paul Katz's earlier books have eminently prepared him for the writing of China's modern religious history. Integrating careful historical research with illuminating fieldwork, he has published extensive works on diverse aspects of the Chinese religious tradition, from hagiographies of Daoist divinities to the empowerment of warriors through bloody sacrifices; from judicial rituals to the exorcistic cult of plague deities.[1] The present volume brings his expertise to bear in the form of three essays, combining three distinct genres of historical writing: the first chapter is an institutional history, examining the fate of Chinese temples under destruction campaigns, which began as early as early as 1898; the second chapter is a history of book publication, charting the introduction of mechanized printing and its impact on the religious publishing industry during the Republican period (1911–1948); finally, the third chapter is a biography (of Wang Yiting, 1867–1938) that in the best tradition of the genre employs its protagonist to illuminate the spirit of the age—in this instance the interplay of modernity and religion in the lives of Chinese elites.

Many of us have been under the mistaken impression that the dividing line in Chinese religious history occurred with the Communist takeover of 1949. We hazily presume that the wholesale attack on Chinese cultural heritage originated with the frenzied youths of the Maoist era. Paul Katz reveals that the destruction of temples began much earlier. Following in the footsteps of such scholars as Vincent Goossaert,[2] he demonstrates that as early as the late nineteenth century, Chinese intellectuals considered their religious tradition an obstacle to modernity. With the rise of the Kuomintang-led party-state in the 1920s, temples (whether Buddhist, Daoist, or belonging to the less easily defined popular religion) became the object of intensive campaigns, which were intended either to convert the edifices into modern institutions, such as schools, or to demolish them altogether. Paul Katz ably charts the general contours of the temple destruction policies, even as he demonstrates the complexities of their implementation under diverse local conditions. He describes in fascinating detail the struggles between state officials, local elites, and religious specialists (such as Buddhist monks and Daoist clerics) over the fate of individual temples. He further seeks to quantify the effects of the Republican-period temple destruction campaigns in one locality: Shanghai. In this respect, his richly documented survey is a microhistory, albeit of a place whose significance far exceeds its geographical borders: Shanghai was a beacon of Chinese modernity, and the fate of its temples signaled trends that were to engulf much of the country as a whole.

If the first chapter of the book is concerned with the destruction of temples, the second examines the rise of new means for religious expression in their stead. Paul Katz describes traditional Chinese religion as communal and territorially based, the members of each village and neighborhood focusing their religious and social activities on the local temple. The wide-scale demolition of temples—accelerated by urbanization and rapid land development—has forced individuals to find new ways of communicating their spiritual goals. Nowadays religious networks are often created via the mass media—from televised Buddhist lectures to virtual congregations on the Internet. Paul Katz deftly traces the contemporary forms of religious communication to their Republican-period antecedents. He tells the story—largely neglected in the history of Chinese printing—of the emergence of the religious press. The Republican period witnessed the proliferation of religious publications—books, periodicals, pamphlets, and newspapers. Katz analyzes the contents of this literature no less than the biographies of its authors: their education, livelihood, and spiritual aspirations. He is careful to keep tabs on circulation numbers and prices, providing a reliable assessment of the impact this literature has had on its devotee readership.

The third chapter is perhaps the most inspiring. Katz portrays a compelling image of an early twentieth-century elite that defies the facile categories of "modern" and "traditional." Wang Yiting was at once an innovative entrepreneur and industrialist, a painter, a science enthusiast, and a firm Buddhist believer, whose large-scale philanthropic works were intimately related to his spiritual aspirations. Wang's close connection to the Japanese Buddhist establishment—out of step with contemporary Chinese trends—is among the most revealing aspects of his career. He maintained close contacts with leading Japanese monks and scholars, and had even rallied his Chinese compatriots to assist the Japanese victims of the Great Kantō Earthquake in 1923. In Wang Yiting we encounter a Chinese philanthropist whose spiritual aspirations transcended national borders.

Religion in China and Its Modern Fate originated in the Menachem Stern Jerusalem Lectures, which Paul Katz delivered in the spring of 2012. To the speaker and his rapt Israeli audience alike, the very location of the lectures aroused comparative questions. As the birthplace of the three monotheistic faiths, Jerusalem invites an examination of the similarities and the differences between the Western religious tradition and the Chinese one. Paul Katz offers illuminating insights on this topic in his concluding chapter. He notes that (notwithstanding exceptions) "in China the practice of religion is central, but the idea of piety is not." There is no denying that even as religion has flourished in contemporary China, its overall tone is very different from the tone familiar in a monotheistic setting. It might perhaps be argued that the Chinese religions lack—at least in daily practice—the "fear and trembling" that a Christian thinker such as Søren Kierkegaard (1813–1855) considered as the defining characteristic of the religious experience.

Religion in China and Its Modern Fate records not only the suppression of traditional religious forms, but also their revival in new and unexpected ways. In this respect, Paul Katz's book teaches a heartening lesson on the power of individuals to resist state oppression, finding ever-new means of self-expression. We are grateful to him for illuminating the modern fate of the Chinese religion, no less than for adding a Chinese perspective to the infinite variety that characterizes the encounter between modernity and tradition worldwide.

PREFACE

I have always had a personal interest in religion, even if I don't come from a particularly religious family. My father (Arnold) is Jewish, but he's not observant, while my mother (Phyllis) is Protestant and not observant either. I never was raised in any sort of religious setting and never had a bar mitzvah, a baptism, or anything like that. But when I attended an Episcopal boarding school (Kent School), I fell in love with church music and joined the choir, and also was struck by the rituals performed at the school chapel (burning incense, processions with candles, and so forth). When my siblings and I joined my parents on their travels throughout Europe (my father is a cardiologist and my mother a classicist), we spent a lot of time visiting different churches and other cultural sites, so I developed an interest in the history of Western religion, not so much the theology but the practice and the ritual side of it. When I went to Yale, originally I was interested in medieval history, so I took courses with John Boswell and started to work on the Reformation with Jaroslav Pelikan. At the time, the main question I hoped to answer was this: Why, in the space of a few decades, did half of Europe lose its cult of saints and other religious traditions so thoroughly and so rapidly? When you go to Germany now, the northern half is almost completely Protestant, while the southern half still has Fasching and other festivals; it's almost like China.

My interests changed dramatically during my sophomore year at Yale, when I decided to take a course on modern Chinese history with Jonathan

Spence. Professor Spence is a brilliant lecturer, and his classes attract hundreds of students. Some of his lectures were about the White Lotus Rebellion, the Taipings, and the Boxers, all of which I found fascinating. I ended up majoring in history (with a concentration in Chinese history), and after graduation I decided that I wanted to pursue a doctoral degree. However, before I could start graduate school, I needed more language training, especially in classical Chinese, so I spent one year (1984–85) at the Stanford Center, which was still located at National Taiwan University. During my stay, I started meeting a lot of Taiwanese students, and they would take me to their homes in central and southern Taiwan. Once you get outside downtown Taipei, it's a completely different world, with all manner of temples. I was really struck by the amazing colorfulness, diversity, and liveliness of it all.

While I was attending the Stanford Center, I met David K. Jordan, who is an anthropologist of Taiwanese religion and society. Like me, Professor Jordan was there to study classical Chinese, but unlike me he had done extensive fieldwork and was fluent in Taiwanese. He took me with him on some of his research trips, most notably to the town of West Haven (Xigang 西港) in Tainan County, where we spent three days observing the triannual plague festival. After watching the procession with its bloody spirit mediums, as well as the Daoist priests performing exorcistic rituals culminating in the burning of the plague boat, I decided that this was what I absolutely had to study. So these two things, the combination of taking courses with Jonathan Spence and spending time in Taiwan observing the religious culture, are the real reasons that I got into this field.

Through the years, I have researched a wide range of topics, including plague festivals, cults to Daoist immortals, religious rebellions, judicial rituals, and now the transhybridity of Han Chinese and Miao 苗 religious cultures. One thing that has struck me about the field of Chinese Studies is the prominence of Jewish sinologists, including Benjamin Elman, Joshua Fogel, Gail Hershatter, Joseph Levenson, Henri Maspero (who perished in Buchenwald), Kenneth Pomeranz, Murray Rubinstein, Vera Schwarcz, Benjamin Schwartz, Meir Shahar, and Madeleine Zelin. On the surface, it might seem a bit odd that so many Jewish scholars would be interested in China, since the vibrant polytheism of Chinese religious life is one of the main sins railed against in the Old Testament. However, I suspect that this is because of the many values that are shared in Jewish and Chinese cultures, such as the importance of family, the value of education, the emphasis on law, and the respect for the written word. One reason for my choice of Chinese religion as the topic for my lectures is my hope that their contents can help further bridge the gap between these two cultures. As Levenson once pointed out, "Chinese history . . . should be studied because . . . it can be seen to make sense in the same world of discourse in which we try to make sense of the West. If we can make this kind of sense, perhaps we can help to make this kind of world."[1]

The topic of this book is the fate of Chinese religions in the modern era, with its title being inspired by Levenson's three-volume classic *Confucian China and Its Modern Fate*.[2] The data represent one result of an Academia Sinica Thematic Research Project entitled "1898–1948: Fifty Years that Changed Chinese Religions," which I have undertaken with Vincent Goossaert.[3] The project's mission has been to accelerate a major transformation in the scholarly understanding of modern China by showing how the fifty years from 1898 to 1948 changed Chinese religion into a modern, globalized religious culture. We chose this time frame because it covers the full course of the first stage in the modern history of Chinese religions, from the first all-out assault on Chinese religions during the 1898 reforms to the eve of the Communist takeover of the mainland, which subsequently ushered in a second stage under very different political and social conditions. This study is based on the idea that the first part of the twentieth century deserves study as much as any other period, and that such research can shed new light on modern Chinese religious life.

This project could not have been completed without the help and support of numerous colleagues and friends. One of the persons to whom I am most indebted is Vincent Goossaert, who is the true pioneer in the study of modern Chinese religions, starting with his 2006 *Journal of Asian Studies* article ("1898: The Beginning of the End for Chinese Religion?") and culminating in the 2011 book he coauthored with David Palmer (*The Religious Question in Modern China*), which just won the 2013 Levenson Prize. Another source of inspiration is Kristofer Schipper, one of the leading figures in both the historical and ethnographic study of Chinese religions. Schipper was born into a family of Dutch Protestants before he became a Daoist, and his parents hid many Jews during the war. His father (Klaas Abe Schipper; 1906–1949) was caught by the Gestapo and imprisoned, so Kristofer spent part of his childhood hiding in Amsterdam. His mother (Johanna Engelberta Schipper-Kuiper, "Hannie"; 1896–1956) escaped from the Germans and continued to save as many lives as she could. Recently she was recognized by the Yad Vashem as a Righteous.

I am deeply grateful to Academia Sinica for the three-year grant that has funded our Thematic Project, and also to my colleagues at the Institute of Modern History (both the academic and administrative staffs) for their intellectual and logistical support. I would also like to express my heartfelt thanks to the following individuals for their generous assistance: Rostislav Berezkin, Chang Ning 張寧, Walter Davis, Fan Chunwu 范純武, Fu Haiyan 付海晏, Huang Ko-wu 黃克武, J. Brooks Jessup, Kang Shih-yu 康詩瑀, Li Kai-kuang 李鎧光, Li Ying-ju 李盈儒, Lien Ling-ling 連玲玲, Lin Pei-jung 林佩蓉, Lin Tsung-ta 林宗達, Liu Wenxing 劉文星, Liu Xun 劉迅, Lo Shih-chieh 羅士傑, Poon Shuk-wah 潘淑華, Qi Gang 祁剛, Gregory Scott, Sun Huei-min 孫慧敏, Wang Jianchuan 王見川, Wang Shih-chun 王世駿, Wu

Cheng-che 吳政哲, Wu Chi-na 吳啟訥, Wu Yakui 吳亞魁, Yau Chi-on 游子安, Yung Sai-shing 容世誠, and Peter Zarrow.

This book also represents the fruits of three talks I gave for the Menahem Stern Jerusalem Lectures, which are under the auspices of and hosted by the Historical Society of Israel. Being able to present the Jerusalem Lectures was a privilege and a joy, and I am forever indebted to my dear friend Meir Shahar for helping make it all possible. The journey to the ancestral home of my father's family proved a dream come true, thanks in large part to the unstinting efforts of my hosts, including Maayan Avineri-Rebhun, Israel Bartal, Ya'ad Biran, Michael Heyd, Yosef Kaplan, Yuri Pines, Shulamith Shahar, Yitzhak Shichor, Heshie Stoffer, Tovi Weiss, Lihi Yariv-Laor, and Zvi Yekutiel. The trip was made even more special by the presence of my parents (Arnold and Phyllis), as well as members of the Schick family (Peter, Vivian, Jon, and Michael).

Most of all I wish to express my undying love for my wife, Shu-fen, our daughter, Emily, and our son, Philip, for all they have done to bring true joy into our lives.

RELIGION IN CHINA & ITS MODERN FATE

INTRODUCTION

The main goal of this book is to assess the important processes of change that shaped the fate of Chinese religion during the last decade of the Qing dynasty and the entire Republican era. Historians of literature, culture, the arts, political thought, and other areas of Chinese culture all have shown abundantly how creative this period was in shaping Chinese modernity and creating the society we now live in,[1] and scholars of religion are rapidly following suit.[2] In this book, I endeavor to place religion at the core of understanding modern Chinese history by assessing three forms of change, which are treated in separate chapters. Chapter 1 considers mutations of the communal structures of religion as seen in the different campaigns that targeted temples, their rituals (especially festivals), and other forms of traditional religious life. Chapter 2 treats the innovative production of knowledge that shaped religious publishing enterprises. Chapter 3 examines new types of religiosity and their roles in the lives of modern Chinese elites. These three chapters cover various forms of change at many different levels and therefore require different types of analysis. The first level of these analytical frameworks is macrosocial and looks at the entirety of Chinese communal life in both rural and urban areas. The second focuses on smaller institutions, in this case religious publishing houses and the associations that supported them, while the third level deals with individuals. The three frameworks are united by a common research agenda, which is to trace the ways in which the vast religious resources (texts, expertise, symbolic capital, material wealth, and so on) that circulated throughout Chinese society during the late imperial period were reconfigured in new ways and new social formations during the Republican era. The book traces these complex processes of destruction and revitalization by following modern Chinese elites as they joined in attacks on communal temples or resisted such campaigns (chapter 1), while also engaging in the dissemination of religious knowledge (chapter 2) and playing active roles in the development of urban-based religious groups (chapter 3). In this introduction, I set the stage for the consideration of these issues by describing the nature of Chinese religious life as well as the challenges these beliefs and practices were forced to confront during the modern era because of the impact of Western culture, especially Christianity. I also assess previous research on these topics, as well as related methodological issues.

ON THE NATURE OF CHINESE RELIGIOUS LIFE

Over the years, scholars have come to realize that, despite the unfortunate use of labels such as "chaotic" or "diffuse," Chinese religions constitute a coherent system that integrated practices for individual self-cultivation, kinship rites, and communal rituals. Religious life is in large part based on the belief that all sentient beings are endowed with spiritual power (*ling* 靈) and can purify themselves through morality and self-cultivation, which shapes their fate after death in terms of being reborn as gods, ghosts, ancestors, or various animal spirits.[3] Another key concept is that of divine retribution (*bao* 報), which can occur both in the afterlife and in this world as well.[4] Conventional wisdom focuses on the role of three leading religious traditions (the so-called "Three Teachings" or *sanjiao* 三教: Buddhism, Daoism, and Confucianism; early forms of Christianity and Islam are ignored), each of which is credited with possessing its own canons, religious specialists, and sacred sites. At the same time, scholars have recognized that the Three Teachings were not merely self-contained institutions that provided exclusive paths to salvation; instead, one of their main roles in Chinese religious life was to serve autonomous religious communities that chose among the texts and specialists of these three traditions as need or preference dictated.[5] Most of these religious communities centered on temples that were built and managed by clerics or local elites. These temples served as key public spaces and, like the communities that patronized them, were largely autonomous, although they could participate in alliances and networks as needed.[6] In terms of religious organizations, one highly useful distinction is between ascriptive communities and voluntary associations. The former included territorial cults, lineages, and corporations such as guildhalls (*huiguan* 會館, *gongsuo* 公所), while the latter ranged from pious societies to devotional incense associations (*xianghui* 香會) to pilgrimage associations to voluntary performance troupes to sectarian groups devoted to individual salvation and philanthropic activities. The latter often are referred to as "redemptive societies," in part to avoid the negative connotations of the term "sectarian," but also because to a certain extent the term "salvationalist" might work better.[7] This book represents a social historical study of the fate of these groups in modern times.

The study of temple cults began to take shape during the 1960s and 1970s, but it was not until the 1980s that scholars undertook detailed case studies of the religious lives of local communities, particularly temple cults and their ritual traditions. The study of Chinese religions at the regional level has been transformed as well, with scholars using interdisciplinary methodologies to conduct in-depth research in China and Taiwan. These data have broadened our understanding of developments in religion and society during the late imperial era and elucidated the challenges with which Chinese religions have grappled in modern times.[8]

At the same time a significant portion of Western research on Chinese communities has been constricted by undue dependence on post-Enlightenment dichotomies such as "religion" and "society." One result of this has been that much late imperial and modern Chinese social history tends to neglect the importance of religion. Perhaps the best-known instance involves the effort to locate a Chinese "civil society" or "public sphere." In considering this issue, previous scholarship has stressed the importance of organizations such as guilds and native place associations, without adequately considering the roles played by temple committees and ritual associations.[9] For example, despite the fact that religious activities associated with temple cults clearly conform to Mary Rankin's definition of "public" in that they entail "the institutionalized, extrabureaucratic management of matters considered important by both the community and the state," Rankin chooses to exclude such activities from her definition by labeling them as private (*si* 私), in contrast with the official administration (*guan* 官) and public (*gong* 公) management by elites.[10] Urban historians have also downplayed the importance of temples in late imperial and modern Chinese cities. In analyzing sites for the discussion of public affairs, for example, such scholars tend to consider only sites such as urban teahouses and wineshops as having been capable of stimulating the debate of public issues similar to that of European cafés or coffee houses.[11] In short, the tendency has been to view temples and temple cults as passive objects in the physical or sacred landscape of a locale that are manipulated by social and economic forces. Events involving or affecting the history of temples and temple cults are seen as reflecting the processes of local development; the ways in which such entities may have shaped communal life in their own right are rarely considered.

All in all, post-Enlightenment analytical frameworks have caused scholars to overlook that one of the most important realms of public activity in late imperial and modern Chinese communities has been popular cults and festivals. This means that any discussion of Chinese public life should not be considered complete until it has taken into the account the immense importance of temples and their religious activities.[12] For example, Prasenjit Duara's research reveals that temple cults constitute one key node of what he terms "the cultural nexus of power,"[13] which consisted of both hierarchical organizations (including temple committees and ritual associations) and informal networks (including those formed or reinforced during festivals and pilgrimages).[14] In addition, the ritual dramas performed during festivals exert a significant impact on popular mentalities,[15] while temple murals possess a clear didactic function with the potential to influence public mores.[16] Finally, temples play an integral role in dispute resolution, including the taking of oaths and the performance of indictment rituals.[17] This indicates that temple cults were one of many resources that the different interest groups used to enhance their power and legitimacy.[18]

More recently, a new body of research has broadened our understanding of developments in religion and society during the late imperial and modern eras. In the field of urban history, for example, Susan Naquin's magnum opus on late imperial Beijing clearly shows that while temples seem to have little in common with European cafés and coffee shops, they do provide a public space available to all citizens in which opinions, beliefs, and values can be formed and debated.[19] The impact of Naquin's approach can be seen in Richard Belsky's recent study of Beijing's native-place lodges (*huiguan* 會館), which devotes an entire chapter to the importance of religion and ritual to their members.[20] Such research has also been supplemented, and at times surpassed, by the work of Kristofer Schipper, Vincent Goossaert, and their colleagues who took part in the Centre national de la recherche scientifique (CNRS) project entitled "Peking as Sacred

City—Liturgical Structures and Civil Society,"[21] while Marianne Bujard has collected valuable new epigraphic data on Beijing's temples.[22]

If we take a more holistic view of this research, we can see that temple cults and their rituals always have been inherently social entities, situated at the heart of triangular networks of power featuring three groups of people directly involved in their management and regulation: officials (who represent the state and attempt to carry out its policies), elites (who control the social and economic affairs of their communities), and religious specialists (who are in charge of the ritual aspects of communal life) (see Figure I.1). Officials attempt to shape communal religious traditions in a number of ways, including legal rulings, the issuance of titles and placards to approved temples, and the provision of monetary and literary patronage. They also work to regulate the activities of the religious specialists by placing restrictions on the numbers of ordinations and temples. Elites rely on temples and their rituals to define territory and shape identity, as well as to reinforce the legitimacy of their dominance over communal affairs. Religious specialists strive to absorb and also reshape the pantheons and rituals of local communities, while looking to the state for patronage and confirmation of the orthodoxy of their traditions. The interconnections between these individuals have been marked by both top-down efforts at control and reform as well as bottom-up assertions of legitimacy and identity.[23]

In addition to studying temple cults and their patrons, a growing number of scholars in Asia and the West have begun to examine the importance of festivals in both reflecting and shaping the development of socioeconomic structures in local communities. Festivals are ideal sites for observing the previously mentioned triangular networks in action, because members of all three groups either sponsor or participate in such ritual events, in the course of which they attempt both to enhance their own legitimacy and to extend their influence over communal affairs. As a

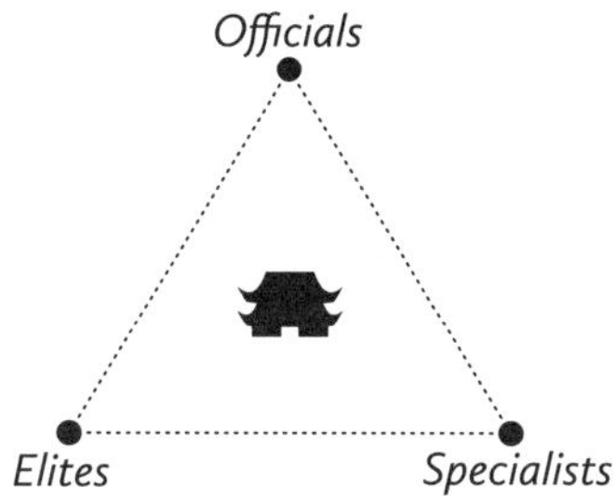

FIGURE I.1: *The Triangle*

result, festivals often become arenas for intense power struggles over whether the state allows a community to hold its festival, who is obligated to pay for it (and how much), which religious specialists are hired to perform rituals, who marches in the procession (and in what order), and so on.

While numerous volumes on "temple fairs" (*miaohui* 廟會) have been published, the history of these ritual events remains difficult to research, particularly because of the paucity of detailed accounts prior to the Qing dynasty (1644–1911).[24] Some scholars have studied the ways in which the state attempted to regulate festivals during the modern era. For example, James A. Flath examined how Nationalist government attempts to appropriate the economic and political resources of temple festivals differed according to the effective might of the local state,[25] while Poon Shuk-wah adopted an approach that centered on symbolical issues and the theme of resistance.[26] In China today, festivals constitute a carefully controlled but legitimate form of religious expression, valued by the state and local communities for their ability to generate tourism yet also possessing the potentially for promoting local agendas that may not always conform to the state policies.[27] In Taiwan and other Han Chinese communities that escaped the ravages of communism and the Cultural Revolution, festivals continue to be occasions for the expression of local identity and the consolidation of power networks.[28]

All in all, festivals featured a dazzling array of contrasts that indicated their integral role in the formation and maintenance of communal life. On the one hand, these ritual events featured lavish symbols of wealth, prosperity, and harmony. On the other hand, they were also arenas for intense competition between the three components of the triangle. Local tensions often bubbled to the surface during the procession, and the state was hard-pressed to maintain a semblance of control. People cleaned the streets in order to display the community's ritual purity, only to have those same streets filled by beggars and penitents expressing their polluted state who wore cangues (*jia* 枷) and called themselves "criminals" (*fanren* 犯人) or "sinners" (*zuiren* 罪人). The community was also considered polluted by the presence of dangerous demons that had to be rounded up by the local protective deities and expelled in the course of these events.[29]

THE IMPACT OF THE MODERN WEST

While the religious traditions described previously had always been in competition with each other and faced occasional campaigns of suppression by the Chinese imperial state, the modern era witnessed graver challenges in the unprecedented impact of modern Western values and organizational modes, especially those linked to Christianity. While traditional elites (particularly the rural gentry) had tended to be hostile toward Christianity during the late imperial era, this was not the case for much of modern China's elite, which was largely composed of civil and military officials, as well as merchants and urban professionals.[30] A sizeable percentage of these men had been trained in modern schools (often founded and managed by Christians) and had close ties with Westerners. Many of modern China's most renowned leaders converted to Christianity, including Sun Yat-sen 孫逸仙 (Sun Zhongshan 孫中山; 1866–1925) and Charles J. Soong (Song Jiashu 宋嘉樹; 1863–1918; an American-educated Methodist missionary). Soong's eldest daughter Soong Ching-ling 宋慶齡 (1893–1981) ended up marrying Sun Yat-sen. Another example is Chiang Kai-shek 蔣介石 (Jiang Zhongzheng 蔣中正; 1887–1975), who had been raised as a Buddhist (see chapter 3) but chose to be baptized as a Methodist in 1929 in order to marry Soong May-ling 宋美齡 1898–2003), one of Soong's other daughters. Many other modern Chinese elites were Christians as well. Of the 274 members chosen in 1912–1913 to serve in China's first national parliament, a total of 60 (nearly 22 percent) were Christians, an astonishing proportion when one realizes that less than 1 percent of China's total population had converted to Christianity. Even if one concedes that many of these parliamentarians were not elected because of their Christian faith, it is essential to recognize that their success resulted in part because many of the elites who supported and actively participated in Republican-era governance were Christians. Similar (but not as pronounced) trends persist in postwar Taiwan, where approximately 7 percent of legislators elected in 2003 belonged to Christian movements.[31]

Apart from the realm of politics, Christianity exerted a profound influence on many facets of Chinese social life. One of the most obvious effects was in the field of education, with almost half of Republican China's institutions of higher learning being run by Christian organizations, the leaders of which viewed traditional temple cults as one of the leading obstacles to their efforts (see chapter 1). In addition, Christian elites launched new forms of religious publishing, while also using the mass media to support their proselytizing enterprises, with their efforts being emulated by non-Christian elites whose actions were also shaped by late imperial precedents (see chapter 2). Finally, Christian groups regularly founded hospitals and initiated other forms of modern Chinese philanthropy. As in the case of religious publishing, non-Christian elites quickly learned to copy such efforts, while also drawing on indigenous forms of these practices (see chapter 3).[32]

One of Christianity's most significant influences on modern China was in the conceptual realm. During the latter half of the nineteenth century, Western and Christian ideas of modern religion, and even the term "religion" itself (*zongjiao*宗教), spread to China from Japan as part of the gradual adoption of modern social science categories,[33] with China's own field of religious studies (*zongjiaoxue*宗教學) being in large part molded by the Christian impact. As a result, by the end of the Qing dynasty many Chinese elites began to adopt Western definitions of religion as part and parcel of their vision for a modern Chinese nation, while also blaming indigenous religious traditions as one of the main factors contributing to China's decline (see the following section and chapter 1). Many of these elites were also influenced by Western ideas of secularization (*shisuhua*世俗化). Admittedly, secularization is a thorny concept because often it is used loosely to refer to a wide range of different historical processes, most notably inexorable "despiritualization" (the loss of religiosity).[34] Yet the concept of secularization proves somewhat relevant for the study of modern Chinese history because of the idea that secularized societies become differentiated or atomized into autonomous subsystems (economy, polity, law, education, and so on) that are highly discrete in relation to each other, with religion being restricted in influence to its own integral sphere. At the same time, however, there is considerable disagreement over the degree of secularization possible, with Talal Asad arguing that the interdependence of the political and religious spheres inhibits total differentiation, as opposed to José Casanova, who steadfastly adheres to the idea of the secular sphere being differentiated (and even emancipated) from the world of religious institutions and ethics.[35] There are also legitimate reasons for caution about applying the concept of secularization to China, especially because many definitions treat secularization as a historical process of the modern West by which the religious system loses its dominance over communal life.[36] In the case of Chinese history, however, religion has continuously interacted continuously with a range of other subsystems from ancient times to the present day, including commercial, philanthropic, and political ones. As we will see in chapter 1, many modern Chinese elites argued in favor of "despiritualization," while others advocated for religion being relegated to its own unique sphere that would be severed from yet also closely regulated by the state. In the end, however, Chinese religious culture did not "secularize" in the same way as the West (even if some of China's modern elites wished for this to happen), with religion continuing to have potential legal and political importance in ways that are rarely seen in the West.[37]

Of far greater interest is what Robert Weller describes as "religionization," namely, "the development of religion as an institutionally and ideologically independent formation" (Goossaert and Palmer refer to this as the "Christian-secular normative model").[38] As noted previously, those modern Chinese elites whose worldviews had been molded by the Christian view of religious life strove to construct a new religious landscape that conformed to Western and especially Protestant mores. The result of these processes was that Chinese religious movements wishing to be deemed worthy of state support or at least tolerance came to be conceived of as voluntary associations possessing shared scriptural and other textual traditions that were led by trained specialists who had received at least a modicum of modern education. Accordingly, while religion could be allowed to exist, the actual freedom to practice religion would only be extended only to groups that could rebrand themselves according to the criteria deemed necessary for China to become a modern and secularized society. Those groups that did not adhere to this criteria were to be labeled as "superstition" (*mixin* 迷信; also a Western neologism) and subject to state suppression.[39] In short, the modern Chinese state's mission of governing based on Western ideas of secularization impelled Chinese religious groups to redefine themselves in ways that the authorities could accept and attempt to regulate, because any separation of "church and state" could only prove viable if "religion" were to be accepted as a legitimate category distinct from other political and social entities. As Weller aptly puts it, "Secularization as a state project thus requires religionization."[40]

The conceptualizations described previously clearly influenced renowned intellectuals such as former Academia Sinica president Hu Shih 胡適 (1891–1962; see Figure I.2), who in 1908 wrote an impassioned editorial against the presence of "superstition" in China using the pen name "Iron Child" (Tie'er 鐵兒). After complaining about the resources people "wasted" on worshipping gods and ghosts, as well as the deleterious impact of such practices on China's youth, Hu Shih concluded that religion and ritual were inhibiting the "evolution" (*jinhua* 進化) of the Chinese people (note the conscious use of Darwinian terminology), with the citizens of otherwise "highly civilized" (*ji wenming* 極文明) urban centers such as Shanghai stubbornly persisting in their performance of annual celebrations and festivals (derided as "barbaric customs" or *yeman de fengsu* 野蠻的風俗). Hu Shih not only advocated for temple destruction campaigns, but also went so far as to propose that religious specialists who lived off the people be expelled, and in some cases even put to death.[41]

In the face of these challenges, if not outright threats, Chinese religious organizations hardly could afford to be idle, and many did take the initiative in responding. One example of these processes was the efforts by indigenous groups to copy the Christians by forming their own national associations that would work to counter state suppression while also promoting religious publishing and philanthropic projects, with the Buddhists proving the most successful.[42] It is these processes of response combined with innovation that are the subject of the three chapters that form this book. Each chapter is comprised of an overall survey and a case study, with each of the case studies covering

FIGURE I.2: *Hu Shih at Age Nineteen. Courtesy of the Hu Shih Memorial Hall, Institute of Modern History, Academia Sinica.*

a specific part of one key area (Zhejiang and Shanghai) so as to encompass the whole of one regional trajectory in the formation of Chinese religious modernity. Work on each overall survey is grounded in a synthesis of the existing literature and published sources on that theme, in order to set up clear parameters (relevant policies and main actors), formulate key theoretical questions, and sketch the various paths followed in different parts of China. The case study itself consists of an in-depth exploration of precisely defined primary sources in order to answer the question in a detailed manner.

This book draws on a wide range of sources (local gazetteers, archives, newspaper accounts, and so forth) in order to trace the evolution, both quantitative and qualitative, of Chinese religious life. Chapter 1 explores how renowned Chinese temples and their extravagant festival cultures were nearly reduced to ruins while also considering the following qualitative questions: What changed in the temples and their ritual functions? What was lost and what was preserved, and why? Who were the key actors in these processes of historical transformation? These questions will be examined by means of case studies focusing on Shanghai and other urban areas in Zhejiang, especially Wenzhou 溫州 and its environs.

Chapter 2 reveals that even as communal religious life was coming under extreme duress, in a novel development related to this process, urban religious centers recycled the religious culture of the temples that were being destroyed and transformed them into new forms of knowledge in the form of books and periodicals. The data presented in this chapter center on the following questions: Who wrote, edited, or reprinted these works? Which texts did they choose and why? What prices did these works sell for, and who were their intended and actual audiences? What networks of production and distribution facilitated their transmission, and what innovations in contents or form characterized their contents? The case study will be based on catalogues of religious books and periodicals produced in Shanghai by the Illuminating Goodness Publishing House (Mingshan shuju 明善書局).

The first two chapters look at the macro level of peoples' participation in communal forms of religion and taking part in religious culture through reading and writing. In contrast, chapter 3 focuses on a narrower but more crucial category of people: urban elites (defined as all of those people who held an elected or meaningful political or military position or a directorship of a large civil body) who, through positions of power in urban city governments or influence through charity, educational boards, and chambers of commerce, called the shots in urban management right up to the People's Republic of China (PRC) takeover. Traditional scholarship has held that these people were modernist and therefore secularist. Modernist they may have been, but case study after case study shows that they engaged in spirit writing (*fuji* 扶乩), converted to a wide range of religions, engaged in self-cultivation regimens, and so on. For many of these people, creating a modern urban China could entail curtailing and otherwise regulating local communal devotion, but certainly did not mean ushering in a totally soulless culture. One particularly important question is when, why, and to what extent local elites shifted from participation in local communal religious institutions (mostly temple committees) to other types of religious engagement such as running charities, organizing religious publishing enterprises, and participating in new forms of religious self-cultivation. This chapter also considers how the religious practices of late imperial local elites (daily self-examination, veneration of written characters, meditation, and scripture recitation) were perpetuated, reformulated, or abandoned by their Republican-period counterparts. The case study centers on an elite whose family came from Huzhou 湖州 in northern Zhejiang, but who spent most of his life in Shanghai, Wang Yiting 王一亭 (1867–1938).

Taken as a whole, this book qualifies as a regional study of modernization, but more innovatively, it is a regional study of *religious* modernization. It attempts to map the transformation of the Chinese religious landscape from the late Qing through the Republican era, both in terms of discourse and of practice. As we shall see, the reformation of Chinese religious life did not result in an inexorable march toward modernity. Despite the effort that the state and those elites who supported its mission made to aggressively promote secularist projects, Chinese communities did not end up being fully secularized.[43]

1

STATE VERSUS SOCIETY

TEMPLE DESTRUCTION CAMPAIGNS

This chapter examines temple destruction campaigns in China from 1898 to 1948, including the tearing down of temple buildings or converting part of their premises into schools or other nonreligious edifices, as well as outlawing their ritual activities and the specialists who participated in them. The chapter is divided into three sections. The first section provides a critical overview of the different campaigns that targeted temples and their rituals (not to mention other forms of traditional religious life), including "build schools with temple property" (*miaochan xingxue* 廟產興學), "eradicating superstitions" (*pochu mixin* 破除迷信), and "rectifying customs" (*fengsu gailiang* 風俗改良), as well as related undertakings such as the New Culture Movement (Xin wenhua yundong 新文化運動) and the New Life Movement (Xin shenghuo yundong 新生活運動). The second section of the chapter considers the roles played by the different actors who supported or opposed these campaigns, as well as the outbreaks of resistance provoked by their efforts. The third section assesses the effects of these campaigns in southern China, especially Shanghai 上海, parts of northern Zhejiang 浙江 (most notably Hangzhou 杭州 and Ningbo 寧波), and Wenzhou 溫州 in southern Zhejiang. We know that during this period China's central, regional, and local governments frequently labeled temples and their rituals (especially festivals) as forms of "superstition" (*mixin* 迷信) and launched a series of campaigns both to seize their property and to assert the state's authority over communal society.

Some of these temple cults have reemerged since the 1980s, but what happened in between is, in the current state of scholarship, anybody's guess. Yet the extent to which these facets of communal religion were destroyed during the fifty years covered by this book makes a vital difference in explaining their revival or lack thereof. In this chapter, I use archival data, newspaper articles, and other primary sources to assess the ways in which China's temple cults and festivals strove to adapt to the challenges of this era.

TEMPLE DESTRUCTION CAMPAIGNS: AN OVERVIEW

In his article about the state regulation of religion in China, Pitman B. Potter observed that, "The relationship between religion and state power in China has long been contested."[1] As scholars such as Hsiao Kung-ch'üan have documented, the Chinese imperial state endeavored to control local society and culture through a combination of coercive and persuasive policies that were essentially a utopian project to enforce a top-down cosmic moral order.[2] Daniel Overmyer's research indicates that during the imperial era the Chinese state possessed a strong commitment to ritual practice, with imperial authority in part deriving from sacrifices to imperial ancestors and nature spirits that only the emperor and his officials could worship. According to the *Book of Rites* (*Liji* 禮記):

> The son of Heaven [the king] sacrifices to Heaven and Earth; to the [spirits presiding over the] four quarters; to [the spirits of] the hills and rivers; and offers the five sacrifices of the house [i.e., to the door, the stove, the middle pillar, the gate, and the well]—all in the course of a year. The feudal princes present oblations, each to [the spirits presiding over] his own quarter, to [the spirits of] its hills and rivers, and offer the five sacrifices of the house—all in the course of the year. Great offi-

> cers present the oblations of the five sacrifices of the house—all in the course of the year. [Other] officers present oblations to their ancestors. A sacrifice that is not proper to offer, and yet is offered, is called an illicit/improper sacrifice [*yinsi* 淫祀].[3] A licentious sacrifice brings no blessings.[4]

By the Ming dynasty (1368–1644), these regulations had been modified to specify that the sacrifices of commoners were to be limited to their ancestors, the unruly dead, and the stove god, with exceptions to be made for the worthy. One 1368 decree ordered officials to seek out and make annual offerings to the spirits of "famous mountains and great rivers, sage emperors, enlightened kings, loyal officials, and brave officers, and all who have performed meritorious service for the nation, and who have acted in loyalty and love among the people."[5]

When it came to specific religious traditions, the state attempted to regulate Buddhist and Daoist clergies,[6] while it also launched suppression campaigns against sectarian religions and the so-called "secret societies," groups that openly espoused millenarian ideologies possessing the potential to overthrow the established order, with such campaigns eventually being directed at some Christian groups as well.[7] As for communal religious traditions, while the state had the authority to label unsanctioned temple cults as "illicit/improper sacrifices," it could also co-opt popular local deities and include them in official registers of sacrifice (*sidian* 祀典), which meant annual offerings and occasional state-funded temples. Temple cults that the state chose to support generally were perceived as adhering to "orthodox" or Confucian ideals and practices (including making meat offerings to the gods) that the state promoted in order to "standardize" local religion and "superscribe" its agendas onto local society.[8] The state generally followed a five-part strategy in dealing with temple cults, which encompassed absorption, patronage, acceptance, tolerance, and suppression, with the success or failure of these efforts varying depending on its strength in a particular region at a certain point in time.[9]

These policies and procedures shifted dramatically during the Republican era because of the adoption of the Western distinction between "religion" and "superstition" described in the introduction, which meant that cults to deities that originally had been approved or simply tolerated were now targeted for state suppression. Be that as it may, the attacks on temples and their rituals during this era did not necessarily constitute one continuous phenomenon, being undertaken more vigorously during some periods of time than in others. Based on his long-term research about these campaigns, Fu Haiyan 付海晏 maintains that they can be divided into the following periods: 1) late Qing (1898–1911), 2) early Republican (1911–1927), 3) Nanjing government (1927–1937), 4) War of Resistance against Japan (1937–1945), and 5) final years of the Republic (1945–1949).[10] Further subdivisions are also possible, as can be seen in research by Chen Jinlong 陳金龍 that categorizes the "build schools with temple properties" campaign from 1928 to 1937 according to three distinct phases. The first phase (beginning in April 1928) had the greatest impact on the Jiangnan region, while the second (November 1930) witnessed the advent of more restrictive policies, and the third phase (August 1935) was more widespread with policies being effectively enforced.[11] However, the campaigns persisted even during wartime and are documented as late as 1948.[12] The temporal flows of these campaigns could also vary by place. In the case of Shanghai, for example, research by Ai Ping 艾萍 delineates three phases, with the first (1919–1927) witnessing a shift from rigid to periodic enforcement of relevant policies, the second (1927–1934) attempting to distinguish between temples to be preserved and destroyed, and the third (1934–1937) assuming a largely laissez-faire attitude toward temple cults and their festivals.[13]

As Vincent Goossaert and David Palmer have observed, the most thorough state effort to destroy temple cults occurred during the decade from 1928 to 1938, when the Nationalist government had reached the acme of its power following the Northern Expedition. Accordingly, the authorities proved willing to recognize the legitimacy of groups that conformed to the Western/Christian category of "religion," especially those possessing elites able to found organizations that would negotiate with the state, while also doing their utmost to eliminate religious phenomena belonging to the "superstition" category.[14] These campaigns, led by officials such as Minister of the Interior Xue Dubi 薛篤弼 (1890–1973) and educators such as Tai Shuangqiu 邰爽秋 (1896–1976), were undergirded by a wide range of policies (described in detailed studies by Rebecca Nedostup and Poon Shuk-wah), including the "Regulations for Registering Temples" (*Simiao dengji tiaoli* 寺廟登記條例, 1928), "Regulations for Managing Temples" (*Simiao guanli tiaoli* 寺廟管理條例, 1929), and "Regulations for Overseeing Temples" (*Jiandu simiao tiaoli* 監督寺廟條例, 1929). These policies were most notable for advocating the establishment of civic committees to oversee temple property, as well as for allowing temples to be declared "abandoned" and then taken over by the state.[15] Perhaps the most influential policy of all was the "Standards to Determine Temples to Be Destroyed and Maintained" (*Shenci cunfei biaozhun* 神祠存廢標準), which was enacted in November 1928. The "Standards" divided temples into four categories. The first two types of temples, dedicated to "former sages" (*xianzhe* 先哲) and deities of the five state-recognized religions (*zongjiao* 宗教: Buddhism, Daoism, Catholicism, Protestantism, and Islam), were to be preserved. The latter two, namely temples for the worship of "ancient deities" (*gushen* 古神, encompassing a wide range of local cults, especially to nature deities and heroes) and those placed in the traditional category of "illicit/improper shrines" (*yinci* 淫祠) were to be eradicated. Regulations were also enacted to eliminate divination and geomancy (for example, the *Feichu bushi xingxiang wuxi kanyu banfa* 廢除卜筮星相巫覡堪輿辦法, 1928) as well as the manufacture and sale of ritual items deemed to be "superstitious" (*Qudi jingying mixin wupin banfa* 取締經營迷信物品辦法, 1929). While actual enforcement of these rules varied considerably by place and time, nonetheless they exerted immense pressure on many forms of Chinese religious life.[16]

At the same time, the Nationalist regime also launched an active and widespread program to reform local customs. According to a lengthy manifesto entitled "The Significance of and Methods for Destroying Superstitions" (*Pochu mixin de yiyi yu fangfa* 破除迷信之意義和辦法), temple destruction campaigns were related to policies such as the adoption of the Western calendar (also one form of "rectifying customs"), encouraging widespread literacy, and launching propaganda campaigns with catchy slogans to attract popular attention.[17] Some of these efforts ranged from the sublime to the ridiculous. For example, one set of regulations about door gods (*menshen* 門神), enacted by the Fujian provincial authorities in 1935, strongly objected to the use of the term "deity" (*shen* 神) but proved willing to allow their continued use so long as the paintings of the door gods were limited to historical exemplars such as Yue Fei 岳飛 (1103–1142), Wen Tianxiang 文天祥 (1236–1283), and Qi Jiguang 戚繼光 (1528–1588). All of this was meant to achieve the goals of not only eradicating superstition, but also "cultivating nationalist consciousness" (*peiyang minzu yishi* 培養民族意識).[18]

The fact that these policies were enacted with particular energy from the 1920s through the 1930s may be in part because of the urgency China's leadership felt in the face of numerous threats, be they immediate or impending, real or imagined.[19] Such threats included warlord armies, peasant uprisings, so-called "Communist bandits" (*gongfei* 共匪), other criminal elements, and especially Japanese imperialist encroachments.[20] Longer-term quests for cultural reform also dated back to the

May Fourth Movement (Wusi yundong 五四運動), most notably the New Culture Movement (Xin wenhua yundong 新文化運動), which in addition to advocating for the adoption of Western models of democracy and science—the so-called "Mr. Democracy" (De xiansheng 德先生) and "Mr. Science" (Sai xiansheng 賽先生")—also emphasized the rejection of superstition as one of its core values.[21] During the May Fourth Movement in 1919, some intellectuals called for the widespread adoption of Western culture, arguing that traditional Chinese culture was preventing China's successful modernization. Such views were highly prevalent, but by no means universal or unchallenged. Other intellectuals continued to advocate the study of Chinese history and traditional culture despite being influenced by Western ideas, while a group of folklorists began detailed research on China's popular culture. For its part, the Kuomintang (KMT) state attempted to find a middle ground between these two positions, while also promoting policies such as the New Life Movement of 1934, which attempted to use traditional Confucian values and Sun Yat-sen's "Three Principles of the People" (Sanmin zhuyi 三民主義) to maintain social stability and unify popular support for the KMT. These ideals had a strong impact on the temple destruction policies of the Republican era, especially those linked to the "eradicating superstitions" and "rectifying customs" campaigns, including the "Standards to Determine Temples to Be Destroyed and Maintained."[22]

In general, while some campaigns proved effective in parts of North China as well as in larger cities, the enforcement of those regulations cited previously appears to have been irregular and inconsistent.[22] In just one example, Yuan Shikai 袁世凱 (1859–1916) initiated a harsh antisuperstition campaign in 1912, only to relent one year later and enact regulations guaranteeing religious freedom (the "Temporary Compacts and Laws" or *Linshi yuefa* 臨時約法) and protecting temple properties (the "Temporary Regulations for Managing Temples" or *Siyuan guanli zhanxing guize* 寺

院管理暫行規則).[24] Even in major urban centers such as Guangzhou 廣州, some schools still contained altars or shrines for the worship of deities from the temples they had occupied or shared space with,[25] while in Shanghai some temples and their festivals proved able not only to survive but even to flourish amidst the heat of some of the most strident campaigns.[26] In late Qing Hangzhou, officials proved reluctant to suppress plague expulsion festivals, particularly when epidemics were raging.[27] Other regulations, such as those governing "superstitious" items, were put on hold in Jiangsu and Zhejiang because of fears about the impact they would have on religious businesses.[28] Official reluctance to follow through on temple destruction campaigns was compounded in the face of organized and at times impassioned outbreaks of resistance.

NEW TERMS AND NEW ACTORS

Underlying the temple destruction campaigns described previously were discursive changes that can be traced back to the waning years of the Qing dynasty and continued throughout the Republican era, particularly the advent of new labels for religious phenomena based on Western (and Christian) categorizations such as "religion" and "superstition" (see the introduction). This new terminology helped inspire the first "build schools with temple properties" campaign, which was initiated by leading elites such as Zhang Zhidong 張之洞 (1837–1909), Zhang Taiyan 章太炎 (1869–1936), and Kang Youwei 康有為 (1858–1927), who once complained that, "Foreigners come in our temples, take photographs of the idols, show these photographs to each other, and laugh."[29] However, data preserved in newspapers such as *Shenbao* 申報 suggest that many new terms, including "superstition" and "reform" (*gailiang* 改良), did not become widespread until the Republican era.[30] One work of Christian authorship, the *Comprehensive Writings for Eradicating Superstition* (*Pochu mixin quanshu* 破除迷信全書, 1929), employs this new term to cover a veritable catchall of religious phenonema, using a combination of traditional and modern categories such as geomancy (*fengshui* 風水), divination (*bushi* 卜筮), physiogamy (*kanxiang* 看相), attaining Buddhahood (*chengfo* 成佛), attaining immortality (*chengxian* 成仙), and so on. The most striking of these categories may be that for "heterodox movements and practices" (*zuodao* 左道), which covers not only various sectarian movements but also festivals (*yingshen saihui* 迎神賽會), pilgrimages (*chaoshan lifo* 朝山禮佛), and exorcistic Nuo rituals (*xiangren Nuo* 鄉人儺).[31] In other words, while the campaigns were a continuous phenomenon, the terminology used to justify their enactment took some time to become a fully accepted component of state and elite discourse.

In addition, it is important to remember that not all of the concepts adopted in modern discourses about religion had a negative impact on temples and temple cults. Some elite authors, including notables such as Dai Jitao 戴季陶 (1891–1949) and Gu Jiegang 顧頡剛 (1893–1980), viewed religion as a form of "folklore" (*minsu* 民俗) meriting both study and protection.[32] Others, using terminology at times strikingly similar to that used in current campaigns to protect religion as a form of intangible cultural heritage (*feiwuzhi wenhua yichan* 非物質文化遺產), argued in favor of designating at least some of China's most venerable temples as historical monuments (*guji* 古蹟; also a traditional term in its own right), with their statues and other ritual artifacts meriting protection as cultural artifacts (*wenwu baohu* 文物保護; the term *wenwu* 文物 is a traditional one as well).[33] Republican-era archives are full of regulations about both monuments and artifacts,[34] while even those officials and elites who most stridently advocated in favor of temple destruction campaigns conceded that some temples and their ritual items deserved to be preserved.[35] One example may be found in Republican-era documents preserved in the Baojing 保靖 County Archives in Western Hunan (Xiangxi 湘西), which I am examining as part of my research project on modern Miao 苗 religion. One 1941 document contained in the archives, promulgated by the provincial authorities, is entitled "Provincial [Rules] for Protecting Temple Properties" (*Sheng baohu simiao caichan* 省保護寺廟財產) and specifies the circumstances under which sacred sites were entitled to state protection.

Finally, it is essential to note the considerable continuity these campaigns evinced in terms of both terminology (positive and negative alike) as well as practices. This is because the temple destruction campaigns of the Republican era represent merely one phase of a centuries-long contest over the control of religious authority and resources, one that has extended into the present day. The work of Sarah Schneewind is especially instructive in this regard, and a poem she has translated that was written in 1478 by the reformist official Zhang Bi 張陛 surely would have earned the approval of Republican-era activists:

> . . . Temple walls and possessions pass into public and
> private hands.
> Gradually I wipe out ancient and deluded customs;
> Saving the people's wealth for full bellies and warmth
> today . . .[36]

While the most common slogan used was "destroying illicit shrines in order to erect community schools" (*hui yinci li shexue* 毀淫祠立社學), late imperial campaigns resembled those of the Republican era in featuring attacks on Buddhist and Daoist temples. In just one example, one district magistrate of Kunshan 崑(昆)山 named Yang Ziqi 楊子奇 (1458–1513) earned praise for turning 110 Buddhist and Daoist monasteries into schools. As in the Republican era, such campaigns also sparked numerous acts of both passive and in many cases violent resistance.[37] Even the "Standards to Determine Temples to Be Destroyed and Maintained" featured its own mix of tradition and modernity, on the one hand advocating for a new manifestation of Chinese religious life inspired by the West, while on the other hand citing historical figures such as Ximen Bao 西門豹 (fl. 446–396 BCE) and Tang Bin 湯斌 (1607–1687) as paradigms of reformist officials who were effective in eradicating temple cults. Moreover, the editors of the "Standards" retained the traditional term "illicit shrines" (*yinci* 淫祠), albeit attempting to broaden its scope to encompass all manner of temple cults that did not fit the modern category of "religion," including those which had once belonged to the imperially approved register of sacrifices (*sidian* 祀典).[38]

As we have seen, the temple destruction campaigns of the Republican era were nothing new to Chinese history, representing merely one phase of an age-old struggle between the state and local communities for the control of economic and symbolic resources, one which has extended into the present day. However, some facets of these campaigns seem relatively unique to the modern age. Apart from the realm of terminology in the form of new labels such as "religion" and "superstition," significant changes may be found in the nature of those individuals and organizations that took part in the campaigns, with many new actors appearing on the scene. As Vincent Goossaert aptly points out in his recent paper presented at the Fourth International Conference of Sinology in Taiwan, ". . . 1910–1912 witnessed a shift from a model where intermediaries (Buddhist, Daoist and Divination officials) managed the local religious scene, to one where new institutions (the Ministry of Education, local civil affairs bureaus, and the police) were supposed to take over, but without the inner knowledge their predecessors had."[39] To complicate matters even more, while the imperial state had come to an end, China was now ruled by a combination of powerful forces, including not only the KMT but also the Chinese Communist Party (CCP) and the Japanese.

Of equal if not greater significance was the advent of the party state. While government agencies such as the Ministry of the

Interior (Neizhengbu 內政部) and Social Affairs Bureaus (Shehuiju 社會局) took charge of formulating many of the policies discussed in this chapter,[40] their actual implementation was often done hand in hand with KMT party cadres and other activists, especially at the local level.[41] Much of the best data on this phenomenon come from the KMT power base of Jiangsu 江蘇 province, where the capital city Nanjing 南京 was located. For example, while Xue Dubi 薛篤弼 played a key role in formulating temple destruction policies, their enactment in Jiangsu depended in part on the support of Jiangsu party chairman Niu Yongjian 鈕永建 (1870–1965).[42] The importance of party-state cooperation was noted explicitly in one key document promulgated by Xue's cohorts, the "Declaration of the Republic of China Committee for Advancing [the Cause] of Temples Being Turned into Schools" cited previously.[43]

He Zhiming 何志明's study of the 1928 "eradicating superstition" campaigns in Yancheng 鹽城 County (Jiangsu) reveals that they were launched by an alliance of provincial government officials from the Department of Civil Affairs (Minzhengting 民政廳) and cadres from the county party offices (Xiandangbu 縣黨部).[44] A similar partnership shaped a 1929 campaign to abolish deity statues (*feichu ouxiang* 廢除偶像) in Baoying 寶應 County (Jiangsu), which KMT party members unanimously voted to support. The county government concurred and instructed the police to escort party activists to their first target, the local City God temple (Chenghuang miao 城隍廟).[45] This was also the case in Zhejiang, one example being KMT party instructions to the local authorities in Fuyang 富陽 County to forbid the use of medicinal divination slips (*yaoqian* 藥籤) in local temples.[46] Relations between party cadres, local officials, and nonparty elites were not always harmonious, however, and could spark tensions or even acts of violence when the latter groups opposed temple destruction policies. Such instances, which clearly merit consideration in the context of the interaction between state and society,[47] occurred sporadically throughout China during the late Qing and Republican eras, and ranged in nature from editorials and other critical writings to lawsuits and even violent actions such as tearing down new schools and thrashing the officials and activists who had helped build them.[48]

Another change involved the age of those individuals who proposed and attempted to carry out temple destruction policies, with many being students or recent graduates of modern Western schools.[49] Their ranks included many highly educated Buddhist monks and nuns, as well as lay Buddhists who, while strongly opposing attempts to expropriate or destroy Buddhist temples, were far less sympathetic to local temple cults.[50] Students (and at times their mentors) were at the vanguard of many of the most violent temple destruction efforts, including one 1929 campaign in Xiaoshan 蕭山 County (northern Zhejiang, near Hangzhou 杭州) that targeted its City God temples.[51]

Christianity and especially Christian activists also played key roles in these campaigns. The iconoclasm embraced by Sun Yatsen may have had its roots in Chinese Christian iconoclastic movements,[52] while the Christian warlord Feng Yuxiang 馮玉祥 (1882–1948; also a patron of Xue Dubi 薛篤弼) gained considerable renown for his efforts at extirpating "superstition" during the 1920s and 1930s.[53] Many ideals underlying modern China's temple destruction campaigns found expression in Christian periodicals such as *Xinghua* 興華,[54] while the preface of the 1929 work *Pochu mixin quanshu* previously mentioned, which was edited and compiled by two leading Methodists named Li Ganchen 李幹忱 and Luo Yunyan 羅運炎 (1890–1938?), also expresses clear Christian agendas.[55]

A final group of actors whose roles recently have begun to be fully appreciated consisted of women practitioners. A number of documents from 1929 preserved in the Buddhist periodical *Sound of the Tide* (*Haichaoyin* 海潮音) expressed the state's profound uneasiness over religious activities undertaken by Buddhist nuns and lay women worshippers.[56] Such concerns dated back to imperial times, with Vincent Goossaert's recent research on the *Shenbao* 申報 and other late Qing sources vividly documenting all manner of bans (or at least attempted bans) against women practicing at Buddhist temples (especially nunneries) and taking part in religious processions as penitents (often in the nude). It is also striking that many of the Shanghai and Hangzhou temples which ended up being turned into schools during the late Qing period were Buddhist nunneries.[57] Many religious women refused to go quietly into the night, however, and did not hesitate to take part in or even lead resistance efforts against temple destruction campaigns.[58]

With so many different actors competing so fiercely for control over the plentiful economic and symbolic resources that temples represented, it is hardly surprising that many tensions and conflicts arose. The interaction between national officials, local officials, and party activists was often marked by friction, as can be seen in Fu Haiyan 付海晏's study of the attempted expropriation of the Iron Mountain Monastery (Tieshan Si 鐵山寺) in Beiping 北平 (Beijing)[59] and Ai Ping 艾萍's analysis of the differing attitudes of KMT cadres and government officials in Shanghai.[60] Such tensions often were most intense outside of the big cities in county seats and market towns, where the elite maintained close ties to traditional religious activities. In the course of the 1928 Yancheng County campaigns described previously, these tensions erupted into outright violence, with the local citizenry wreaking its wrath on KMT party offices and new schools that had once been temples, but *not* local government offices.[61] Another example took place in Gaoyou 高郵 County (also in Jiangsu), where antisuperstition campaigns during the 1930s were wracked by fractious ties between party and local officials.[62]

Considerable strain also existed between urban intellectuals and more rural elites. As Vincent Goossaert and David Palmer perceptively point out, relatively few modern Chinese elites chose to promote religion as a form of national identity, a phenomenon markedly different from what occurred in many other Asian countries. Numerous Western-educated urban elites, including Hu Shih and Chen Duxiu 陳獨秀 (1879–1942), felt a profound sense of crisis about China's future and became especially concerned with "superstition" in the aftermath of the Boxer Rebellion. Their support of temple destruction campaigns contrasts sharply with elites in more rural areas and also in market towns. While some (especially those not holding formal office) may have supported temple destruction campaigns in order to side with what they perceived to be the winning power of the state, many others steadfastly defended their local religious traditions.[63] Both sides proved adept at using the mass media (what Nedostup aptly refers to as a "toolbox of modernity") to their advantage.[64] One fascinating case study of how these tensions played out on the ground is Poon Shuk-wah's recent paper on the "ancestral temple" (*zumiao* 祖廟) of the Dragon Mother (Longmu 龍母), located in the market town Yuecheng 悅城 (Deqing 德慶 County, Guangdong 廣東) on the northern bank of the West River. While this cult and its festival were subjected to constant and vehement attacks by modern intellectuals in Guangzhou 廣州 (often being derided as a "vulgar custom" (*louxi* 陋習) or a "superstition of divine power" (*shenquan mixin* 神權迷信)), the town's officials and local elites had far more ambiguous feelings, being torn between the pressure for political correctness and the need for economic development.[65]

The differing and at times conflicting agendas embraced by different actors in modern China's temple destruction campaigns lie at the heart of another key issue, namely, the extent to which these campaigns were actually enforced. Some of the best organized and most effective resistance to temple destruction campaigns was led by renowned Buddhists such as Wang Yiting 王一亭 (1867–1938), who during the late 1920s and early 1930s successfully negotiated with Chiang Kai-shek not to implement many of the harshest regulations against Buddhist institutions (see chapter 3).[66] Wang and other members of his Buddhist elite also composed a powerful rebuttal to the "Declaration of the Republic of China Committee for Advancing [the Cause] of Temples Being Turned into Schools" in September 1931, which culminated in the following hard-hitting conclusion:

> What is the state of our field of education today? Cries of its bankruptcy echo throughout the land. If we consider the reasons for this sorry state of affairs, we should admit that many educators have blindly believed in the omnipotence of material things [*wuxin wuzhi wanneng* 誤信物質萬能], thereby obliterating the cultivation of the spirit [*mosha jingshen xiuyang* 抹殺精神修養]. Mistakenly trusting in the "treasures" [*fabao* 法寶] of Western utilitarianism [*gongli zhuyi* 功利主義], they have abandoned our traditional morals [*biqi jiuyou daode* 鄙棄舊有道德], which has led editorialists to opine that today's schools are little more than centers for the production of high-level vagabonds [*gaodeng youmin* 高等遊民]. This is a true cause for sorrow. With the national crisis [*guonan* 國難] ever magnifying, educators need to engage in profound self-reflection, while citizens should oversee those responsible. Buddhist doctrine provides a limitless and beneficial medicine [*wushang liangyao* 無上良藥] and is the supreme means for cultivating morality . . . We believe that promoting Buddhist doctrine in our educational system can eliminate the selfish and self-serving consequences of individualism and increase the cultivation of a pure and lofty spirit. If today's educators are unable to be enlightened on this point and seize solely on materialism [*weiwu rangduo* 惟務攘奪], should they be considered as beneficial or harmful to our cause?[67]

Buddhist elites often were able to persuade the state to accept their arguments, as can be seen in a number of decisions by the Ministry of the Interior and other government organizations to delay the implementation of laws advocating the destruction or expropriation of temples, or to protect their artifacts.[68] These elites also took the lead in filing petitions or lawsuits, which happened in 1929 when workers seized control of the Iron Mountain Monastery in Beijing. After a three-year lawsuit, the courts ruled in the temple's favor, and its properties were restored.[69]

In addition, research by Vincent Goossaert shows that other groups of elites, particularly those with close ties to guilds and other commercial organizations, took the lead in resisting state attempts to ban festivals. This was especially important in the Jiangnan region, where temple cults and their festivals represented a key economic resource that could also stimulate commercial activities. As a result, when officials and party activists strove to eliminate the festivals or block attempts to revive them, their efforts often ran head-on into the agendas of commercial elites who were trying to do the opposite. Inasmuch as the state lacked sufficient resources to enforce bans on festivals, and police were reluctant to strictly enforce relevant regulations since doing so often resulted in violence and casualties, the end results tended to follow intricate processes of negotiation, with both sides working to find mutually agreeable solutions, including using festival funds for worthy philanthropic causes and reducing the scale of celebrations during times of crisis.[70]

Still other elites argued in favor of carefully distinguishing between legitimate religious practices (especially self-cultivation) and indiscriminate worship of deities for personal gain (which even they considered to be a form of "superstition"). Adopting forms of discourse at times strikingly similar to those espoused by the state, they nonetheless used writings published in their own religious periodicals to warn the authorities against recklessly implementing antisuperstition policies. One example may be found in a spirit-writing text attributed to the Song-dynasty Buddhist monk Jigong 濟公, published in 1922 in *Morality Magazine* (*Daode zazhi* 道德雜誌), which was produced by the Society of the Way (Daoyuan 道院, also known by the name of its philanthropic branch, the World Red Swastika Society or Shijie hongwanzihui 世界紅卍字會) (for more on religious periodicals, see chapter 2):

> [Jigong]: Sit down and listen. What you refer to as superstition is not those beliefs and practices to which we devote ourselves. Those people whom our elders [*fuzi* 夫子] refer to as superstitious include both ignorant men and women [*yufu yufu* 愚夫愚婦] who engage in idolatry [*bai ouxiang* 拜偶像], as well as those who claim to believe in gods and buddhas but fail to live by their teachings. Today, we adhere to the true principles [*zhenli* 真理] of the sages, immortals, and buddhas. We incorporate the Five Teachings [*wujiao* 五教: Buddhism, Daoism, Catholicism, Protestantism, and Islam] as one great way [*dadao* 大道], practicing internal and external cultivation, saving ourselves while also providing salvation for others. As such, we hardly compare to those who blindly engage in various practices. What do you have to say to that?[71]

Texts such as this also point to the growing importance of new religious movements in Republican China, especially since some of them assumed the functions of temple cults in areas where temple destruction campaigns had been effective. As recent research has begun to show, these voluntary religious associations (generally referred to as "redemptive societies" or *jiushi tuanti* 救世團體) helped contribute to a reconfiguration of Chinese religious life during the Republican era.[72] Research by David Ownby and other scholars reveals that, during this period of flux and instability, these groups attracted large numbers of adherents because of their ability to voice lay salvationist ideals that had flourished in China for centuries, while doing so independently of more established religious movements such as Buddhism and Daoism. In addition, they gained notoriety for their emphasis on proper moral conduct, acceptance of all major world religions, engagement in philanthropic activities, and practice of spirit-writing rituals (variously referred to as *fuji* 扶乩, *fuluan* 扶鸞, or *feiluan* 飛鸞).[73] Only now are scholars beginning to appreciate the extent to which these movements challenge conventional dichotomies such as elite/popular or institutionalized/diffused, because of their national organization, hierarchical structure, systematized doctrine, and canon formation. Redemptive societies also call into question the traditional/modern dichotomy because of their commitment to a "new civilizational discourse" embracing Asian solutions to the problems of the modern world, as well as their attempts to define self-cultivation practices (including meditation, the martial arts, and healing) as fitting the categories of both "religion" and "science."[74]

Some of the largest and best-organized of these societies gained legitimacy by being allowed to register with the state from 1912 to 1949, including not only the previously mentioned Society of the Way, but also the Fellowship of Goodness (Tongshanshe 同善社), the Universal Morality Society (Wanguo daodehui 萬國道德會), the Teachings of the Abiding Principle (Zailijiao 在理教), and the Way of Pervading Unity (Yiguandao 一貫道).[75] The success of such groups in being recognized as legitimate religious groups was partly because they boasted among their membership some of the leading military figures of that age, including Yan Xishan 閻錫山 (1883–1960), Lu Yongxiang 盧永祥 (1867–1933), and most notably Duan Qirui 段祺瑞 (1865–1936, ROC President 1923–1924; Duan's anti-Buddhist stance does not seem to have precluded his participation).[76] Many KMT leaders were also active members, including former premier Xiong Xiling 熊希齡 (1870–1937), who presided over the Red Swastika Society. As a result, some modern Chinese leaders proved willing to condone a wide range of religious activities, including spirit writing, which could avoid the "superstition" label if associated with religious associations that had gained the sanction of the authorities. In the case of redemptive societies, many such groups registered with the authorities as philanthropic associations or organizations devoted to the practice of self-cultivation, which facilitated state approval. At the same time, however, while the state often embraced such groups for their charitable actions or adherence to traditional Chinese culture, it could also end up denouncing the very same groups as heterodox manifestations of superstition. As for the elites who led these societies, while they may not necessarily have been affected directly by the temple destruction campaigns described in this chapter, texts such as the passage just quoted reveal that they were concerned about the ways in which the state's attempts to regulate temples and festivals might influence the future of Chinese religious life as a whole.[77]

ASSESSING THE IMPACT OF TEMPLE DESTRUCTION CAMPAIGNS

When considering the impact of temple destruction movements, one needs to distinguish between campaigns aimed at utilizing a portion of the temple's properties for other-than-religious uses and those that resulted in the temple's utter destruction. The original goal of the "build schools with temple property" movement, as articulated by Zhang Zhidong 張之洞 in his "Essay Advocating [the Construction of] Schools" (*Quanxue pian* 勸學篇), stipulated that at most 70 percent of a temple's assets were to be used for this purpose, with the rest being left in the hands of those religious specialists who owned or resided at the temple. Other campaigns focused on extracting revenue from the temples via taxes and fees.[78] Such nuances also are reflected in a second slogan used in the course of such movements, namely, "destroy temples and found schools" (*huimiao banxue* 毀廟辦學). The distinction between "build schools with temple property" and "destroy temples and found schools" was hardly a rigid one, and the two phrases could be used interchangeably in some contexts, yet many people did distinguish between the two. Even activist educators such as Tai Shuangqiu and the officials who promulgated such policies as the "Regulations for Overseeing Temples" tended to favor using temples and their resources for education without utterly demolishing them, especially if the temples in question were Buddhist ones. Despite the fact that the Shanghai city government went so far as to recommend that all temple properties under its jurisdiction be confiscated for educational uses, such policies never were effectively implemented.[79]

There also were differences in the targets of various temple destruction campaigns. For example, those movements that aimed at turning temples into schools had to focus on those religious establishments possessing sufficient resources for such a purpose, especially the monastic centers and large communal temples.[80] In particular, wealthy Buddhist monasteries and nunneries often were the initial targets of these campaigns, but once Buddhism proved successful in defining itself as a "religion" meriting state protection, activists tended to turn their attention to local temple cults.[81] Apart from the Buddhist sacred sites, many of the earliest temples to be transformed into schools had belonged to the state cult. These sacred sites had ample resources on a par with (or even exceeding) those belonging to other temples, but local residents rarely worshipped on their premises and thus were much less likely to intercede on their behalf.[82] In contrast, many sacred sites that were targeted during antisuperstition campaigns tended to be smaller shrines with little property and far fewer backers. For example, when the Shanghai city government made up an admittedly perfunctory list of fifty-two "illicit shrines" (*yinci* 淫祠) to be destroyed (discussed in detail later in the chapter), the vast majority were small and recently founded altars (*tan* 壇) that tended to practice spirit writing.[83] It is also necessary to differentiate between destroying temples and their statues and banning festivals. In just one instance, the diary by a Wenzhou elite named Zhang Gang 張棡 (1860–1942) contains an entry noting that while one City God's statue was destroyed in the spring of 1928, the temple's festival still was held as planned.[84]

Another key issue that has yet to be addressed adequately is how temple destruction campaigns influenced the lives and careers of the religious specialists. These men and women certainly were targets of discourses aimed at reforming or eradicating aspects of Chinese religious life, with texts such as "The Significance of and Methods for Destroying Superstitions" criticizing both religious specialists and the rituals they performed.[85] In general, it seems that religious specialists tended to come out on the losing side of struggles against the state,[86] but the roles they played during such campaigns have been overlooked.[87] Fortunately, however, Qi Gang and I have located some promising data from Ruian (in southern Zhejiang), which will be discussed later in this chapter.

Only recently have scholars begun to examine the actual impact of temple destruction campaigns in modern China, and the limited amounts of data collected to date make it difficult to advance any definitive conclusions. However, it appears that such policies tended to be enforced more strictly in northern China. Recent research by Vincent Goossaert and David Palmer reveals that in Dingxian 定縣 (central Hebei 河北) the number of active temples belonging to a cluster of 62 villages dropped from 432 in 1900 to just 116 in 1915. In Changli 昌黎 County (northern Hebei), 34 of 42 temples possessing landed endowments had these assets expropriated by 1933, with 17 becoming the property of the village government, 17 being converted to schools, and 8 properties continuing to be used by the temples. In Liangxiang 良鄉 County (near Beijing), most temples were turned into schools by 1923, with all temple lands being confiscated by village assemblies.[88]

Other scholars have come up with similar figures for North China as well. For example, research by Liu Xun 劉迅 and Mei Li 梅莉 reveals that in Nanyang 南陽 (Henan), one renowned

Daoist temple known as the Dark Mystery Monastery (Xuanmiao Guan 玄妙觀) and its affiliated temples had accumulated approximately 77 *qing* 頃 of farmland prior to 1911 (1 *qing* = 6.7 hectares). However, during the first year following the birth of the Republic, the monastery suffered the loss of nearly half its lands, much of which was used as part of an endowment for new educational agencies and schools. By 1949, the monastery's remaining land holdings had shrunk to barely 20 *mu* 畝 (1 *mu* = 1⁄15 of a hectare or 1⁄6 of an acre) as a result not only of state expropriation but also of private takeovers, illicit pawning, and overall mismanagement.[89] Liu Chengyou 劉成有's study of the 1929 gazetteer for Tai'an 泰安 County (Shandong 山東) reveals that of the 348 schools constructed by 1929, a total of 328 (94.25 percent) were built in temples, including 67 in Buddhist temples, 203 in "communal temples" (*minsu miaoyu* 民俗廟宇), 20 in lineage halls (*citang* 祠堂), and 10 in mosques (*qingzhensi* 清真寺).[90] In addition, data in Xu Xiaozheng 許效正's doctoral dissertation indicate that all 169 new schools built in Yuxiang 虞鄉 County (Shanxi 山西) between 1902 and 1920 were located in temples, while in Xinyang 信陽 County (Henan 河南) 38 of 45 new schools were built in temples, with 31 of these operating using temple funds.[91] Whether all of these temples were completely destroyed or were simply forced to share some of their space and funding with the new schools has yet to be determined.

This does not mean that temple cults in North China had disappeared from the scene, however. Temple surveys undertaken from 1941 to 1948 by Willem A. Grootaers (1911–1999) and a Fu-jen University (Furen daxue 輔仁大學) research team that included Li Shih-yu 李世瑜 and Wang Fu-shih 王輔世 revealed an average of between 4.2 and 6.5 temples per village in Xuanhua 宣化 and Wanquan 萬全, while Sidney D. Gamble's (1890–1968) surveys counted a total of thirty-eight temples in six Hebei "sample villages," with fifteen in one village alone.[92]

Temple destruction campaigns seem to have been relatively

less effective in southern China. In Taihe 太和 County (Anhui 安徽), for example, only two of its five late Qing schools were built in temples; for the period covering the years from 1912 to 1916, the figures were eleven of twenty-one (just over 50 percent).[93] Xu Yao 徐躍's study of late Qing Sichuan 四川 reveals that while as many as three-fourths of the province's new schools may have been established in temples, their income rarely exceeded 50 percent of these temples' properties, meaning that coexistence rather than destruction was the norm.[94] Hundreds of Guangxi 廣西 temples survived into the twentieth century despite the depredations of Taiping and warlord soldiers, and while many new schools were constructed, only limited data exist on the numbers of temples turned into schools. If data from Guixian 貴縣 are representative, many temples may have continued to survive, as only eleven of this county's forty-two new schools were built in temples from 1917 to 1932.[95] Such trends continued into the 1940s, with Fu Haiyan 付海晏's research indicating that 207 of 286 Hubei temples survived from 1936 to 1949.[96] The factors underlying the discrepancies in the impact of temple destruction campaigns in North and South China have yet to be fully ascertained, but may have been tied to local geographical and especially socioeconomic conditions, with the tightly knit temple cults and lineages of the south often able to mount substantial resistance to state policies, something that proved less feasible in the scattered and loosely organized northern communities.[97]

The main exceptions to the southern patterns just described center on large urban areas. Detailed information from the Jiangnan region follows, but one other relevant example comes from Minhou 閩侯 County in Fuzhou 福州. Its Republican-era county gazetteer lists a total of ninety-five temple reconstruction projects, but not one was undertaken between 1911 and 1933, which suggests that Fuzhou temples either had been expropriated or were falling out of use.[98] In one other instance, city government officials in Kunming 昆明 took control of sixty-one temples, justifying their actions by quoting from the "Standards" as to why each seized temple (including the Buddhist and Daoist ones) had not been deemed sufficiently "religious."[99]

Apart from the apparent north-south differences, significant rural-urban ones existed as well. By now the largest amounts of primary source data about temple destruction campaigns (especially archives and newspaper reports) already have been collected for major metropolises such as Beijing, Nanjing, Shanghai, and Hangzhou. We know almost nothing about the details of these campaigns at the village level, and relatively little about county seats such as those in southern Zhejiang that the "Fifty Years" project is current examining, such as Pingyang 平陽, Ruian 瑞安, and Yueqing 樂清.[100] It would also be interesting to examine the fate of temples in older and more "traditional" cities such as Yangzhou 揚州.[101] The question of spatial differences is of critical importance to research on this topic, because the "eradicating superstitions" and "rectifying customs" campaigns appear to have centered on cities and large market towns, while the "build schools with temple property" movement was undertaken throughout China, including in cities, towns, and villages.[102]

One of the most thought-provoking investigations of these issues has been undertaken by Poon Shuk-wah, who confirms that Republican-era officials and elites viewed cities as bastions of modernity, meaning that the antisuperstition drives they organized tended to take place in urban areas. This did not spell the end of religious life for urban dwellers, however, as many citizens took advantage of new transportation networks to visit sacred sites in nearby towns and villages, as was the case for Yuecheng's Dragon Mother Temple. Poon's research has important implications for our understanding of possible spatial variations in Republican China, particularly in light of scholarship that postulates a growing rural-urban divide and the advent of an autonomous urban culture.[103] While the representativeness of the Dragon Mother Temple case study remains to be fully ascertained, the data that Poon has collected suggest that while the rural-urban divide seems quite vivid in much elite discourse, religious activities provided one important link between cities and the countryside. Urban dwellers may not have wished to trade in their modern material culture for a rustic one, but the numerous temples that survived in towns and rural areas constituted integral components of their spiritual lives.[104]

Despite the resistance efforts that have been delineated, the number of temples throughout China did continue to decline during the Republican era. Temple destruction campaigns appear to have become more widespread and more thoroughly enforced during the 1930s,[105] as was also the case for policies against festivals and other ritual activities deemed to be "superstitious."[106] Other factors apart from the policies themselves appear to have been at play, however. The first was warfare, most notably the War of Resistance against Japan. On the one hand, the devastating destruction of this period ravaged many rural areas that previously had escaped the temple destruction campaigns unscathed. On the other hand, wartime needs prompted the state (and especially local governments) to be much more proactive in seizing temples and their assets, at times even going beyond the scope of central government regulations.[107] Policies enacted immediately after the war also had harsh consequences for some temples, especially those whose leaders or religious specialists stood accused of collaborationist activities.[108]

The second factor had to do with economic decline. As numerous scholars have noted, temples lay at the heart of many local economies, including various forms of gift exchange, local investment, and marketing networks.[109] Festivals and other ritual activities were also highly commercialized activities that could help spark economic growth.[110] On the one hand, these factors made temples and their festivals attractive targets for state expropriation and taxation policies;[111] on the other hand, temples and festivals were also highly sensitive to economic downturns.

The severe deterioration of the Chinese economy during the 1930s and 1940s had a major impact on both temple cults and the elites who supported them. As remains the case today, bad years resulted in lower incomes for temples, which in turn meant delayed reconstruction projects and much smaller festivals.[112]

CASE STUDY 1: THE JIANGNAN REGION

The Jiangnan region lay at the heart of the Nationalist government's sphere of control and was also a major publishing center (including religious publishing; see chapter 2). Accordingly, this region is home to a wealth of data about local temple campaigns, some of which have already been discussed previously. Jiangnan boasted its share of thriving temple cults as well as mammoth festivals, but many of these had been devastated during the Taiping Rebellion, while the decimation of this region's population and destruction of both private and communal property caused many cults and festivals to wither away without any form of state intervention. The temple destruction campaigns enacted during this time period put further pressure on communal religious life, especially in large cities.[113]

The limited amount of statistical evidence that has been collected thus far suggests that temple destruction campaigns were not undertaken as thoroughly in this region as was the case for North China. During the late Qing, for example, slightly over half (fifteen out of twenty-five) of the autonomous offices (*zizhi gongsuo* 自治公所) erected in the prefectures of Suzhou 蘇州, Songjiang 松江, Changzhou 常州, and Zhenjiang 鎮江, as well as the subprefecture of Taicang 太倉, had originally been temples. Moreover, as late as the 1920s, only twenty-two of eighty-one popular educational institutions built in Wu County had been temples.[114] Similarly, attempts to ban festivals often proved fleeting and highly difficult to enforce, especially in the face of firmly entrenched elite interests. Goossaert's research on this topic has already been discussed, while additional evidence may be found in Xiaotian 小田's study of Republican-era attempts to ban the Fierce General Liu (Liu Mengjiang 劉猛將) festival in Suzhou 蘇州 in the course of antisuperstition campaigns. In the end, such policies were not thoroughly enforced, and the failure of state-sponsored efforts to catch locusts (*buhuang* 捕蝗) only contributed further to popular sentiments to perpetuate the festival.[115]

As one would expect, some of the best (yet also highly problematic) statistical data come from the Shanghai area, much of which has been compiled in the *Comprehensive Overview of Shanghai Religion* (*Shanghai zongjiao tonglan* 上海宗教通覽). This source, recently used to great effect by Vincent Goossaert,[116] draws on archival data to show that by 1949 Shanghai city and its suburbs remained home to a total of 2,186 temples of various types and sizes, ranging from Buddhist and Daoist institutions to small local shrines (see Table 1.1). As one would expect, the relative abundance of open space in suburban areas meant that far more temples were built in the suburbs than in the city itself (1,841 versus 345), and one future task for this project will attempt to determine how these temples differed and whether the suburban temples were more likely to survive temple destruction campaigns than the urban ones.[117]

The *Overview* also contains detailed tables documenting the historical development of 1,952 temples, including 1,135 labeled as "Buddhist" (*fosi* 佛寺) and 817 labeled as "Daoist" (*daoguan* 道觀). As is the case for postwar Taiwan, these categories are utterly arbitrary, usually being based on the identity of each temple's main deity. As the editors of the *Overview* noted themselves, the deities of many "Buddhist" temples could be Daoist or communal gods, while the religious specialists who resided in them or performed rites on their premises were not necessarily members of the Buddhist *sangha*.[118] The vast majority of these sacred sites appear to have been lay Buddhist halls or even communal temples; only a few were formal Buddhist institutions. Similar problems can be found for the "Daoist" temples, many of which

TABLE 1.1. Temples in Shanghai and Surrounding Counties (1949)

District	*Temples*	*County*	*Temples*
Huangpu	24	Shanghai	76
Nanshi	68	Chuansha	236
Jing'an	45	Nanhui	62
Hongkou	52	Chongming	30
Zhabei	38	Qingpu	462
Yangpu	29	Jinshan	9
Putuo	26	Songjiang	307
Changning	22	Fengxian	85
Luwan	31	Baoshan	57
Xuhui	10	Jiading	517
Total:	345	Total:	1,841

were also communal temples or spirit-writing centers, some of which were probably managed by redemptive societies. A few were former state cult sites as well, including many of those for the City God and Guandi 關帝.[119]

Despite the presence of these methodological pitfalls, however, some potentially significant trends can be observed:

1. Shanghai witnessed an initial peak in turning "Buddhist" temples into schools during the late Qing (1898–1907), which was followed by a gradual decline through the first years of the Republican era (1908–1927). Most instances of "Buddhist" temple destruction during the former period of time were because they were being turned into schools. The rates of turning "Buddhist" temples into schools remained relatively steady from the 1920s to the 1940s, with even fewer cases occurring thereafter.

2. While the rates of turning "Buddhist" temples into schools declined over time, the overall destruction of such sacred sites actually increased from 1918 through 1927 and on. This was

mainly because of their being converted into government offices or police or fire stations, but the ravages of warfare also took a heavy toll, with temples being either utterly destroyed or used as hospitals, clinics, and eventually refugee centers. Another rapid increase in the destruction of "Buddhist" temples took place after 1949 and persisted through the Cultural Revolution (see the concluding section of this chapter).

3. There was also a rapid rise in turning "Daoist" temples into schools from 1898 through 1907 and reaching its acme from 1908 through 1917, with rates of destruction exceeding those for "Buddhist" temples. This was followed by a precipitous decline from 1918 through 1927, and then by another increase (albeit less rapid) between the 1920s and 1950s. "Daoist" temples seem to have suffered less than "Buddhist" ones after 1949, with the destruction campaigns occurring at a slower pace and lasting for a shorter period of time.

4. Trends for the overall destruction of "Daoist" temples roughly paralleled those for such sacred sites being turned into schools, but with two exceptions: The first occurred during the early 1910s, when large numbers of these temples were transformed into township offices (*xianggongsuo* 鄉公所). The second exception occurred during wartime, following patterns similar to those for the "Buddhist" temples discussed previously.

5. Overall, there appear to have been two peaks in Shanghai campaigns to turn temples into schools, both of which marked times of profound political transition. The first occurred during the late Qing and early Republican eras, while the second took place as the Republic of China collapsed and the People's Republic was established.[120]

In the case of the "Buddhist" temples, data in the *Overview* indicate that prior to 1949 125 out of the 1,135 Shanghai temples placed in this category were turned into schools, including 64 before the year 1900, with 94 being turned into elementary schools.[121] A total of 61 such instances occurred between 1911 and 1949, including 3 in 1911; 1 in 1912; 1 in 1913; 4 in 1914; 2 in 1916; 2 in 1917; 2 in 1920; 3 in 1922, 1 in 1923; 1 in 1925; 1 in 1926; 2 in 1927; 2 in 1928; 1 in 1929; 1 for the 1930s ("1930年代"); 3 in 1930; 1 in 1931; 4 in 1933; 2 in 1935; 2 in 1936; 2 in 1937; 1 after 1940 ("1940 後"); 1 in 1942; 1 in 1943; 2 in 1944; 4 in 1945; 4 in 1946; 2 in 1947; and 2 in 1948.[122] An additional 34 temples were used for other purposes, including 4 for hospitals, 5 for clinics, and 5 to house refugees (in 1937). Only 19 "Buddhist" temples were destroyed during wartime, far fewer than the 97 that suffered the same fate during the Taiping Rebellion. An additional 93 simply were listed using such terms as "abandoned" (*fei* 廢), "ceased to function" (*ting* 停), or "occupied" (*zhan* 佔), including 4 in the 1910s, 1 in the 1920s, 76 in the 1930s (most likely destroyed during wartime), and 12 in the 1940s (before 1949). In all, 270 temples were affected, or 23.7 percent of the total. Some of these temples ended up being rebuilt, only to suffer further devastation following CCP rule.

Those temples labeled as "Daoist" also suffered intense devastation during the Republican era. A total of 214 of the 817 such temples placed in this category were turned into schools, of which 183 were elementary schools.[123] Only three of these instances took place prior to 1898, including one case of a temple being turned into a community school (*shexue* 社學) in 1537, but later rebuilt as a temple (consider the trends Sarah Schneewind examined in her research, discussed previously). A total of 103 "Daoist" temples were turned into schools between 1911 and 1949, including 6 in 1911; 7 in 1912; 9 in 1913; 2 in 1914; 8 in 1915; 3 in 1916; 3 in 1917; 1 in 1918; 2 in 1919; 1 in 1920; 1 after 1920; 1 in 1921; 3 in 1923, 1 in 1925; 1 in 1926; 3 in 1927; 2 after 1927; 2 in 1928; 1 in 1929; 4 in 1930; 13 after the 1930s; 1 in 1931; 1 in 1932; 2 in 1933; 1 each in 1934, 1935, and 1937; 2 in 1938; 3 in 1939; 1 in 1940; 1 in 1941; 2 in 1942; 1 in 1943; 3 in 1945; 5 in 1946; and 2 in 1947.[124] A total of 41 temples were put to other uses, including 26 that were turned into township government offices (*xianggongsuo* 鄉公所; only one such instance occurred for "Buddhist" temples), while another 27 ended up being destroyed during wartime. An additional 19 were simply listed as "abandoned," "ceased to function," or "occupied," including 2 in the 1910s, 12 in the 1930s, and 6 in the 1940s. A total of 301 temples (36.8 percent) suffered some form of destruction or appropriation.

The statistical evidence in the *Overview* merely provides a broad sketch of what was going on, however. The processes of attempting to destroy urban temples could be highly complex and also tied into intricate networks of power. This was the case for the Abbey of Sagely Longevity (Shengshou An 壽聖庵), a highly popular Buddhist sacred site founded in 1861 and patronized by Huzhou 湖州 elites, including members of an organization they founded known as the Huzhou Society (Hushe 湖社). In 1928, following the successful completion of a reconstruction project, the abbey's resident monk, Disong 諦松, asked Yang Kuihou 楊奎侯 (the Huzhou banker in charge of managing the temple) for all contracts and other legal documents necessary to register the abbey with the authorities, only to learn that Yang had transferred control of the temple to the Huzhou Society. After repeated attempts to get the documents back, Disong took his case to court. Legal wrangling dragged on for over three years, accompanied by frequent accusations of corruption and other forms of malfeasance. The city and even national authorities attempted to intervene, but to no avail, and the entire incident was the subject of frequent reports in *Shenbao* 申報. In the end the monks lost their case, and control of the abbey remained in the control of Huzhou's elites until it was shut down for good in 1954.[125]

The *Overview* also tends to overlook the existence of smaller shrines built during the late-Qing and Republican eras. Some of these sacred sites are listed in a "Table of Investigations on Illicit Shrines and Heterodox Sacrifices in Shanghai City" (*Shanghaishi yinci xiesi diaochabiao* 上海市淫祠邪祀調查表), compiled in 1930 during one of the city's antisuperstition campaigns. Of the fifty-two shrines listed in this table, a total of thirty-eight were built during the Republican era, while six others date back to the reign of the Guangxu 光緒 emperor (1875–1908). None of these shrines had any property, and the vast majority were altars (*tan* 壇) dedicated to Lü Dongbin 呂洞賓 and Huang Daxian 黃大仙. These deities tended to be worshipped by members of spirit-writing groups, and it is possible that some of these shrines had links to redemptive societies.[126]

Shanghai was also a major center of "rectifying customs" (*fengsu gailiang* 風俗改良) campaigns, some of which focused on temples and their festivals.[127] In 1929, for example, the Shanghai Buddhist elite Qin Xitian 秦錫田 (1861–1940) led a campaign to forbid rituals for the City God taking a concubine.[128] However, such rituals and the festivals that often accompanied them persisted into the 1930s, as can be seen in bans enacted as part of the New Life Movement.[129] There were also attempts to abolish activities of specialists deemed to be "superstitious,"[130] most notably the spirit mediums generally referred to as *shiwu* 師巫 or *taibao* 太保, albeit accompanied by a three-month grace period in order to allow them sufficient time to find new lines of work.[131] The effectiveness of such policies has yet to be determined.

Temple destruction campaigns also were carried out with great alacrity in the urban parts of Zhejiang, which put the provincial government in a somewhat awkward position. On the one hand, it made numerous attempts to limit the construction of new temples or the repair of old ones. On the other hand, it had to respond to frequent complaints from elite groups, especially Buddhist practitioners, about overzealous acts of destruction by young intellectuals and party activists.[132] The provincial capital of Hangzhou was the site of many temple destruction campaigns, including those conducted as part of the antisuperstition or customs rectification movements. At the same time, however, many temples also were torn down or taxed out of existence in order to make way for major urban planning projects.[133] Temples in the market towns surrounding Hangzhou suffered grievously as well. In Tangqi 塘棲 (just north of Hangzhou), for example, twenty-five out of twenty-nine temples were slated for destruction, with only nine surviving into the 1940s.[134]

The impact of temple destruction campaigns varied significantly in other parts of Zhejiang. Officials and party activists in Shaoxing 紹興 went so far as to organize their own Committee for Building Schools with Temple Property (Miaochan xingxue weiyuanhui 廟產興學委員會), but the fruits of their efforts are still unclear.[135] In Dinghai 定海 County (Zhoushan 舟山), only 8 out of 146 temples were restored during the Republican era (as opposed to 29 during the late Qing period), which suggests that the campaigns might have been somewhat effective.[136] This contrasts with what happened in Wenling 溫嶺 (in Taizhou 台州, southern Zhejiang), when only 7 of the 21 elementary schools founded from 1924 to 1934 were built using temple property.[137]

As in Shanghai, temple construction movements often sparked complex conflicts of interest. This was the case in Huzhou 湖州, when, during one of the "build schools with temple properties" campaigns, a local nunnery known as the Abbey of Blessings in this Lifetime (Fuchen An 福塵庵, popularly referred to as the "little temple" or *xiaomiao* 小廟) was converted into a public school and the nuns sent home. However, much of nunnery's property was not used for the school but rented out for profit. The nuns filed a complaint, while some residents petitioned the county government to have the nunnery preserved as a historical monument (*guji* 古蹟). Their petition was rejected, but the authorities did decide to evict all of the illegal tenants.[138]

Some of the most controversial temple destruction campaigns, which also sparked frequent clashes, took place in and around the venerable port of Ningbo 寧波. Efforts to destroy these sacred sites commenced in 1929, when party activists, police, and soldiers in Ningbo, Yuyao 餘姚, and Cixi 慈谿 declared special dates for destroying deity statues, and organized troupes of students to attack local temples, starting with the Temple of the Eastern Peak (Dongyue Gong 東嶽宮). The participants in this onslaught, including KMT party members, students, and members of the local chapter of the Boy Scouts (Tongzijun 童子軍), gathered in Ningbo's Sun Yat-sen Park (Zhongshan gonguan 中山公園), where they were issued small flags inscribed with the words "eradicate superstition" (*pochu mixin* 破除迷信) and "overthrow the idols" (*dadao ouxiang* 打倒偶像). After listening to speeches by the county magistrate, mayor, and other officials, they marched to the Temple of the Eastern Peak, where, after considerable effort, they smashed its statues to smithereens.[139] The abuses that resulted from these campaigns, as well as the conflicts that ensued, prompted state attempts at reconciling the interested parties, but to no avail.[140] By 1931, the elites concerned about the extent to which the situation had deteriorated began to publish articles pointing to the positive aspects of religious values and criticizing the wanton destruction of temples without providing viable spiritual and psychological alternatives.[141]

Four years later, one of Zhejiang's most dedicated education officials, Huang Shiling 黃式陵 (1911–1951; a Hunan native who helped edit and frequently published in the *Zhejiang jiaoyu yuekan* 浙江教育月刊), wrote a five-page article describing the violence that regularly accompanied local temple destruction campaigns while also analyzing its causes and possible solutions. In this article, Huang conceded that educators had misjudged the situation and had overlooked the need to cope with local elites and the networks of power that undergirded their authority. He also appreciated the need to recognize local concerns, as well as realities on the ground such as poverty and slow economic development, not to mention thorny issues such as what to do about the religious and ritual specialists who stood to lose their livelihoods. He concluded by pointing out that the entire antisuperstition movement was both a cultural and social issue and that officials responsible for undertaking such campaigns would have to adapt at least partially to local conditions.[142]

Despite the fury they aroused, these campaigns seem to have enjoyed only a limited success. According to the highly detailed records of Ningbo's temples preserved in the Republican-era edition of the *Yinxian tongzhi* 鄞縣通志, of the 517 communal temples that had existed there prior to the twentieth century, only 57 had been turned into schools by 1935, with an additional 57 being used for government offices. Apart from 2 that had fallen into ruin and 6 that had been converted into private facilities such as guildhalls, the remaining 391 temples (over 75 percent of the total) had survived.[143]

CASE STUDY 2: WENZHOU

Similar tribulations beset the temple destruction campaigns in the treaty port of Wenzhou 溫州, with Lo Shih-chieh's doctoral dissertation convincingly demonstrating that these policies caused great disruption to local cults and festivals, but ended up doing little to change the ways in which Wenzhou natives worshipped their deities.[144] As was the case in much of China, the campaigns began in earnest during the early 1900s, with reformist officials attempting to turn local temples into schools and even imposing new taxes (such as one on oranges) in order to help pay for them, all of which served to augment tensions between the Qing state and local society.[145] One of Wenzhou's first temple destruction campaigns took place in Ruian 瑞安 County (just south of Wenzhou City), where the local magistrate, assisted by sympathetic or at least sycophantic local elites, transformed four local temples from the official register of sacrifices (*sidian* 祀典) into the first new-style schools in the county.[146] One of these elites, who also provided support for subsequent anti-superstition campaigns, was none other than the prestigious late-Qing literatus Sun Yirang 孫詒讓 (1848–1908), who also inspired a younger generation of Western-educated students to commit themselves to the causes of reform and modernization.[147] Other activists attempted to ban official worship of state cult deities such as Confucius, Guandi 關帝, and Yue Fei 岳飛, while also transforming state temples to Confucius (the Wenmiao 文廟) into Sun Yat-sen memorial shrines.[148]

As was the case in Xiaoshan and Ningbo, the pattern of students taking the lead in attempting to reform communal religious traditions persisted into the 1920s, one new wrinkle being that they had gained the assistance of KMT party leaders. One example took place in Yueqing 樂清 County (northern Wenzhou) in 1928, when a local Nationalist cadre named Chou Yuesan 仇約三 led a group of students to express their commitment to the creation of a new and modern culture by organizing a "deity demolishing troupe" (*daoshen tuan* 搗神團) with the express goal of smashing temples and the statues of deities they housed within. In one instance, this troupe even took one temple's statues of horses back to their school to rebuild as athletic equipment, while using the bell from a local Buddhist monastery for their school's clock.[149] And again, as had happened throughout other parts of China, such campaigns sparked an array of resistance tactics, including posting anonymous poems accusing officials or party members of corruption, telling stories about those who had taken part in the campaigns dying sudden and horrible deaths, bribing the police to look the other way, insisting on holding festivals even if the relevant temples or statues had been destroyed, and tearing down the new schools that had been built in place of the temples.[150]

My assistant Qi Gang 祁剛 and I are working on a statistical analysis of the impact of these campaigns on temples, beginning with Ruian County (we are also in the process of gathering data on other counties as well). One promising item that we have acquired is a 1957 survey of Ruian's "Buddhist" temples and specialists undertaken by the county's Buddhist Studies Association and presented to the local authorities.[151] Of the 340 temples covered by this survey, only 16 had been turned into schools and 26 used for other government offices (in 11 cases, the temple was allowed to coexist with the new establishment). There were many more cases of temples being taken over by individuals (71, including 3 by Daoist priests (*daoshi* 道士)), especially in areas farther from the county seat.[152] In terms of spatial features, Ruian seems similar to the Yin County case discussed previously, with more temples being turned into government offices in areas closer to the county seat. At the same time, however, there was an even distribution of temples being turned into schools (see Map 1.1). Overall, just over 63 percent (216/340) of the Ruian temples had survived intact, slightly lower than the 75 percent rate for Yin County. Qi Gang and I have just begun to analyze these data, so it will take some time to fully ascertain the factors underlying these trends.

The impact of these campaigns on Wenzhou religious specialists is even more difficult to assess, especially in light of the paucity of gazetteer and archival sources on this topic. Evidence from Ruian, while still awaiting further investigation, also suggests that at least some religious specialists were able to survive the campaigns of the Republican era. The first piece of the puzzle is the Republican-era *Draft Edition of the Ruian County Gazetteer* (*Ruian xianzhigao* 瑞安縣志稿, 1937), which contains information on a total of 843 local temples, including the amount of property in their possession and the number of religious specialists residing on their premises. These data, apparently derived from two surveys undertaken during the reign of the Jiaqing 嘉慶 emperor (1796–1820) and the early years of the Republican era, list a total of 829 such individuals (including monks and nuns, as well as male and female laypeople and temple workers). The second, a survey of all 83 of Ruian's towns and townships undertaken in 1937, lists a total of 1,942 specialists. However, it would be unwise to take these sources at face value and simply assume

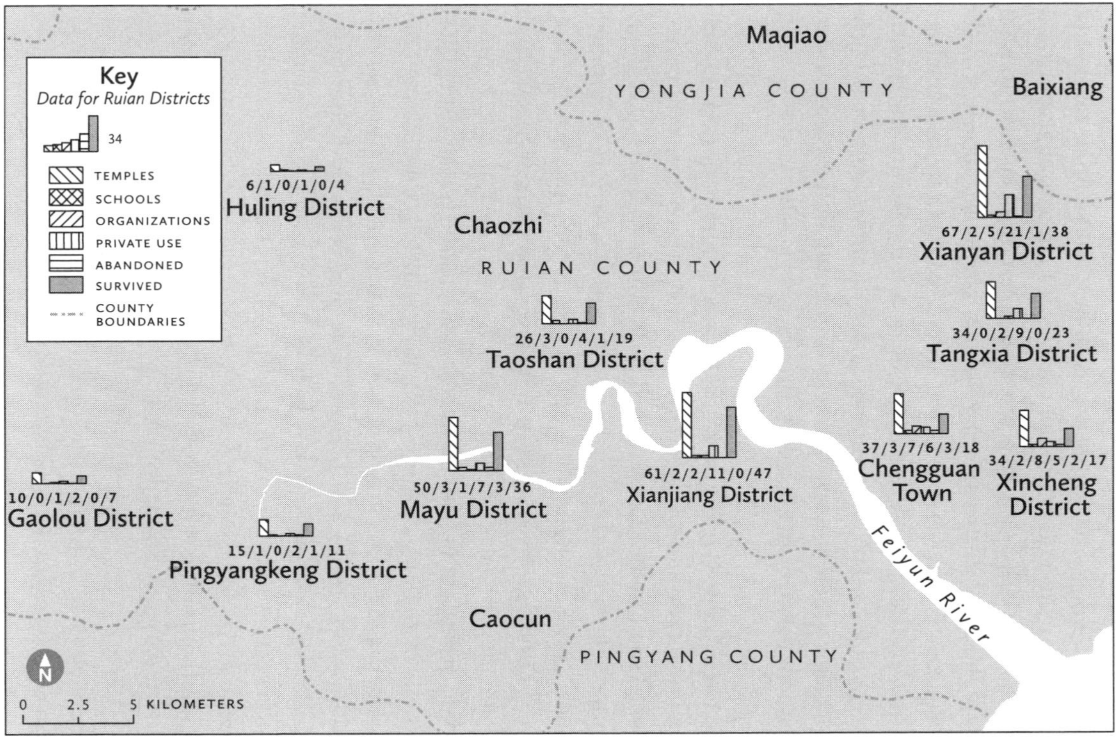

MAP 1.1: *The Fate of Temples in Ruian County, Wenzhou (1957). Based on map designed by Center for GIS, Research Center for Humanities and Social Sciences, Academia Sinica.*

that the number of religious specialists had actually doubled. The latter set of data appears to be based on a more recent and thorough survey, and additional factors such as changes in administrative districts also must be taken into account. In addition, because portions of the Ruian archives are currently in the process of being digitized, we are not yet able to double-check their accuracy.[153] Nonetheless, even after allowing for the discrepancies mentioned previously, it remains striking that the number of religious personnel living in Ruian temples does not appear to have decreased over time.

■ The evidence vividly indicates that the temple destruction campaigns of the late-Qing and Republican eras marked a significant watershed in the modern history of Chinese religions. While the imperial state had consistently attempted to assert its authority over Chinese religious life, the fifty years covered by this chapter witnessed the advent of new discourses to describe temple cults, new policies of varying effectiveness designed to regulate or extirpate them, and new actors committed to achieving these goals. In the face of these new and potentially devastating challenges, those elites, religious specialists, and worshippers who supported traditional temple cults and festivals undertook a wide range of responses as well as innovations, some of which proved more successful than others. The impact of these campaigns on Chinese religious life varied significantly from one region to another, and also in terms of whether the temples were located in urban or rural areas.

Research on religion in modern China, especially on the Republican era, is largely in its preliminary stages, and numerous questions remain to be addressed. For this research project, some of the most important are as follows:

1. *How organized were these campaigns?*
How much overlap occurred between them?

Based on what we know today, it seems clear that the "build

schools with temple property," "eradicating superstitions," and "rectifying customs" campaigns were not structured, organized movements (with the possible exception of the antisuperstition campaigns undertaken between 1927 and 1937). Nonetheless, they did exhibit considerable historical continuity in terms of both discourse and practice. The discourse of using temples to build schools was a constant presence in Chinese history, as was that of rectifying customs. As for the term "superstition," while it was a neologism taken from the West via Japan, it was also used alongside the traditional labels that the state and elites applied to unacceptable religious traditions, most notably "illicit cults."[154]

In addition, considerable overlap between these movements occurred. Research by Zheng Guo 鄭國 reveals that activists promoting the "eradicating superstitions" campaigns also viewed one of their goals as "rectifying customs," while those advocating in favor of the latter campaign classified "build schools with temple property" as a form of "rectifying temples" (*miaoyu gailiang* 廟宇改良).[155] Tai Shuangqiu and those officials and activists who supported his cause also viewed the eradication of all superstitions as constituting an integral component of the using temples to build schools campaign. Such forms of overlap should not cause us to overlook the qualitative differences in all three campaigns, however. In general, the "build schools with temple property" campaigns tended to be largely peaceful, regardless of whether they were undertaken in urban or rural areas. Antisuperstition campaigns often proved to be more violent and largely urban in nature, in part because they attracted the support of a younger generation of students inspired by revolutionary ideology. As for customs reform movements, these covered the broadest range of social and cultural phenomena (including etiquette, marital and mortuary rites, geomancy, and so on), meaning that religion was only one of many goals they espoused, and one not always at the top of their list of priorities. However, it is essential to recognize that the one common denominator linking all three of these movements was the vital importance of temples, both as material and symbolic resources.[156]

2. *To what extent were these campaigns carried out in non-Han parts of China?*

I began considering this issue while undertaking my Academia Sinica Investigator Award, which examines the issue of change and continuity in Miao 苗 and Tujia 土家 religious life in Western Hunan (Xiangxi 湘西) during the past century.[157] Viewed from the perspective of discourse, it is clear that terms such as "superstition" were applied throughout Hunan beginning in the late-Qing period and throughout the Republican era.[158] This was also the case in Western Hunan, as can be seen in documents that used the term to describe religious practices ranging from festivals to divination to the employment of local religious specialists.[159] In addition, the provincial official Zeng Jiwu 曾繼梧 (1878–1944) labeled a wide range of Miao and Tujia religious practices as superstitious, as did other contemporary observers such as Wang Jinghuan 王靜寰 and Yang Lixing 楊力行, as well as the Chinese missionary Chen Xinchuan 陳心傳 (fl. 1917–1937); these individuals also used other derogatory terms such as "backward."[160] Such terminology has persisted in CCP official publications to the present day.[161]

These were not the only terms that could be applied to Miao or Tujia religious culture, however. When some of Academia Sinica's founding scholars, Ling Chunsheng 凌純聲 (1902–1981) and Rui Yifu 芮逸夫 (1899–1991), undertook fieldwork in this very area, they chose to rely on Bronislaw Malinowski's (1884–1942) dichotomy between "religion" (*zongjiao* 宗教) and "magic" (*wushu* 巫術). This was also the case for one of their partners in the field, a Miao elite named Shi Qigui 石啟貴 (1896–1959), who only applied the term "superstition" to a very narrow range of ritual specialists.[162] A new generation of scholars and local experts is becoming increasingly wary of using such pejorative language, although there remains a tendency to rely on such terms as "shamanistic religion" (*wujiao* 巫教) or "primitive religion" (*yuanshi zongjiao* 原始宗教).[163]

As for actual practice, temples appear to have been far less common in the Miao areas of Western Hunan, with religious life centering on rites performed by religious specialists in worshippers' homes or small shrines that tended to be overlooked in government investigations. For example, one survey of temples conducted in Baojing in 1931 identified only eleven such sites. Accordingly, antisuperstition campaigns in this region tended to center on forcing religious specialists to abandon their trades and destroy their ritual implements. Perhaps even more important, KMT (and subsequent CCP) policies toward China's non-Han peoples gave considerable leeway to indigenous cultural traditions, including religious ones, with many practices that would have been labeled "superstition" in Han areas being allowed to exist and even gaining protection as forms of "ethnic customs" (*minzu fengsu* 民族風俗). Current state discourse and policy have led to non-Han religious traditions being defined as acceptable customs belonging to the category of "intangible cultural heritage" (*feiwuzhi wenhua yichan* 非物質文化遺產).[164]

3. *How do the campaigns of 1898–1948 compare to those undertaken after 1949?*

While this chapter has focused mainly on KMT policies, it would be remiss not to note the importance of CCP policies enacted in the areas of China that it controlled prior to assuming control over all of China in 1949.[165] While New Culture Movement spokespersons such as Chen Duxiu 陳獨秀 (1879–1942) had taken extreme secularist positions (such as arguing that religion would disappear following advances in technology and modern life), during its formative years the CCP proved willing to establish alliances with a wide range of religious movements in order to achieve its goals. The CCP made every effort not to needlessly alienate peasant support while also working to establish its own grassroots associations that would replace temple cults.[166] By the 1940s, however, many religious groups who sided with the KMT spread apocalyptic rumors about impending Communist rule, and the CCP responded by labeling such groups as "reactionary secret societies" (*fandong huidaomen* 反動會道門) and ruthlessly persecuting them during the 1950s. In contrast, communal religious traditions proved to be a lower priority and were less actively suppressed during the early 1950s; there was even a minor revival in some areas, with temples being rebuilt.[167] All of this changed during the Great Leap Forward (Dayaojin 大躍進; 1958–1961) and Cultural Revolution (Wenhua dageming 文化大革命; 1966–1976), which featured the wholesale destruction of temples and the persecution of religious specialists as "rightists" during "political education" sessions. Throughout most of China, the result was that most religious activity came to an end, with temples becoming shells of their former glory and restoration efforts not taking place until the reforms launched during the late 1970s.[168]

In many areas of southern China, including Wenzhou, elite support proved vital to the preservation of local temple cults, and the ambiguous stance of these elites toward traditional religious life remained apparent even in writings compiled after 1949. One powerful example of these sentiments may be found in a lengthy account (two volumes exceeding one hundred thousand Chinese characters) entitled *Historical Materials on Wenzhou's Old Customs* (*Wenzhou jiusu shiliao* 温州舊俗史料), produced in response to a nationwide summons issued by the CCP government in 1959. On the one hand, such works asserted that "superstitions pertaining to gods and ghosts have hindered social development"; on the other hand, they acknowledged the positive function temple cults could make toward sustaining moral order and "checking improper behavior." In short, such elite writings but accomodated state discourse but also strove to manipulate it in order to advance local agendas.[169]

Based on the limited amounts of data collected so far, it seems that in the major metropolises such as Shanghai the campaigns after 1949 may have caused much more damage, but far fewer temples ended up being converted into schools. Evidence for such trends may be found in the *Comprehensive Overview of Shanghai Religion* (*Shanghai zongjiao tonglan* 上海宗教通覽), which, as noted earlier in the chapter, states that 2,186 temples still existed in Shanghai and its environs in 1949. However, a survey undertaken in 1951 recorded that the number of temples had plummeted to just 624 (this figure may include only the larger temples that had registered with the authorities). By 1961, just over 500 temples were still standing, and only 220 remained as sites where rituals were performed. The launching of the Cultural Revolution in 1966 spelled the end for all of these sites except the Jade Buddha Monastery (Yufo Si 玉佛寺), and even after the enactment of more liberal policies by the 1980s, only 57 temples (47 "Buddhist" and 10 "Daoist") have been officially recognized and allowed to reopen.[170]

Exactly what happened to those temples that were destroyed after 1949? According to the *Overview*, only 20 of the "Buddhist" temples were turned into schools, including 1 in 1949, 3 after 1949, 3 in 1950, 1 in 1951, 1 in 1953, 2 in 1957, 2 in 1958, 1 in 1960, 1 in 1962, 1 in 1968, 2 in 1971, and 2 in 1973. An additional 25 were turned into other buildings such as government offices or police or fire stations, including 3 after 1949; 3 during the first years after Liberation; 10 during the 1950s; 6 during the Cultural Revolution; and 3 after 1977. In sharp contrast, however, a total of 475 temples are listed as having been "abandoned" (*fei* 廢), "ceased to function" (*ting* 停), or "occupied" (*zhan* 佔), including 1 in 1949, 368 after 1949 ("1949後"), 70 in the 1950s, 26 in the 1960s, and 10 in the 1970s. An additional 21 temples were "torn down" (*chai* 拆). In short, Shanghai's "Buddhist" temples suffered grievously after 1949, with 541 or 47.6 percent of the total being destroyed or otherwise appropriated, but only a minor percentage ended up being turned into schools, all of which differs strikingly from what had taken place during the late Qing and Republican eras.

A sizeable percentage of "Daoist" temples also suffered after 1949 (197 or 24.1 percent). A total of 88 were turned into schools, considerably more than had been the case for the Republican era. These instances of conversion included 8 in 1949, 4 after 1949, 6 after Liberation, 5 in 1950, 5 in 1951, 4 in 1952, 2 after 1952, 2 in 1953, 2 in 1954, 3 in 1956, 4 in 1957, 11 in 1958, 4 in 1959, 5 in 1960, 4 in 1964, 2 in 1965, 10 in 1966, and 1 each in 1968, 1970, 1971, 1974, 1976, and 1977.[171] A total of 10 were turned into other buildings, while 66 were listed as having been abandoned, ceased to function, or occupied, including 6 in 1949, 4 after 1949, 13 after Liberation, 21 in the 1950s, 19 in the 1960s, and 3 in the 1970s. Another 33 were "closed down" (*guanbi* 關閉), almost all during the 1950s and 1960s. Only 10 "Daoist" temples had reopened by 1995.

When we consider the fate of those temples for which we have location data, some rather striking patterns emerge (see Table 1.2 and Map 1.2). Of the 1,007 temples for which we have such information that still existed in the Shanghai area by 1898 (the starting date of the "Fifty Years" project), only 67 (6.7 percent) had survived by 1958 (when even more rigorous temple destruction campaigns were launched), with the vast majority being turned into schools (280 or 27.8 percent), used by other organizations (82 or 8.1 percent), destroyed during warfare (22 or 2.2 percent), or totally shut down because of government policies, most notably in the years 1930, 1949, and 1956 (556 or 55.3 percent).[172] In terms of spatial patterns of destruction, the largest numbers of Shanghai temples that ended up being utterly destroyed were located in the city's center (414 of 568 in Shanghai County, at a rate of 72.9 percent), with only a few ending up being used as schools (76 of 568, or 13.3 percent). In contrast, temples located in Shanghai's suburban areas seem to have been able to avoid

TABLE 1.2. The Fate of Shanghai's Temples (1958)

County	*Temples*	*Schools*	*Organizations*	*Warfare*	*Abandoned*	*Survived*
Shanghai*	568	76	36	6	414	36
Jiading	182	53	21	10	93	5
Songjiang	25	9	5	4	3	4
Qingpu	19	15	2	0	0	2
Jinshan	47	16	12	1	10	8
Chongming	19	11	2	0	2	4
Baoshan	31	15	2	0	14	0
Fengxian	21	20	1	0	0	0
Nanhui	57	44	1	1	8	3
Chuansha	38	21	0	0	12	5
Total:	1,007	280	82	22	556	67

* Includes the ten municipal districts and Shanghai County listed in Table 1.1.

total destruction, with their property and other resources (which might have escaped unscathed during the early campaigns) apparently being used for communal needs. For example, in Qingpu 青浦 County, 15 of 19 temples were converted into schools (78.9 percent), with none being utterly destroyed, but only 2 surviving completely intact. Similar data exist for Nanhui 南匯 County: 44 of 57 (77.2 percent) turned into schools, 8 intact. The figures for Fengxian 奉賢 County are even more extreme: 20 of 21 (95.2 percent) turned into schools, 0 intact. But more balanced patterns can be found in counties such as Jinshan 金山: 16 of 47 (34 percent) turned into schools, 8 intact; and Chongming 崇明: 11 of 19 (57.9 percent) turned into schools, 4 intact. In short, while

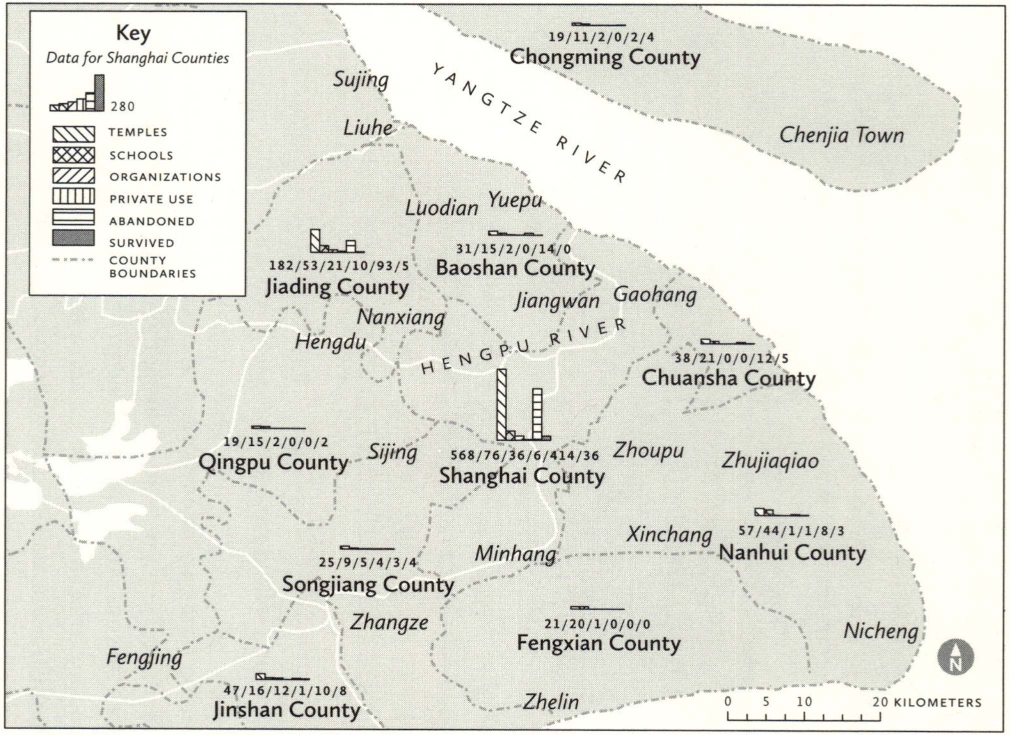

MAP 1.2: *The Fate of Temples in Shanghai (1958). Based on map designed by Center for GIS, Research Center for Humanities and Social Sciences, Academia Sinica.*

temples throughout the Shanghai area suffered grievously during the time period covered by this project (1898–1948), those located outside of urban centers had a greater chance of surviving at least partially intact.

When compared to the other case studies covered in this chapter, Shanghai's rate of temple survival proves significantly lower than those for Yin County (77.9 percent, albeit based on 1935 data) and Ruian (more comparable because of the 1957 survey date and having a temple survival rate of 63.5 percent). On the one hand, this might be because state policies were enforced more thoroughly closer to urban areas. On the other hand, the support of local elites could prove critical to a temple's survival, and as the data in this paper reveal, such support was at the ready throughout much of Zhejiang during the late Qing and Republican eras. Wenzhou elites also made every effort to preserve temple cults and other aspects of traditional culture after 1949. One example is the 1959 *Historical Materials on Wenzhou's Old Customs* discussed previously. While this was a state-initiated project, with one of its goals being to identify local customs for subsequent destruction, the compilation of this text provided an arena in which Wenzhou elites could engage in a form of creative adaptation to CCP hegemony,[173] while also expressing a strong sense of local identity. One might even conjecture that the roots of the religious revival in Wenzhou and other parts of China today can be traced in part to the elite discourses described in this chapter.[174]

The impact of the temple destruction campaigns already described appears to differ significantly from those campaigns that involved the temporary appropriation of these sites by the authorities during times of political transition. One striking case study may be found in the first decade of Japanese colonial rule over Taiwan (1895–1905), when the authorities appropriated only 226 (12 percent) of the island's registered temples. Of these, the highest rates of appropriation involved temples being used as military barracks (69 temples, or 4 percent of the total) or police stations (63, or 3 percent). Only 27 temples (just over 1 percent) ended up being converted into schools. Moreover, many temples were returned to their ritual communities once the colonial state had consolidated its rule over Taiwan.

The relationship between the state and Chinese religious groups continues to be one of contestation and adaptation, with the fate of temple cults and festivals remaining uncertain. In Taiwan, the democratization processes initiated during the 1980s have led to temple cults becoming more than passive observers of government policy, as they now play important roles in furthering local interests and asserting communal identity.[175] Moreover, data in my recent book *Divine Justice* demonstrate the roles temples play in local elections as places where candidates take oaths of innocence (and at times even behead chickens) in order to prove that they have not engaged in vote buying, while also noting that police and prosecutors worship judicial deities when dealing with crimes that prove difficult to solve.[176]

In contrast with Taiwan, the Chinese government has allowed only a few select urban temples to reopen, mostly Buddhist and Daoist monasteries that serve as tourist sites and symbols of intangible cultural heritage, with religious practice in cities becoming increasingly centered on vegetarian restaurants, bookstores, and the Internet. Temple, festivals, and ritual practices still exist and even flourish in some suburban and rural areas, but their continued survival depends on delicate negotiations between the state and local communities that largely center on their being labeled as tourist sites or intangible cultural heritage (as opposed to the traditional tactic of absorbing temples into the state cult or register of sacrifices).[177] As Adam Chau observes in his introduction to the edited volume *Religion in Contemporary China*, the interaction between the Chinese state and various religious groups has shifted from one of confrontation to that of negotiation centering on the "politics of legitimation," with legitimation being achieved by means of two different strategies: 1) "getting into the party fold" (becoming recognized as a religion or *zongjiao*), and 2) "creative dissimulation" (practicing religion but disguising such activities as something more acceptable to the state such as folklore or intangible cultural heritage. Chau also points to the importance of local activists who gained power after decollectivization stripped the authority from production teams, particularly the ways in which they work both to legitimize religious practice and to expand the space for such activities.[178] Kenneth Dean and Zheng Zhenman conclude that, because of their importance in communal life, many temples end up functioning as "China's second government," with elites adapting state institutions and ideas while also constituting new regimes of power from the bottom up.[179] As we continue to observe and assess the religious revival in China today, we need to pay close attention to the tensions and agendas that shape the interaction between all three sides of the previously mentioned triangle (members of the central, provincial, and local officialdom, different groups of elites, and various religious specialists), as well as the real needs they represent.

2

TIME AND A WORD

NEW FORMS OF RELIGIOUS PUBLISHING

While many temple cults were teetering on the edge of elimination during the fifty-year period covered by this study, the same era witnessed astounding growth in the realm of religious publishing. Previous scholarship on the history of modern Chinese printing techniques and the mass media has tended to overlook their impact on indigenous Chinese religious movements.[1] However, one key aspect of Chinese religion during the Republican era was its highly public nature, with believers using various forms of the mass media to transmit their views. Inspired by the example of using the printed word in Christian proselytizing, yet also drawing on the indigenous Chinese traditions of publicizing morality and philanthropy, numerous Republican-era elites devoted themselves to using the mass media for the transmission of Chinese religious traditions. This chapter focuses on five main issues: 1) the ways in which religious groups strove to publicize their beliefs and practices in mainstream outlets (books, newspapers, magazines, radio stations, and so on), 2) the types of texts they chose to publish and the categories used to classify religious knowledge, 3) the messages contained in these media, 4) their intended and actual audiences, and 5) the overall historical significance of these phenomena, including late imperial precedents and the ways in which they continue to shape Chinese religious life today.

RELIGIOUS PUBLISHING IN MODERN CHINA: AN OVERVIEW

While handwritten manuscripts consistently have proven to be the main means of transmitting liturgical manuals and other forms of esoteric knowledge,[2] the printing of scriptures and other doctrinal or ritual texts became a core activity for Chinese religious groups as early as the Tang dynasty (618–907 CE). The earliest Chinese printed book for which we have a clear date is a Buddhist scripture, and the various editions of the Buddhist Canon were among the most mammoth publication projects in early modern history.[3] Printed texts continued to shape the development of Chinese religions during the late imperial era,[4] especially among sectarian movements. Some sources describe sects printing hundreds of morality books (*shanshu* 善書) and precious scrolls (*baojuan* 寶卷),[5] while state crackdowns on these groups resulted in the confiscation of thousands of texts, both handwritten and printed.[6] Be that as it may, during the late imperial era commercial printers played only a minor role in religious publishing, choosing instead to publish texts that possessed inherent market value such as novels, textbooks, manuals for examination candidates, and so on. Even when commercial printers did choose to take on a religious project, they tended to do so only on a commission basis, not as a regular activity.[7]

All this changed during the modern era, when religious publishing was transformed into a major commercial enterprise. During the late Qing and early Republican eras, the adoption of Western printing techniques such as metal movable type made it possible to print high-quality texts on a much greater scale yet at lower cost, all of which had proven impossible using xylographic systems. Chinese religious publishing also benefited from the introduction of stone-based lithographic printing and especially the cylinder printing machine (brought to China in 1847 by Western missionaries), which in six months could print the entire yearly output of hand-operated presses. Improved speed of production, quality of products, and economies of scale were augmented further by the implementation of a modern postal system, which allowed publishers in urban centers such as Beijing and Shanghai to exert their influence in a broad range of regional markets. These innovations made a profound impact on the history of modern Chinese religions by sparking the growth of new forms of religious print culture that consisted of mass-produced books and periodicals, often written in the vernacular (*baihua* 白話) and accompanied by illustrations (*tu* 圖). Such works were produced by new organizations, namely, modern religious publishing houses that depended on lay support and established wide-ranging distribution networks to market their products. By the Republican era, nearly all major religious organizations and their leaders were involved in publishing enterprises.[8]

The development of religious publishing in modern China was in large part because of the influence of the Christian missionaries who worked in China during the eighteenth and nineteenth centuries (for more on the Christian impact, see chapter 1). Mindful of the impact that printing had made on the Reformation in Europe, missionaries such as Robert Morrison (1782–1834) of the London Missionary Society took the lead in promoting modern forms of religious publishing in China. One of the first Christian periodicals was the *Eastern Western Monthly Magazine*, established by Karl Friedrich August Gutzlaff (1803–1851) in Canton during the years 1833 to 1838, followed by the *China Serial* in Hong Kong from 1853 to 1856. Beginning in the late 1850s, however, Shanghai became host to over 50 percent of the Chinese religious press, starting with works such as the *Shanghai Serial* (1857–1858). Numerous other Christian magazines came into being during the 1860s and 1870s, one of the most important of which was the *Chinese Scientific Magazine* (founded in 1876). Of all these publications, however, by far the most influential was the *Church News*, founded by Young J. Allen (1836–1907)[9] in 1868 and renamed *The Chinese Globe Magazine* in 1876. This periodical, which was published continuously until Allen's death, helped to shape the lives and thoughts of many Chinese elites. Printer missionaries such as Walter Henry Medhurst (1796–1857), Samuel Dyer (1804–1843), and William Gamble (1830–1886) used modern publishing techniques to further the efforts of the London Missionary Society Press and the American Presbyterian Mission Press, organizations that quickly gained the attention of many Chinese urban elites.[10] These men and the organizations they founded had a profound effect on Chinese religious publishing, with their achievements actively being emulated by non-Christian elites who also continued to adhere to the ideals and values expressed by late imperial publishers.[11] A number of other foreign religions also pursued publishing enterprises in China, including Islam and Judaism, but their endeavors will not be discussed here.[12] One other topic that merits further exploration is the impact of new technologies on religious organizations in modern Japan (including Christian revivalist groups), especially their innovative use of new media and visual technologies (art, large-scale exhibitions, photos, and even documentary and narrative movies) in order to promote their mission.[13]

The fifty years covered by this study were marked by the publication of astounding numbers of religious books and periodicals. In the case of Buddhism, scholars have estimated that between 150 and 300 Buddhist periodicals were published during the Republican era,[14] with Shanghai serving as a leading center of such activity. This was also the case for scriptures and other books. For example, Gregory Scott's "Digital Bibliography of Modern Chinese Buddhism" (Jindai Zhongguo Fojiao dianzi shumu 近代中國佛教電子書目; http://bib.buddhiststudies.net/) has a total of 2,051 entries, with 1,021 of these works (nearly 50 percent) being published in Shanghai, including 9 for the Illuminating Goodness Bookstore, the latest being from 1947. These texts were produced by numerous Buddhist publishing houses sponsored by lay elites, most notably the Society for Propagating the Dharma

(Honghuashe 弘化社; founded in 1930) and Shanghai Buddhist Books (Shanghai Foxue shuju 上海佛學書局; literally "Shanghai Buddhist Bookstore"; founded ca. 1929–1930). Buddhist proselytizing was not limited to the printed word, however, and also included the circulation of Buddhist records and broadcasts by Buddhist radio stations.[15] Such trends continued up to the CCP's rule over China in 1949, with organizations such as the Deer Park Buddhist Study Society (Luyuan foxuehui 鹿苑佛學會) buying ad space in Shanghai's major newspapers from 1946 to 1947 to publicize Buddhist teachings and try to convert readers directly. This method was much discussed in contemporary Buddhist periodicals, with leaders claiming that such methods were especially effective among China's youth.[16] Gregory Scott has completed a doctoral thesis on how these new techniques of printing and distribution transformed both the ways in which monastic and lay Buddhist elites propagated new ideals and values, as well as the criteria they used to define their own religious traditions.[17]

Scholars currently researching the development of modern Buddhist publishing are grappling with a number of thorny methodological issues, starting with the question of whether new forms of religious media modified or even transformed the messages contained in Buddhist texts. In a recent conference paper (and his doctoral thesis research), Scott argues that mechanized printing not only enabled the production of cheap, high-quality texts on a scale that had been impossible using traditional techniques, but also reshaped the legacy of Buddhist thought and practice, particularly in terms of the types of texts placed at the core of modern Buddhism, as opposed to those that ended up being marginalized.[18] In addition, recent research by J. Brooks Jessup maintains that the collaboration among Buddhist publishers may have promoted national integration and shared discourse in this religious movement (a phenomenon that also influenced other religious groups).[19]

An equally nettlesome issue centers on the intended and

actual audiences of modern Buddhist printed texts. Because as many as two-thirds of such titles continued to be canonical scriptures, religious publishers soon realized that new types of texts were needed to be able to meet the needs of lay readers. One example involves the lay Buddhist exegete, physician, and polymath Ding Fubao 丁福保 (Ding Zhongyou 丁仲祐, 1874–1952), who devoted five years (1918–1922) to producing a series of books entitled *Buddhist Studies Collectanea* (*Foxue congshu* 佛學叢書). This series was especially noteworthy for including annotated scriptures that explained complex doctrinal concepts, as well as reference tools for lay readers such as dictionaries of Buddhist terminology. The series became highly popular and was regularly reprinted during the Republican era. Other religious publishers imitated Ding's effort by producing their own "books for beginners" and other reference works that attempted to simplify Buddhist subjects. Overall, the most popular Buddhist works appear to have been noncanonical books produced by modern authors and editors that were intended for a mass market of general readers, especially vernacular and illustrated works.[20]

The scholarship discussed in the previous paragraphs has achieved important breakthroughs in terms of demonstrating how Buddhism became an integral facet of modern Chinese public life, yet is somewhat limited in scope because of its exclusion of other religious traditions. One reason for this limitation may be that far less work has been done about the media's impact on non-Buddhist groups during this time period. One of the most important accomplishments to date is Liu Xun 劉迅's recent book on Chen Yingning 陳攖寧 (1880–1969) and lay Daoist circles in Shanghai, which describes the role of journals such as the *Immortals' Way Monthly* (*Xiandao yuebao* 仙道月報) and the *Biweekly to Promote the Good* (*Yangshan banyuekan* 揚善半月刊). Liu's research reveals that Daoist elites such as Chen and his colleagues viewed journals as a vital means of attracting popular support, and made every effort to improve communication between themselves and their readers by designing their journals to be more palatable to a general readership, including the introduction of new columns and letters to the editor. Their success can be seen in the fact that thousands of copies of these journals circulated throughout Chinese communities, including as far away as Manila, being distributed in large part by means of mail-order subscriptions, with subscribers allowing family and friends to borrow copies for their own use, which further enhanced the impact of these texts. All in all, new mass media such as journals proved essential for publicizing self-cultivation techniques that originally belonged to the private realm, and doing so in ways that could attract new converts, solidify bonds between practitioners, and overcome gender barriers.[21]

As in the case of Buddhism, books proved as important as journals for Daoist publishers, with renowned enterprises such as the Yihuatang 翼化堂 (literally "Hall of Assisting in Transformations") and the DanDao kejinghui 丹道刻經會 (Society for Carving Daoist and Alchemic Scripture), as well as the Qingyuntan 青雲壇 (Blue Cloud Altar) located in Beijing, printing works that contributed to the formation and maintenance of connections among Daoist monastic communities and lay Daoist practitioners, and even to the spread of nationalist discourse in the face of Japanese aggression. Different types of texts were produced for a range of intended audiences and featured different strategies for reaching them. In just one example, in early 1935 the Yihuatang published four different series of books that treated the subject of Daoist learning and inner alchemy (*neidan* 內丹). The first, entitled *The Little Daoist Learning Series* (*Daoxue xiaocongshu* 道學小叢書), featured five titles that had been transformed into primers for all interested readers as a result of extensive editing and annotation by Chen Yingning and other Daoist elites. While the second set of books (*The Daoist Learning Series* or *Daoxue congshu* 道學叢書) centered on two rare inner alchemy texts produced for more skilled adepts, the third (*Little*

Daoist Learning for Women or *Nüzi Daoxue xiaocongshu* 女子道學小叢書) was aimed exclusively at female practitioners and also featured extensive editing and annotation. The final series, entitled *The Collection of the Immortals' Way* (*Xian Dao congshu* 仙道叢書), consisted of two works by Chen that treated the historical, doctrinal, and technical facets of Daoist inner alchemy. Liu Xun's research is especially important for noting the tension between public and private in Daoist publishing, with works such as the series described previously both promoting Daoism to the general public and also stressing the value of intimate personal experience for individual practitioners.[22]

A few scholars, most notably Fan Chunwu 范純武, Wang Jianchuan 王見川, and Yau Chi-on 游子安, have begun to assess the media's impact on sectarian movements.[23] On the one hand, redemptive societies and spirit-writing associations (often referred to as "phoenix halls" or *luantang* 鸞堂) in China, Taiwan, and overseas Chinese communities used modern printing techniques effectively to publicize the morality books they produced.[24] On the other hand, these groups also made use of newspapers and periodicals to publicize their religious ideals and philanthropic deeds (see the case study of the Illuminating Goodness Bookstore that follows).

Highly useful but somewhat skewed information on these trends may be found in Rudolf Löwenthal's *The Religious Periodical Press in China*, compiled in 1940 for the Synodal Commission in China.[25] Based on a series of articles written in the course of undertaking fieldwork, surveys, and questionnaires during the 1920s and 1930s, this work provides valuable insights into the state of religious publishing in Republican China, albeit limited to the realm of religious periodicals. In terms of Buddhist journals, *The Religious Periodical Press* identified 155 works, of which only 61 still were being published. Prices for these journals ranged from 1 to 45 cents per copy or 50 cents to 4 dollars per year, with the circulation figures averaging 1,000 to 3,000 copies per issue, with the exception of publications such as *Sound of the Tide* (*Haichaoyin* 海潮音; published in China from 1920 to 1949 before moving operations to Taiwan), which totaled about 20,000 copies per month. Approximately 2.5 million copies of these Buddhist periodicals were published on an annual basis, with each copy being read by an estimated 5 to 10 individuals (some subscribed to more than one journal, while others shared journals among friends and fellow worshippers).

Periodicals identified as "Daoist" tended to be published by new religious movements currently referred to as "redemptive societies" (see chapter 1).[26] *The Religious Periodical Press* lists forty-one such publications, of which only eighteen still existed, the oldest being the *Journal of Moral Learning* (*Daode xuezhi* 道德學誌; 1917–1918) and the [*Red*] *Swastika Daily News* (*Wanzi riri xinwen* 卍字日日新聞; 1926–1937). These periodicals cost between 1.5 and 15 cents per copy or 30 cents to 5 yuan per year, with their circulation largely limited to initiated elites. While print runs for more popular periodicals could reach two thousand copies per issue, most totaled only a few hundred, for an overall circulation of between five thousand and ten thousand copies. Actual Daoist publications included those published by Chen Yingning (discussed previously), as well as the *Daoism Quarterly* (*Daojiao jikan* 道教季刊; founded in 1932) and the *Daoism Monthly* (*Daojiao yuekan* 道教月刊; founded in Shanghai in 1936).

The Religious Periodical Press also provides data for a total of twenty-one "Confucian" periodicals founded from 1913 to 1936. Most were published by associations dedicated to the worship of Confucius, and all were defunct by the time Löwenthal's team was conducting its survey. These works proved to be more expensive (10 to 35 cents per copy or \$1.80 to \$5 per year, with prohibitive advertising rates of \$15 to \$100 per page) and possessed limited circulation (mostly educated elites; approximately two hundred to five hundred copies per issue at most). In addition, a total of thirty-six Jewish and one hundred Islamic periodicals were published during the time period covered by the Löwenthal survey.

Overall, *The Religious Periodical Press* identified 400 religious periodicals still in circulation by 1939, including 211 Protestant, 74 Catholic, 61 Buddhist, 39 Islamic, 17 Daoist, and 2 Confucian (both founded after 1936). China's religious press was distributed throughout 21 provinces and 103 cities. However, the authors of this survey data also noted that these periodicals had a limited impact because of that era's poor literacy rates, unreliable communications networks, and low purchasing power of the populace. They also pointed out that the existence of many publications depended on the efforts of individual elites. If one key figure were to die or move away, the periodical's continuity could be at risk. Other publishing enterprises had to cope with labor disputes, while the outbreak of the Second Sino-Japanese War in the fall of 1937 and the subsequent disruptions of China's postal networks severely hindered the journals' circulation. Some Chinese publications (including a few religious ones) were able to survive in Japanese-controlled territories (especially those that were at least partially owned by Japanese), and their contents also addressed such issues as the temple destruction campaigns described in chapter 1.[27]

When it came to publishing religious books and periodicals, religious publishers faced a number of challenges in attempting to establish a viable business model. One key issue was whether to print books or journals. Conventional wisdom maintains that journals were essential for Buddhists, but they appear to have been more secondary for Daoist groups and redemptive societies. The latter groups look weak when we focus on journals, but when it came to book distribution, their importance appears overwhelming. Such arguments are not without merit, especially for the Buddhist magazines previously mentioned, which were printed using a newspaper format, had low costs, and attracted numerous subscribers. These periodicals encouraged active reader participation by including local reports from Buddhists around the country, personal accounts of miraculous events, and question and answer dialogues (*dawen* 答問) between authors and readers.

However, journals also shaped the development of modern Daoist groups and redemptive societies. Liu Xun's research, discussed earlier in the chapter, reveals that Daoist publications were an integral component of modern China's public space which contributed to the formation and maintenance of connections between and among monastic communities and lay practitioners, allowed interaction between authors and readers in the form of letter exchanges, and even participated in the spread of nationalist discourse in the face of Japanese aggression.[28] Moreover, while recent work on redemptive societies confirms their reliance on scriptural and liturgical texts, as well as leaders' autobiographical accounts, there is also ample evidence for the importance of journals such as the *Morality Magazine* (*Daode zazhi* 道德雜誌) and the *Morality Monthly* (*Daode yuekan* 道德月刊).[29]

A related problem was how to generate sufficient revenue to cover the costs of publishing religious texts. Such costs could be substantial. In one instance noted in *The Religious Periodical Press*, the 1916 initiation of publishing operations for the previously mentioned *Journal of Moral Learning* required the Morality Society to invest $4,705 for printing machinery, $3,800 for paper, and $2,030 for printing costs. Funds came from advertisements ($12 per page), subscriptions (2.5 cents per issue; 75 cents per year), and especially from membership fees and donations.[30] This problem was exacerbated further because most religious publishers were reluctant to charge exorbitant rates for their works. In the case of the Yihuatang, for example, managers charged only a minimal price or subsidy (*jintie* 津貼) to cover the printing and labor costs (postage often cost extra). These works could then be purchased wholesale by philanthropists throughout China, who usually distributed them free of charge.[31] Religious publishers also could choose to sell their works for a relatively high price, but use most of the proceeds for charitable enterprises. In one such instance, in 1921 the Jinan 濟南 (Shandong) branch of the Society of the Way (Daoyuan 道院) marketed ten thousand copies of a religious text entitled *True Scripture of the Shanghai Rescuing Life Association* (*Shanghai Jishenghui zhenjing* 上海濟生會真經) for $2 per copy.[32] Apart from 20 cents to cover printing costs and 40 cents for society-related expenses (*yuanfei* 院費), the rest of the revenue raised from selling this text was to be used for disaster relief efforts.[33]

Buddhist publishers often proved highly adept at raising the necessary funds. For example, Brooks Jessup's research on Shanghai Buddhist Books shows that its leaders raised $10,000 from the sale of one thousand shares of stock and established a board of directors. However, they encountered difficulties attracting investors after its level of capitalization stabilized at $50,000, which prompted them to collect donations for an endowment fund that generated interest. Buddhist publishers also successfully challenged conventional wisdom about distributing religious works for free as an act of merit by selling their books to the reading public, maintaining that this strategy made more sense commercially and also reached people who were truly interested in their contents. Shanghai Buddhist Books even took the initiative in founding a book club (reading association) for morality books (*zengyue shanshuhui* 贈閱善書會), the members of which signed up to pay for the regular delivery of its various publications. Buddhist publishers also came up with the idea of selling religious works to research libraries (starting with the Buddhist Canon (Tripiṭaka, *Dazangjing* 大藏經), which was imitated by the publishers of the Daoist Canon (*Daozang* 道藏). This reveals a combination of commerce and philanthropy, with some Buddhist elites arguing that investments in religious publishing helped accumulate merit.[34]

Buddhist publishers used similar marketing strategies for

their periodicals, with Shanghai Buddhist Books distributing three leading journals of the Republican era. Apart from the renowned monthly magazine *Sound of the Tide*, it also published 43 seasonal issues of the *World Buddhist Householder Grove Magazine* (*Shijie Fojiao jushilin linkan* 世界佛教居士林林刊) from 1923 to 1937, while also founding its own periodical entitled *Buddhist Studies Bi-Monthly* (*Foxue banyuekan* 佛學半月刊) in 1930, which published 313 issues until 1944. By 1937, it was printing well over 3,000 Buddhist books and periodicals on an annual basis, with branch offices throughout China, as well as in Hong Kong, Singapore, and even Rangoon. Shanghai Buddhist Books also took the initiative in pursuing even more diversified investments, including sponsoring radio programs and eventually launching its own radio station (the Shanghai Huaguang diantai 上海華光電台).[35]

Non-Buddhist publishers also strove to commercialize their operations, while finding the proper balance between accumulating merit and staying economically viable. Rostislav Berezkin's research reveals that throughout the imperial and modern eras, as well as in the present day, many religious groups consistently favored the free distribution of their works, with the covers of such texts containing expressions such as "this is not a commercial item" (*feimaipin* 非賣品), "reprints are welcome" (*huanying fanyin* 歡迎翻印), and even "we welcome printing and distribution [of this text]; it brings immeasurable merits" (*huanying yinsong, gongde wuliang* 歡迎印送，功德無量).[36] However, some modern religious publishers that specialized in lithographic editions of texts such as morality books and especially *baojuan* adopted a different approach, printing commercial catalogues with price lists and embracing the Western concept of copyright, adding notes to that effect (*banquan suo you* 版權所有) in the works that they published for sale.[37] Such efforts to blend religious and commercial concerns also marked the development of the Illuminating Goodness Bookstore.

THE ILLUMINATING GOODNESS BOOKSTORE: A BRIEF HISTORY

This part of the chapter presents a preliminary examination of one leading religious publishing enterprise in modern China, the Illuminating Goodness Bookstore (Mingshan shuju 明善書局), which was founded in Shanghai in 1931 and continued to operate there up to 1949.[38] Originally it was located at 284 Kraetzer Road (Kaizier lu 愷自邇路) in the French Concession,[39] but by the late 1940s had moved to the corner of Xiafei 霞飛 and Songshan 嵩山 Roads.[40] We shall pay particular attention to the elites who founded and managed the Bookstore, the religious movements to which they belonged, their motivations for engaging in religious publishing, and the categorization systems that they brought to the dissemination of religious knowledge. In contrast to the Buddhist publishing houses studied by previous scholars, which tended to produce works belonging to that religious tradition, the Illuminating Goodness Bookstore printed all manner of Buddhist, Daoist, Confucian, and redemptive society texts (see Figure 2.1). Some of its works have been reprinted in Taiwan,[41] while others are still being sold as rare books on websites such as the online bookstore Kongfuzi 孔夫子.[42]

The Bookstore's growth, including the reasons for its having been founded in the French Concession, cannot be understand fully without taking into account the advent of the redemptive societies described in chapter 1, most notably the Fellowship of Goodness (Tongshanshe 同善社).[43] This religious movement arose in Sichuan during the early twentieth century, apparently having developed from religious traditions linked to the Way of Former Heaven (Xiantiandao 先天道). The Fellowship's most renowned leader was Peng Huilong 彭回龍 (original name Peng Ruzun 彭汝尊, also known as Shugu laoren 述古老人; 1873–1950), who was born in Dazu 大足 (Sichuan) as the eldest of three

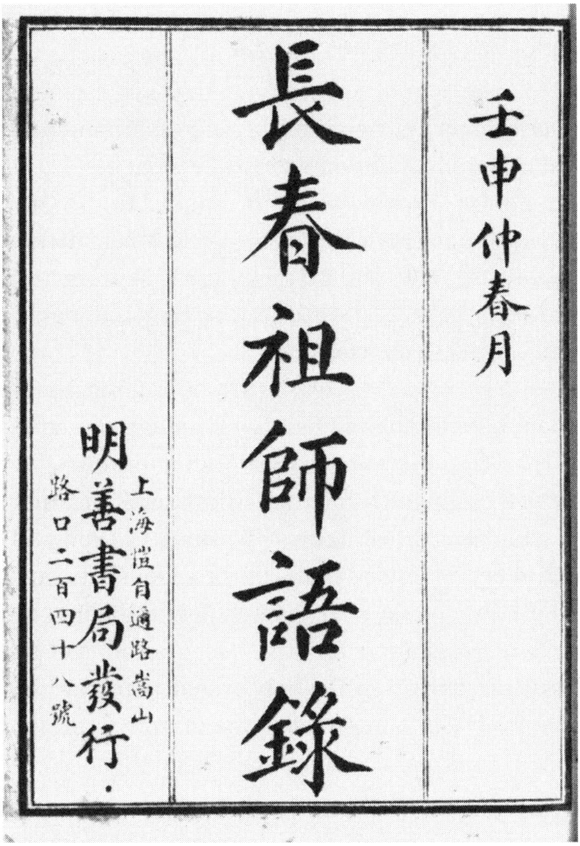

壬申仲春月

長春祖師語錄

明善書局發行

上海愷自邇路嵩山路口二百四十八號

FIGURE 2.1: *Daoist Text Published by the Illuminating Goodness Bookstore. This work, published in 1932, is a collection of sayings by the Perfect Realization (Quanzhen 全真) Daoist master Qiu Chuji 丘處機 (Qiu Changchun 丘長春; 1148–1227).*

sons of a local dyer. Peng received a rudimentary Confucian education (reading the works of Confucius and Mencius), and a number of his followers enjoyed success in the Qing examination system. Peng became patriarch of the Fellowship in either 1909 or 1912, and under his leadership the movement quickly attracted extensive gentry support, being introduced to the Qing court in 1910 and earning recognition as an officially sanctioned "religion" (*zongjiao* 宗教) with the Beiyang 北洋 government in Beijing on November 6, 1917, while also gaining the patronage of leading politicians such as Duan Qirui.[44]

By 1920, the Fellowship had grown into a national organization claiming over one million members, who practiced meditation and scripture recitation (referred to as "inner discipline" or *neigong* 内功) as well as philanthropic activities ("exterior fruits" or *waiguo* 外果). This division between self-cultivation and philanthropic activities characterized many of the redemptive societies mentioned previously (see also chapter 3). These values are clearly visible in the application for state recognition that the Fellowship submitted to the Beiyang authorities in 1917, which stressed the importance of moral development and charitable deeds during times of natural and man-made calamities:

> In China, the six years that have passed since the 1911 revolution have been full of natural and human disasters. Throughout the country, the people are dispersed, and their pain and suffering hardly can be exaggerated. This year there were battles in the west and floods in the north. It is too much to bear . . . The plan is to establish the Fellowship in the capital, to correct the mind and cultivate the body, and to encourage one another in diligence. Should our efforts permit it, we will extend our program to others, giving lectures so as to save the people and return them to heaven's intentions. We hope that the suffering of the people will convince the authorities to grant our petition and allow the registration of the Fellowship

> so that we may carry out our work throughout all the provinces of China.[45]

These sentiments also found vivid expression in the Illuminating Goodness Bookstore's own publications, with the Bookstore's establishment reflecting a trend among Fellowship members to expand from giving public lectures to managing publishing enterprises, the general sentiment being that the latter activity would have a more sustained and long-term impact.

The Fellowship and many other redemptive societies were proscribed by the Nationalist state in 1927, but these policies were not enforced stringently, especially since the authorities benefited from these groups' charitable activities. As a result, the Fellowship was able to remain active underground, with branch organizations referring to themselves using commercial designations and their leaders describing themselves in public documents using titles such as "owner" and "manager." All of the features are apparent in the Illuminating Goodness Bookstore's history. During the 1950s, the Fellowship and all other redemptive societies were harshly persecuted by the Communist authorities allegedly for having taken part in anti-CCP activities, but the Fellowship still survives in Taiwan and part of Southeast Asia, often under the guise of Confucian study societies (including at the renowned Baoan Gong 保安宮 in Taipei).[46]

By at least the first decades of the twentieth century many members of the Fellowship had begun to devote themselves to religious publishing, one of their earliest presses being the Celestial Flower Printing House (Tianhua yinshuguan 天華印書館) located in Beijing.[47] However, when the Printing House was forced to close during the 1927 suppression of the movement, the Fellowship's leadership decided to shift the publishing operations to Shanghai. Thus, it may have been no coincidence that the Illuminating Goodness Bookstore was located in the French Concession, as this would have provided a measure of protection from further state suppression. Fellowship members would have been further heartened by the fact that the Bookstore was one of only a few buildings in that neighborhood to escape unscathed during the Japanese bombing runs accompanying the "January 28 Incident" or "Shanghai Incident" of 1932, which was popularly attributed to divine protection of the Bookstore's efforts in printing morality books.[48] By the time of these events, the Bookstore also had started to publish its own periodicals. The first, entitled *Reports for Protecting Life* (*Husheng bao* 護生報), was published from 1932 until at least 1935,[49] serving as the voice of China's nascent animal rights movement.[50] The second was a biweekly entitled *Collected Reports of Philanthropy* (*Cishan huibao* 慈善彙報), which was founded in 1933 and claimed to have a readership of over ten thousand by its tenth issue.[51]

A number of Chinese elites, including members of the Fellowship of Goodness, played key roles in the Bookstore's founding and subsequent development. One of these men was Zhang Zaiyang 張載陽 (1873–1945), who gained renown for his martial prowess and rose through the ranks of the military and civil officialdom to serve as governor of Zhejiang in 1922 and major general in 1923. A successful entrepreneur as well, Zhang established one of Shanghai's largest places for the pursuit of leisure, the Great World Amusement Park (Dashijie youlechang 大世界遊樂場). He also was a well-known calligrapher, and many of his works still adorn temples and scenic sites in Hangzhou 杭州. As governor, Zhang won praise for his efforts in local public works and philanthropic enterprises, but apart from that reference his standard biographies provide little hint of his religious devotion.[52] At the same time, however, Zhang was a leader in the Hangzhou branch of the Fellowship of Goodness, which he helped to establish after its spread there in 1918 and continued to support up to his death in 1945.[53] A November 12, 1927, article in *Shenbao* 申報 describes Zhang's relationship with a wealthy Huzhou elite surnamed Cai 蔡, who had joined the Fellowship in 1923 and whose home (like the Bookstore eight years later) was left untouched by local bandits. Amazed at this news, Zhang, who was then serving as governor of Zhejiang, visited his home and listened to him preach about the intricacies of Fellowship doctrines.[54]

One surprising aspect of Zhang's religious life was that he ended up being on distinctly bad terms with the Buddhist establishment. One 1931 letter from Dharma Master Yinguang (Yinguang fashi 印光法師; 1861–1940) to a lay devotee named Zhou Shanchang 周善昌, which has been preserved in the *Yinguang fashi wenchao* 印光法師文鈔, mentions Zhang and another elite named Cai Zhenshen 蔡振紳 as being in charge of the Bookstore, while also castigating them for publishing "fake" scriptures.[55] These negative feelings might derive from an incident that occurred in early 1921, when Zhang became embroiled in a land dispute with Great Master Taixu (Taixu dashi 太虛大師; 1887–1947) that resulted in Taixu's losing control over the renowned Jingci Si 淨慈寺 in Hangzhou.[56]

The other Fellowship of Goodness member cited as helping to run the Bookstore was Cai Zhenshen (also known as Cai Liulong 蔡六龍), a native of Huzhou and disciple of Peng Huilong, who may have been related to the wealthy Mr. Cai mentioned previously (both were from Huzhou, but lived in different parts of the prefecture). Cai Zhenshen came from an elite family committed to the promulgation of traditional values such as filial piety. According to a preface Cai wrote for one of the morality books he compiled, entitled *Essential Knowledge of the Eight Virtues* (*Bade xuzhi* 八德須知), his father's first wife and son both had died young, and the second wife did not give birth to Cai until his father was thirty-eight years old. Treasuring this late blessing in his life, the elder Cai personally instructed his son in the Confucian classics when he was but four years old, beginning with the *Classic of Filial Piety* (*Xiaojing* 孝經). Day and night they studied together, their only "holidays" falling on Lunar New Year's Eve and Lunar New Year's Day. This experience molded Cai for life, and he devoted extensive effort to instructing others in the values he had learned, gaining renown for his role in promoting educational reform.[57] The date that Cai joined the Fellowship is unknown, but he was an active member and helped to manage its affairs in both Shanghai and Hangzhou. Some claim that he might have been the actual founder of the Illuminating Goodness Bookstore.[58]

Another leading figure was Sun Mianzhi 孫勉之 (b. 1901), a self-identified native of Haiyan 海鹽 County (Jiaxing 嘉興, Zhejiang), who served as the Bookstore's manager (*jingli* 經理) during the early 1930s, assisted by individuals such as Jiang Lü 姜履 (also a Haiyan native). Sun was succeeded by Gu Daxiao 顧達孝, who managed the Bookstore up to the early 1940s.[59] Finally, I should also mention that the famed Shanghai elite Wang Yiting 王一亭 (1867–1938) provided at least literary patronage to the Bookstore, writing the calligraphy for its 1932 catalogue's title pages as well as a couplet for the inside cover that read, "While you can use speech to admonish people for one generation, you can admonish them for a hundred generations with the written word" (*Yishi quanren yi kou, baishi quanren yi shu* 一世勸人以口，百世勸人以書).[60] Wang's links to the Fellowship still are unclear, but he is known to have joined redemptive societies and other religious groups during the 1920s and 1930s, the most notable being the Teachings of Celestial Virtue (Tiandejiao 天德教) and the China Rescuing Life Association (Zhongguo jishenghui 中國濟生會) (see chapter 3).

What motivated these men to devote so much effort to the field of religious publishing? Some answers may be found in the Bookstore's own catalogues, two of which have been preserved in an extremely valuable reference work entitled *Collected Catalogues of Republican-Era Publishing* (*Minguo shiqi chuban shumu huibian* 民國時期出版書目彙編). The last two volumes of this twenty-volume compilation contain numerous catalogues compiled by religious publishing enterprises. Volume 19 mainly is devoted to Buddhism, especially the catalogues for Shanghai Buddhist Books. Volume 20 contains catalogues representing a wide range of Republican-era religious groups, including the first and sixth catalogues published by the Illuminating Goodness Bookstore in 1932 and 1935. These catalogues are especially significant because they contain far more than mere lists of books, but also writings that express the agendas of those elites who became involved in religious publishing.

One example may be found in a 1931 "Declaration" (*xuanyan* 宣言) composed by Sun Mianzhi to mark the occasion of the publication of the Bookstore's first catalogue shortly after its founding. This work reveals that, like the Fellowship of Goodness members who had applied for state recognition back in 1917, Sun and his peers had been deeply moved by the natural and man-made calamities ravaging China during the early years of the Republican era, believing that practicing the tenets contained in the morality books could provide succor to the afflicted or even prevent future outbreaks. Accordingly, these men strove to use the Bookstore as a means of promulgating the values they hoped would help save the world. The "Declaration" opens by describing the multitudinous disasters afflicting China by 1931, before turning to the need to encourage people to do good deeds, especially via religious publishing (Wang Yiting's statement about admonishing people for a hundred generations by means of the written word is quoted verbatim). According to Sun:

> In a nation such as ours, which is so vast with such a huge population yet lacks widespread education, it is extremely difficult to change people's customs. Organizations that publish morality books must devote themselves to promoting these virtues, in order to achieve the goal of reform by moral uprightness [*ganhua* 感化; a Bookstore category for its catalogues]. Moreover, in this age of incessant disasters, we need

> to encourage ourselves further to perform acts of goodness and strive to guide [people away from] vulgar customs [*yongsu* 庸俗] . . . How can the younger generation [*qingnian zhi liu* 青年之流] consider our acts to be superstitious and corrupt? [Note the importance of the concept of "superstition" discussed in the previous chapter.][61] At the very least, our works can help the common people practice self-cultivation and keep their families in order, and at most aid the nation in its hope to achieve peace.[62]

Similar sentiments are also expressed in a "Declaration" written by Zhang Zaiyang to mark the inaugural issue of the *Collected Reports of Philanthropy*, which advocated for saving the world via moral instruction.[63]

The "Declaration" also provides detail on the Bookstore's organizational structure, which included staff responsible for collecting works to be reprinted, as well as editing them and then distributing them after their publication. It further reveals that Sun was well aware of the problems cited by Löwenthal in the conclusion to his survey of Chinese religious publishing, especially high illiteracy rates.

Four years later, Sun wrote a preface for the Bookstore's sixth catalogue in 1935, which in contrast to the "Declaration" devotes more space to discussing the Three Teachings (Sanjiao 三教), the importance of spirit writing, and the need for engaging in acts of philanthropy. At the same time, however, this work echoes Sun's earlier concerns with spreading proper moral values:

> The words "illuminating goodness" [*mingshan* 明善] derive from Confucian texts [*Rushu* 儒書], yet all books belonging to the Three Teachings have been written with the goal of admonishing people to do good [*quanshan* 勸善]. Confucianism is for ruling the world, Buddhism for converting it, and the [Way of the] Immortals [Daoism] for saving it [*Ru zhishi, Fo dushi, Xian jiushi* 儒治世，佛渡世，仙救世]. All of this rep-

> resents the same principle . . . Our Bookstore is willing to do its part [literally "happy to exert its feeble strength" or *lejin mianli* 樂盡綿力]. Its prices are low yet its products are beautiful, all produced with the aim of promoting goodness.[64]

It is to these acts of production that we now turn our attention.

THE PRODUCTION OF RELIGIOUS KNOWLEDGE

One of the essential elements of religious publishing was the interaction between media and message, particularly the extent to which new technologies such as lithographic printing as well as the growth of modern education systems shaped both the form and content of religious texts. This is because religious publishing entailed not only the production and transmission of beliefs and practices, but also the attempt by religious groups to assert the authenticity of their teachings and persuade the rest of the world of their inherent value.[65] Such concerns also shaped the publishing agenda of the Illuminating Goodness Bookstore, which, while largely relying on traditional woodblock editions, dedicated itself to producing illustrated works that were written in the vernacular, while promoting both Chinese and Western moral values and attempting to reach out to women and youths.

The best evidence of these phenomena may be found in the Illuminating Goodness Bookstore's catalogues, which contain a striking variety of texts. I have been able to locate three such catalogues: The first, which dates from 1932 and is preserved in the *Collected Catalogues* mentioned previously, lists a total of 109 publications. The second, a partial catalogue from the 1930s generously supplied by Yao Chi On, lists 239 works. The third, also in the *Collected Catalogues* but dating from 1935, is the largest and most complete, containing a total of 331 works.

In considering the significance of the works contained in these catalogues, one might start by analyzing their dates. This is a tricky issue, however, since many of these works are undated and have gone through numerous revisions and modifications over time. Nevertheless, some interesting trends are apparent. Of the thirty-six datable texts from the 1932 catalogue, one was said to have been written during the Three Kingdoms (Sanguo 三國) era (220–265), five during the Qing dynasty (1644–1911), and thirty during the Republican era. For the 1930s catalogue, however, the totals for the fifty datable works are three from the Tang dynasty (618–907), two Song dynasty (960–1279), one Yuan dynasty (1279–1368), two Ming dynasty (1279–1368), sixteen Qing dynasty, and twenty-four Republican era. Figures for the 1935 catalogue (sixty-eight datable works) are one Three Kingdoms, three Tang, two Song, one Yuan, three Ming, twenty-three Qing, and thirty-three Republican. This indicates that the elites who managed the Illuminating Goodness Bookstore chose to go back in time, with the percentage of Republican-era works declining and that of Qing-dynasty texts increasing. This may have been because of a trend among Fellowship of Goodness leaders to emphasize the movement's origins and early development, especially in light of the increasing suppression by the state.[66]

As for the contents of those works published by the Bookstore, one is struck by the immense variety. Some texts were related to Buddhism and Daoism, while others stressed traditional moral values and practices. A few publications included collections of both Chinese and Western aphorisms, while there also were numerous works opposing the killing of sentient beings, condemning immoral behavior such as gambling, and reminding readers of the inevitability of divine retribution. The Bookstore's catalogue also featured sectarian scriptures popular among groups in China and Taiwan, medicinal texts, and works on women's education and health.

The Bookstore's catalogues also provide insights into how modern religious groups attempted to categorize sacred knowledge. For example, the 1932 catalogue lists 107 texts (not including 2 uncategorized works), divided according to the following six categories:

1. Compassion and Love (*Ci'ailei* 慈愛類): A total of eight texts, mostly devoted to injunctions against killing sentient beings (*jiesha* 戒殺) that were written by Republican-era lay Buddhist elites such as Huang Hanzhi 黃涵之 (Huang Qinglan 黃慶瀾; 1875–1961) and Feng Zikai 豐子愷 (1898–1975) (for more on these elites, see chapter 3).
2. Eight Virtues (*Badelei* 八德類): Seventeen texts, the titles of which invariably begin with the words "Eight Virtues" that are devoted to promulgating the traditional moral values espoused by the Fellowship of Goodness.
3. Buddhist Scriptures (*Fojinglei* 佛經類): Twenty texts that for the most part are standard Buddhist works, but also include more recent texts by Republican-era lay Buddhists such as Xu Zhijing 許止淨 and Wang Shuyun 王書雲.
4. Daoist Texts (*Daoshulei* 道書類): Thirteen texts, generally treating of Taoist forms of self-cultivation and internal alchemy.
5. Confucianism (*Ruxuelei* 儒學類): Eight texts, largely standard Confucian works such as the *Classic of Filial Piety*, but also more modern texts such as the *Newly Annotated Vernacular Commentaries on the Four Books by Child Prodigy Jiang* (*Jiang shentong xinzhu Sishu baihua jieshuo* 江神童新註四書白話解說) by Jiang Xizhang 江希張 (1907–2004), the youthful leader of the Universal Morality Society (Wanguo daodehui 萬國道德會).
6. Guiding Customs (*Daosulei* 導俗類): The largest category (thirty-nine texts), most of which are venerable morality books such as the *Folios of the Most High on Retribution*

(*Taishang ganying pian* 太上感應篇). However, this category also includes collections of literati writings such as *biji* 筆記 as well as a number of medicinal texts.

The 302 texts (not including 29 uncategorized works) from the 1935 catalogue (the largest and most complete of those that survive) were categorized according to a new system that abandoned the Three Teachings framework in favor of stressing a wider range of moral values, the works being classified as follows:[67]

1. Classics (*Jingdianlei* 經典類): Sixty-eight texts representing the leading works of the Three Teachings. This category consists mainly of Buddhist scriptures, but also includes morality books such as the *Folios of the Most High on Retribution* mentioned previously.
2. Inner Nature and Universal Principles (*Xinglilei* 性理類): Forty-two texts ranging from Confucian works such as the *Four Books* to Daoist writings by Bai Yuchan 白玉蟾 (1194–?), Zhang Sanfeng 張三丰, and Wang Changyue 王常月 (?–1680). This category also includes spirit-writing texts such as the *Golden Needle of Instructions for Guiding the Lost* (*Zhimi jinzhen* 指迷金箴) and the *Golden Basin of Jade Dew* (*Yulu jinpan* 玉露金盤).
3. Eight Virtues (*Badelei* 八德類): Twenty-six texts.
4. Miscellaneous (*Zazulei* 雜組類): Forty-four texts that may not have been viewed as completely "pure" (*chuncui* 純粹), yet could still prove valuable to the pursuit of a religious lifestyle. This category encompasses works ranging from the *Writings of Guanyin for Admonishing People to Do Good* (*Guanyin quanshan wen* 觀音勸善文) to a hagiography of Quanzhen 全真 Daoist patriarchs entitled *Illustrated Collection of the Seven Perfected* (*Huitu Qizhen ji* 繪圖七眞集).

5. Reform by Moral Uprightness (*Ganhualei* 感化類): Sixty-seven texts designed to inspire readers to achieve goodness, including the *Three Character Classic* (*Sanzijing* 三字經) and a women's version thereof (the *Three Character Classic for Women to Study*, or *Nüxue sanzijing* 女學三字經), as well as other textbooks for children plus works about filial piety. There are also collections of aphorisms (*geyan* 格言), as well as the classic *Book of Instructions for Sons by Master Yuan Liaofan* (Yuan Huang 袁黃; 1533–1606) (*Yuan Liaofan xiansheng xunzi shu* 袁了凡先生訓子書).
6. Karmic Retribution (*Yinguolei* 因果類): Thirty texts devoted to the inevitability of divine retribution, especially spirit codes (*lü* 律 and *ke* 科), as well as works describing the consequences of lascivious (*yin* 淫) deeds, most notably the *Records and Tales of the Jade Regulations* (*Yulu chaozhuan* 玉歷鈔傳). There are also a number of books that treat the favorable karmic consequences of cherishing lettered paper (*xizi* 惜字).[68]
7. Compassion and Philanthropy (*Cijilei* 慈濟類): Twenty-five texts largely exhorting readers to avoid killing sentient beings, including the classic *Tears of the Plough Ox* (*Gengniu lei* 耕牛淚).[69] However, this category also includes medicinal texts such as the *Discourses on Cholera* (*Huoluan lun* 霍亂論), as well as those focused solely on women's health, such as the *Writings on Attaining Life* (*Dashengbian* 達生編; a Qing-dynasty work containing essays about coping with pregnancy).[70]

The prevalence of these categorization systems among other religious publishers has yet to be determined,[71] but note that a roughly similar system was used for the mammoth collection of morality books Wang Yiting helped to compile in 1936, entitled

A Treasury of Blessings and Longevity (*Fushou baozang* 福壽寶藏).[72] What is most striking about the Bookstore's catalogues, however, is the consistent use of the category Eight Virtues (Bade 八德), the second category of the 1932 catalogue that was preserved in third place in subsequent catalogues. Only now are scholars beginning to consider the importance of the Eight Virtues in the history of the Fellowship of Goodness, but preliminary investigations by Vincent Goossaert, Fan Chunwu, and Liu Wenxing indicate that for the Fellowship the term "Eight Virtues" referred to a specific corpus of texts, based on nineteenth-century revelations composed during spirit-writing rituals (*fuji* 扶乩). Entitled *Essential Elements of the Golden Code* (*Jinke jiyao* 金科輯要) and *Essential Elements of the Code of the Wheel* (*Lunke jiyao* 輪科輯要), these revelations were composed in the form of two celestial penal codes produced by spirit-writing groups in Hunan between the 1850s and 1880s. These works, which differ from earlier codes in terms of being written in the vernacular and aimed at popular consumption (one preface advocated preaching their contents not only through lectures and dramas but also through movies and radio broadcasts), were eventually adopted as key Fellowship scriptures. It is also essential to note that these Eight Virtues differ from the set most familiar to people today, especially those who have spent time walking the streets of downtown Taipei, namely, *zhongxiao* 忠孝 (loyalty and filial piety), *renai* 仁愛 (benevolence and love), *xinyi* 信義 (trustworthiness and righteousness), and *heping* 和平 (harmony and peace). In contrast, for the Fellowship the Eight Virtues consisted of *xiaoti* 孝悌 (filial piety and respect for one's elders), *zhongxin* 忠信 (loyalty and trustworthiness), *liyi* 禮義 (propriety and righteousness), and *lianchi* 廉恥 (honesty and shame). This set of values—and especially the latter two pairs—helped shape Nationalist cultural policies, especially the New Life Movement (Xinshenghuo yundong 新生活運動),[73] and also were used by protestors during the "Depose President Chen Shuibian" (DaoBian 倒扁) movement of 2008. Cai Zhenshen, one of the elite managers of the Illuminating Goodness Bookstore, played a leading role in promulgating these virtues by means of his *Essential Knowledge of the Eight Virtues*, which was printed in numerous vernacular and illustrated editions featuring print runs of tens of thousands of copies that were distributed throughout China and among overseas Chinese.[74]

Another way to appreciate the diversity underlying the Bookstore's publishing projects involves the authors whose works were selected. Again, one sees a broad spectrum of historical figures, starting with redemptive society leaders such as Jiang Xizhang, who helped found the Universal Morality Society along with his father, Jiang Shoufeng 江壽峰 (1875–1926).[75] A sizeable percentage of Republican-era Buddhist elites also was selected, including well-known figures such as Huang Hanzhi, Nie Yuntai, Feng Zikai, Wang Yunshu, and Xu Zhijing. Daoist authors from the Qing and Republican eras were highly represented, including Wang Changyue 王常月 (?–1680) and Liu Huayang 柳華陽 (1736–?). In addition there were numerous authors of texts traditionally classified as "Confucian," including Chen Xiequ 陳燮樞 (1874–1958), Lu Yiting 陸一亭 (Qing), and Zhu Bolu 朱柏廬 (1627–1698). Other elites whose works defy ready classification according to Three Teachings criteria included the novelist Wang Diaosheng 汪調生, the political leader He Yunqiao 何芸樵 (He Jian 何鍵; 1874–1956; served as governor of Hunan), and the artist Tong Zhifeng 童之風 (1892–1960). The works of leading Ming religious figures such as Lianchi dashi 蓮池大師 (Yunqi Zhuhong 雲棲袾宏; 1535–1615) and Yuan Liaofan 袁了凡 (Yuan Huang 袁黃; 1533–1606) were chosen for inclusion as well.

These data, while hardly comprehensive, reveal that the elites who managed the Bookstore endeavored to collect and transmit a wide range of works possessing a highly eclectic nature. This reflects the cosmopolitan belief systems of redemptive societies such as the Fellowship of Goodness, as well as values centering not only on proper moral conduct but also on the self-cultivation, education, and healing that were espoused by their members. The inclusion of works on women's education and health is particularly fascinating. While the actual impact of these works on modern women remains unclear, this effort to reach out to a female readership provides vivid evidence of the importance of women's religiosity in modern China.

BUSINESS MODELS AND OPERATIONS

The lofty goals of promoting morality inevitably clashed with the realities of trying to manage a publishing enterprise. In the case of the Illuminating Goodness Bookstore, its managers strove to attain these goals through a sophisticated internal organization, including staff members specifically in charge of the distribution process (*liutong zhuanzezhe* 流通專責者), employees in charge of arranging for works to be printed (*chengyin zhuanzezhe* 承印專責者), staff in charge of printing (*fanyin zhuanzezhe* 翻印專責者), and people in charge of editing and other matters related to the Bookstore's publishing efforts (*bianji dengdeng zhi zhize* 編輯等等之職責).[76] Together, these individuals worked to ensure that the collection, production, and distribution of the Bookstore's texts proceeded as smoothly as possible.

The Bookstore's 1935 catalogue contains five pages of detailed information about how its operations actually ran, including data on postage and handling costs (such as via express or registered mail, or with the proper insurance), as well as procedures for sending payment in cash, using stamps in place of cash, or sending payment by wire. There were also explanations about how the Bookstore could arrange to help customers buy books from other publishers. In addition, provisions existed for returning money in cases of overpayment, but no returns of actual books or journals were allowed, and no compensation was provided for lost orders (although the Bookstore would assist in the search for these items). The Bookstore placed great emphasis on the need for providing clear mailing addresses, as well as giving proper notification in cases where a new address had to be used. The 1935 catalogue also delineates the conditions under which people could contact the Bookstore in order to arrange for the printing and distribution of religious texts. First the parties had to negotiate a mutually agreed estimate, following which a payment of at least two-thirds of the total amount was required. In order for any such effort to be economically viable, customers had to agree to the Bookstore printing at least five hundred copies of individual texts or one thousand copies of more than one volume. If negotiations failed, the Bookstore would return works free of charge via registered mail. In all such enterprises, the Bookstore emphasized that its main goal was to make ends meet, not achieve a profit. This attitude can be seen in statements such as, "Prices are more economical than elsewhere, with the goal of covering expenses" (*hejia jiao tachu cong lian, yi zufu kaixiao wei zhun* "核價較他處從廉，以足敷開銷為準).[77] This in turn suggests that while previous scholars have tended to view religious printing as a noncommercial, devotional endeavor, the Bookstore seems to have operated along the lines of a semicommercial, semidevotional organization.[78]

One key question involves the extent to which potential readers could afford the works that the Bookstore was publishing. This is a difficult question to answer without possessing detailed knowledge of wage and price figures from the 1930s, but the Bookstore's catalogues do provide considerable data on how much these texts actually cost (426 works in these catalogues have prices listed). Such works were sold by the hundred, with 62 instances of books costing between $1 and $2 per hundred copies, 89 instances of between $2 and $3, 47 instances of between $3 and $4, 25 instances of between $4 and $5, and 20 instances of between $5 and $6. A total of 18 books cost as much as $10 per hundred copies, while 10 books cost $20, 2 books cost $30, 5 books cost $40, and 2 books cost $80. There were even

2 books that cost $240 per hundred copies. To put this in perspective, in 1932 one copy of the Shanghai newspaper *Xinwenbao* 新聞報 cost 4.5 cents and a full subscription cost $4.50 per year, while prices for elementary school textbooks ranged from 6 to 15 cents, indicating that the Bookstore's publications could be quite affordable.[79] In terms of wages and prices, in 1930 an elementary school teacher's monthly salary was $24, while workers in pharmacies could make between $20 and $22 per month. Based on statistical data indicating that approximately 25 percent of a worker's wages could be used as spending money, it would seem that many workers might be able to afford the Bookstore's cheaper publications.[80] Moreover, the fact that the texts were sold by the hundred indicates that the Bookstore operated along the lines of other religious publishers such as the Yihuatang, distributing its publications in bulk at wholesale prices which could then be passed out for free, thus further confirming its semicommercial nature.

Similar concerns and procedures shaped the publication of the Bookstore's two periodicals, *Reports for Protecting Life* and *Collected Reports of Philanthropy*. The *Collected Reports*' by-laws, published as part of the Bookstore's 1935 catalogue, provide data on its cost, distribution, honoraria for authors, and so forth. This journal was published twice a month, with each issue costing 50 cents and postage and handling being included if one subscribed for six months or one year. For individual issues of the journal, the price remained 50 cents, but a surcharge of at least 10 cents was added to cover postage and handling. Discounts were offered to subscribers who ordered multiple copies that would be sent to the same address (10 percent for 5 copies, 20 percent for 10 copies, and so on), but only if the payment was made in advance. Authors whose works were published in the *Collected Reports* would not receive any royalties, but would be entitled to free copies of the Bookstore's morality books. The Bookstore was also willing to engage in gratis exchanges of journals with other philanthropic organizations (presumably including other redemptive societies).[81]

It is especially important to note that, apart from marketing religious books and periodicals, religious publishers such as the Illuminating Goodness Bookstore and other enterprises including Shanghai Buddhist Books also sold religious goods (statues, paintings, and so on) and recordings of scriptural and liturgical texts. In the case of the Bookstore, its 1932 catalogue contains a price list for such items,[82] while nearly half of its 1935 catalogue was devoted to advertisements for statues, paintings, calligraphy, and other religious artifacts.[83] For example, a five-foot scroll of Fellowship of Goodness patriarch Peng Ruzun's calligraphy written on fine coral-patterned paper (*shanhujian* 珊瑚箋) cost 50 cents, while having it mounted (*lingbiao* 綾裱) would increase the total cost to $1.30. Prices were lower if five feet of white paper (*yubanjian* 玉版箋) was used (40 cents or $1.20), and even lower for only three feet of the same type of paper (15 cents or 60 cents). Costs were roughly identical for calligraphic couplets (*duilian* 對聯), including those extolling the Eight Virtues written by Peng: a five-foot scroll written on fine coral-patterned paper cost 50 cents, while having it mounted would increase the total to $1.30. A print of the deity Jigong 濟公 cost 40 cents, while having it mounted upped the total to $1.20. All prices did not include postage and handling, but at times a discount of 10 percent was offered.[84] These prices might seem a bit high, but they were much lower than those charged by Shanghai artists for their works. For example, lists of remuneration rates (*runli* 潤例) for painters, calligraphers, and seal cutters published in *Shenbao* 申報 in 1935 (the date of the Illuminating Goodness Bookstore catalogue containing the artifacts previously described) indicate that the cost for one foot of calligraphy often started at $1 and worked its way up, with some artists charging $2 or more per character.[85] These figures provide additional evidence suggesting that the Bookstore's business model was a semicommercial one, with religious artifacts being sold to recoup publishing costs but not necessarily to make a profit.

NETWORKS OF TRANSMISSION AND DISTRIBUTION

Once production and marketing obstacles had been overcome, religious publishers also had to deal with the problem of how to arrange for these texts to reach their intended audiences. While some works could be read by individual worshippers, many others were meant to be chanted or otherwise performed for mass audiences, including scriptures, liturgies, and *baojuan* 寶卷. Accordingly, the expression "to be used exclusively for chanting and recitation" (*zhuanggong songdu* 專供誦讀) appears after many of the titles listed in the Bookstore's catalogues. Illustrated morality books were said to be especially worthwhile because of their appeal to less-educated readers.[86] Recent research by Rostislav Berezkin clearly demonstrates the presence of a wide range of reading practices during the Republican era (and most likely earlier time periods as well), ranging from silent reading by educated individuals to different types of amateur and professional performances (*nianjuan* 念卷). Despite the assumption by some authors of religious texts that people could read such works, most publishers were well aware of the importance of recitation and simple language. This was especially the case for women, who were often one of the main intended audiences for many such works, albeit generally by group recitation rather than by individual reading.[87] Elite families had their share of literate women,[88] and their numbers rose steadily during the late Qing and Republican eras with the founding of more public schools for girls.[89] Berezkin's research reveals that evidence for such trends may be found in the writings of intellectuals such as Zhou Zuoren 周作人 (1885–1967), who in a 1934 essay described how one girl was forced to abandon her education after elementary school but continued to read novels and *baojuan* at home, probably having been first exposed to the latter during performances she attended with her mother.[90] Moreover, an autobiographical essay by Hu Shih (who, as we saw in chapter 1, helped lead the charge against traditional Chinese religions) tells the story of the mother-in-law of one of his elder brothers, who not only was literate and liked to read morality books, but also would make the effort to recite their contents to other women or use the books to tell stories to younger generations.[91] Women writers also attested to the importance of such practices, such as Pan Xizhen 潘希珍 (pseudonym Qijun 琦君; 1917–2006) of Yongjia 永嘉 County (Zhejiang), who in an autobiographical story entitled "Mom's Hands" (*Mama de shou* 媽媽的手) movingly recounted how her mother would, after finally finishing all the household chores, soak her hands in a basin of hot water before devoting herself to reading *baojuan*. According to Pan, that was the most relaxing time of her mother's long day.[92] All of this suggests that religious works could find their way into the hands of their intended readers and audiences, including women, but the overall success of publishing enterprises such as the Illuminating Goodness Bookstore remains to be determined.

Another problem involved the ways in which religious texts were distributed. In his survey of Republican-era religious periodicals, Löwenthal maintained that the dissemination of free or low-cost religious publications "[did] not necessarily reflect the real interest of the population, but rather the financial strength and ability to organize on the part of the distributing agency."[93] This cautionary point clearly has merit in terms of assessing the impact of religious publishers such as the Illuminating Goodness Bookstore, but it is also essential to consider that these publishers could often rely on sophisticated distribution networks in order to achieve their goals. In the case of the Bookstore, its works were intended to reach their readers via a series of twelve distribution outlets that ranged from nearby Zhejiang and Fujian provinces all the way north to Liaoning 遼寧, Jilin 吉林, and Inner Mongolia, as well as westward to Sichuan 四川 and Yunnan 雲南. Of these, the distribution center for morality books (Shanshu liutongchu 善書流通處) located in Quanzhou 泉州 was especially important for the religious history of modern Taiwan, with leading publishers such as the Ruicheng Bookstore (Ruicheng shuju 瑞成書局), Lanji Bookstore (Lanji shuju 蘭記書局), and Yuzhen Bookstore (Yuzhen shuju 玉珍書局) reprinting Illuminating Goodness Publishing House works and including them in their own catalogues.

One example of how cross-Strait interaction shaped the transmission of religious knowledge in Japanese colonial Taiwan may be found in the case of Taiwan's oldest religious publishing enterprise, the Ruicheng Bookstore, founded in the city of Taizhong 台中 in 1912 by Xu Kesui 許克綏 (1892–1983). Born into a poor peasant family in Xianxi 線西 Township in today's Zhanghua 彰化 County, Xu was a fifth-generation descendant of migrants who had come to Taiwan from Quanzhou. His family's financial circumstances prohibited Xu from receiving any formal education, but he tried to learn as much as he could by attending local schools (*xueshu* 學塾) when the opportunity presented itself. Xu married at age eighteen and then moved to Taizhong, where in 1912 he first set up a shop for selling seeds and other agricultural products. His commitment to studying the Chinese language and culture persisted unabated, however, so later that year he expanded his storefront to include a space for selling books, journeying to Shanghai and Amoy on a regular basis to collect not only works of fiction and drama but especially Buddhist and Daoist scriptures as well as morality books such as those published by the Illuminating Goodness Bookstore. After many long years of hard work, in 1928 Xu finally proved able to rent a separate storefront for use as an independent bookshop and set up his own printing press in 1932. Such progress entailed considerable hardship, however, including regular inspections by the colonial authorities (who were concerned by his promotion of Chinese culture), and the tragic death of his son in 1931 while on a business trip to Shanghai. Contact with Chinese publishers came to an abrupt end with the outbreak of the Second Sino-Japanese War in 1937, but Xu continued to publish the religious texts he had acquired by using his own printing press, and his descendents continue to manage the Ruicheng Bookstore to this day.[94]

Cross-Strait religious ties also shaped the growth of the Lanji Bookstore, which was established in 1925 by a Jiayi 嘉義 elite named Huang Maosheng 黃茂盛 (1901–1978). Huang was deeply committed to both preserving traditional Chinese culture and transmitting moral values, not only inviting Chinese elites to take part in literary contests, but also setting up his own distribution center for morality books. Huang also took regular journeys to religious publishing centers such as Shanghai, where he collected, brought back to Taiwan, and reprinted a wide variety of religious works and periodicals in order to distribute them free of charge.[95] Huang's efforts attracted the support of Chinese religious elites, including the renowned Shanghai businessman, philanthropist, and religious practitioner Wang Yiting. Huang met Wang during his trips to China and became a member of a charitable-religious organization that Wang had helped found (the Association of Conscience for Upholding Goodness or Zhongguo liangxin chongshan hui 中國良心崇善會). One result of this friendship was Wang's composing a preface for a morality book entitled *Record of the Spirit* (*Jingshen lu* 精神錄), compiled by the renowned East Haven (Donggang 東港) physician and philanthropist Chen Jiangshan 陳江山 (1899–1976) and published by the Lanji Bookstore in 1929. Wang also composed a calligraphic couplet for this work, which read, "Do nothing that is evil; practice all forms of philanthropy" (*zhu'e mozuo, zhongshan fengxing* 諸惡莫作，眾善奉行; see Figure 2.2). The *Record*, which also includes a preface by Huang, subsequently spread back across the Strait to Shanghai, with five editions totaling 6,700 copies being produced in both Taiwan and China prior to

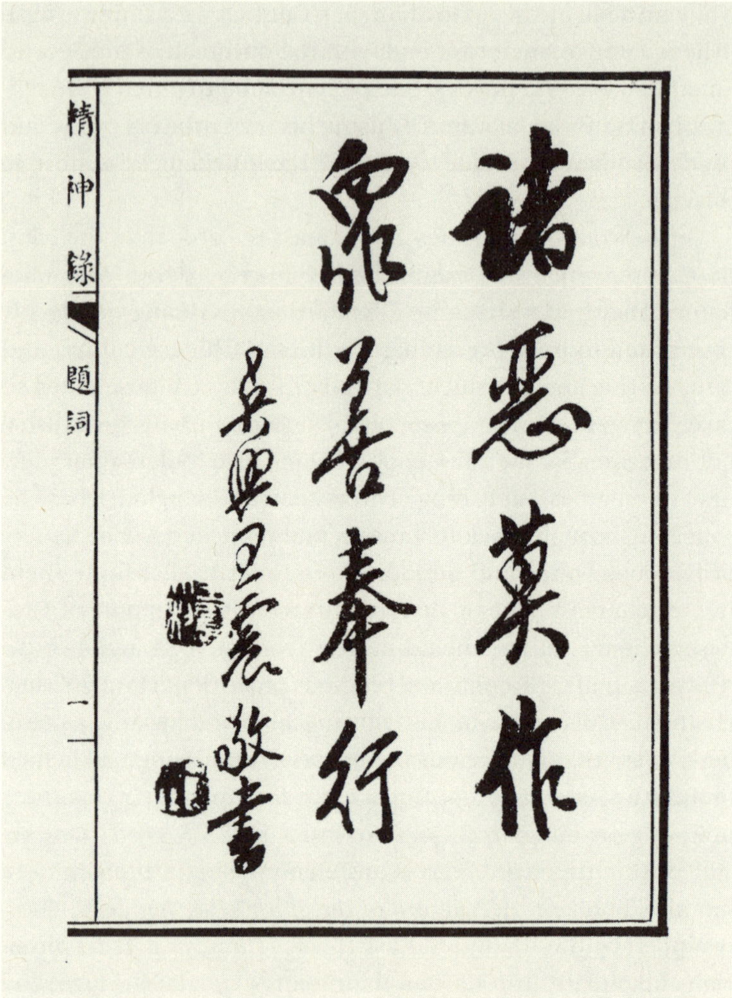

FIGURE 2.2: *Wang Yiting's Calligraphy for the* Record of the Spirit.

the outbreak of the Second World War.[96] One final example involves Chen Yuzhen 陳玉珍 (1897–1972), the founder of the Yuzhen Bookstore (also located in Jiayi), who dedicated himself to publishing many different Chinese works when he opened for business in 1926, including Illuminating Goodness Publishing House religious texts.[97]

■ This evidence, while admittedly limited in both scope and depth, may help shed some light on the importance of religious publishing in modern Chinese history. This is a relatively new area of research, so much work remains to be done, but in my opinion there are two issues that will require further attention. The first entails the formulation of typologies of religious publishers that illustrate their diversity while also allowing for the overlap and competition between them. The second centers on the problem of change and continuity.

The achievement of the first goal will require the completion of more case studies along the lines of what was done for the Illuminating Goodness Bookstore in this chapter, and especially the collection of data on the agendas pursued by the managers as well as the ways in which they ran their operations. It will also be essential for scholars to transcend the limitations of focusing on a single religious tradition, since clearly such limits had little impact on religious publishing itself. In just one example, Buddhist publishers such as Shanghai Buddhist Books produced more than just the texts of that particular religion,[98] which is hardly surprising when one considers the fact that some redemptive society leaders actively supported Buddhist organizations.[99] Some Buddhist groups, and especially lay ones, also practiced spirit writing and did not hesitate to publish the results of their efforts.[100] In short, religious groups in Republican China were not passive respondents to state policies and social changes, but actively strove to create new spaces, including in the publishing industry.

This is also the case for religion and the mass media today, especially in nations such as Taiwan, where democratization has allowed for a multiplicity of beliefs and practices to flourish. Further research also needs to be done on how Republican-era trends helped lay a foundation for the rapid religious publishing in Taiwan today. As Yang Chao 楊照 (Li Ming-chun 李明駿; b. 1963) noted in an essay published in the *United Daily News* (*Lianhe bao* 聯合報) on October 1, 2010, Taiwanese cultural life has been shaped partially by trends that occurred in Republican-era China.[101] This is clearly the case for the relationship between religion and the mass media in modern Taiwan. While the phenomenal growth of Buddhist television stations, Daoist magazines, and redemptive society morality books (including in comic book form) during the postwar era may result in part from trajectories that arose during Japanese colonial rule, there would seem to be little doubt that the roots of what we are witnessing in Taiwan today lie deep in Republican-era history as well.

To conclude, many questions remain to be answered, most notably the impact of new technologies on religious publishers, the texts they produced, and the audiences and readerships they actually reached. This chapter has attempted to break new ground by examining how the interaction between religious movements and the mass media contributed to the development of modern Chinese religious life. In the future, I hope that this research can also reach out to the growing worldwide scholarly discourse on religion's role in the formation of cultural traditions today.

3

SECULAR YET SACRED

THE RELIGIOUS LIVES OF MODERN CHINESE ELITES

In the first two chapters, we have examined the fate of Chinese temples and explored how modern innovations shaped the development of religious publishing. It is now time to turn our attention from places and presses to people, namely, the elites whose efforts were a driving force behind these and many other trends. While current scholarship has delineated the overall development of modern Chinese religions, relatively little research has been done on individual elites. This chapter attempts to fill this gap by examining the religious lives of modern Chinese elites, based in large part on a case study of Wang Yiting 王一亭 (Wang Zhen 王震; 1867–1938), a renowned Shanghai businessman, philanthropist, and religious practitioner during the late Qing and Republican eras. The chapter's main goal is to consider the importance of different beliefs and practices for modern Chinese elites, particularly the ways in which religion helped mold both their professional careers and personal experiences.

In addition, this chapter considers the broader issue of religion and modernity in urban China. Although they lived during an age when many intellectuals who strove to create a secularized society viewed religion as one of the main forces obstructing their efforts,[1] many modern Chinese urban elites do not seem to have suffered a similar sense of disillusion. Instead, they dedicated themselves to a religious lifestyle, which suggests a need for rethinking the very nature of modern Chinese life. That most previous scholarship has tended to overlook the importance of religion seems to be symptomatic of a serious bias in the field of Chinese history, which has at times uncritically adopted Weberian models of modernity. This is especially true for arguments centering on the disenchantment of modern life (*tuomei* 脱魅), with "enchantment" (*meihua* 魅化) being seen as roughly equivalent to "superstition" (*mixin* 迷信). A related view is that to be a member of the modern elite includes treating the religious with a sense of indifference.[2] For nearly a generation, social and cultural historians were influenced by Peter Gay's classic study of the Enlightenment, which argued that the decline of religion (in this case Christianity) marked a harbinger of secular modernity (see also the discussion of secularization in this book's introduction).[3] Such views have constricted our ability to fully describe the complexities of the past, especially when it comes to non-Western cultures that experienced very different processes of modernization. As Michael Saler notes, "The seeming 'universal' distinctions championed by the Western metropole between modernity and tradition, or secularism and superstition, often do not hold up when viewed from the 'periphery' of non-Western cultures negotiating processes of modernization in complex ways."[4] As this chapter endeavors to show, such "negotiations" were an integral part of the Chinese experience of urban life, including its religious forms.

It is also essential to note that even in the West the pursuit of modernity did not mean the abandonment of the religious. Recent research has revealed that modern Western elites were hardly unified in their opposition to religious practices.[5] Many elites actively negotiated the balance between science and religion, not to mention finding a clear sense of compatibility between the two.[6] One striking example of this behavior involves elite fascination with the transcendental, including mesmerism, occultism, and scientism, which at times could transcend gender and class divisions to provide the adherents with a legitimately "modern" sense of enchantment that did not reject the essence of science or reason.[7] Such phenomena had distinct parallels in modern China as well, particularly when it came to practices such as spirit writing (*fuji* 扶乩).[8] In short, be it Western Enlightenment or Chinese modernization, it now seems clear that their manifold processes of historical development cannot be fully understood outside the context of religious beliefs and practices.[9]

THE MEANING OF RELIGION FOR MODERN CHINESE ELITES

Let us consider a few examples of what religion could mean for Chinese elites during the modern era, starting with the life of Great Dharma Master Hongyi (Hongyi dashi 弘一大師; 1880–1942).[10] Born as Li Shutong 李叔同 to the youngest of four wives of a wealthy Tianjin 天津 salt merchant who had gained renown for being a lay Buddhist and avid philanthropist, Li enjoyed a life of wealth and privilege, growing into an intellectually and artistically talented young man. He married two wives, the second of whom was from Japan, and spent considerable time in Tokyo, where he cross-dressed to play the leading lady in dramas such as *Uncle Tom's Cabin*. Li was also the first Chinese artist to use nude models (including, perhaps, his Japanese spouse) and one of the first to train in Western-style oil painting. However, Li eventually chose to become a monk (literally "leave the family" or *chujia* 出家) and take the dharma name Hongyi after suffering from an illness identified as "neurasthenia" (*shenjing shuairuo* 神經衰弱 in Chinese). During long years of asceticism and self-cultivation, Hongyi developed a profound interest in deathbed protocols and wrote many short works on this topic. In his will, he asked not to be commemorated by a stupa, but by printing two thousand copies of his writings on the Buddhist Vinaya (*lü* 律). As Raoul Birnbaum's research reveals, Hongyi's life vividly reflects the role of religion in modern Chinese culture. Hongyi started life as a wealthy elite who also took part in China's intellectual and artistic revolution (he fled to the French Concession in Shanghai after the failed Hundred Days of Reform in 1898) and experienced the fruits of modernization in Japan. Even his illness was defined as something that young men at the intellectual forefront of modern Chinese culture were particularly susceptible to. Yet Hongyi did not engage in a wholesale and uncritical adoption of Western culture, instead choosing to seek enlightenment in Chinese religious traditions, which, as we have seen in this book's first two chapters, were also being reformed partly because of the influence of Christianity. This intricate amalgam of Chinese and Western cultures is also apparent in the religious life of Wang Yiting.

While eminent monks such as Hongyi devoted themselves to preparing for the hour of their death, many elite lay Buddhists found comfort in this religion on the deaths of their loved ones. This can be seen in the case of Huang Hanzhi 黃涵之 (Huang Qinglan 黃慶瀾; 1875–1961). A native of Shanghai, Huang earned a tribute student (*gongsheng* 貢生) degree during the Qing dynasty and subsequently studied modern learning in Japan, serving as a local official during both the Qing and Republican eras and gaining renown for his philanthropic endeavors. He was also a devoted lay Buddhist and one of the most prominent disciples of Dharma Master Yinguang (Yinguang fashi 印光法師; 1861–1940), not only playing an active role in Buddhist publishing enterprises such as the Society for Propagating the Dharma, but also composing numerous commentaries, handbooks, and vernacular versions of Buddhist scriptures, many of which continue to circulate today.[11] Huang faced a tragic life crisis in the spring of 1923, when his beloved wife fell gravely ill and slowly passed away. In a series of letters, Huang and Yinguang engaged in moving discussions about how best to prepare for the inevitable, with Yinguang stressing that Huang and other family members devote themselves to reciting the name of the Buddha (*nianfo* 念佛) because of this action's salvific powers. For his part, Yinguang took the time to chant scriptures (*songjing* 誦經) for Huang's wife in order to achieve the "transfer of merit" (*huixiang* 回向) of this act to her. Huang's wife died on June 6, 1923, with Huang providing a detailed description of her passing to Yinguang, who assured Huang that she had attained rebirth in the Buddhist Pure Land (Jingtu 淨土).[12]

In addition, as was noted in the introduction, the religious lives of many other modern Chinese elites were profoundly influenced by Christianity. One example involves none other than Chiang Kai-shek, who studied Neo-Confucianism and learned of Buddhism from his mother, but then chose to convert to Methodism in order to marry Soong May-ling in December 1927 (he was not baptized until October 1930). We know that Chiang regularly read the Bible and that his faith provided him with much-needed strength during the difficult days of the Xi'an Incident (Xi'an shibian 西安事變).[13] Apart from the Bible, another important source of inspiration for Chiang was a collection of Christian testaments entitled *Streams in the Desert* (*Huangmo ganquan* 荒漠甘泉), which stressed unwavering faith in the face of failure. Chiang is known to have devotedly jotted down his thoughts next to the book's daily inspirational messages. One testament of the power these beliefs exerted on Chiang may be found in his March 26, 1937, Good Friday message to the Eastern Asia Conference of the Methodist Episcopal Church at Nanjing, which contains the following statement: "Without religious faith there can be no real understanding of life . . . Without faith, human affairs, both great and small, are difficult to achieve. Often when we [are] face to face with opposition and possible danger, we mortals are prone to retreat and abandon our work halfway. Such lack of confidence in ourselves is often because of the absence of strong religious faith."[14]

Further evidence for the importance of Christianity in Chiang's life may be found in his diary, with the recent publication of parts of this work shedding new light on his private world, including his hopes and fears, and above all his self-doubts and desire to repent for his failings.[15] Recent research by Huang Kowu 黃克武 on Chiang's diary reveals that, whenever possible, Chiang would devote two hours of each morning (usually from 6:00 to 8:00 AM) to various forms of self-cultivation and self-discipline (he referred to this as "morning instruction" or *chaoke* 朝課), including calisthenics (*ticao* 體操), Bible study (*dujing* 讀經), meditation (*jingzuo* 靜坐), and prayer (*daogao* 禱告). The goal of these exercises was the achievement of atonement, and Chiang did not hesitate to come clean with what he perceived as his many flaws, including sloth, impatience, physical abusiveness, lust, and masturbation.[16] One plaintive statement of his self-doubt may be found in the April 1, 1934 (Easter Sunday) entry of a portion of his diary entitled "Record of Self-Reflection and Self-Control" (*Xing-ke ji* 省克記), which reads as follows: "Today is Easter. While I believe in Christ, I have yet to achieve self-control. How can I enter the state of sanctity (*rusheng* 入聖)? How can this task be completed (*chengshi* 成事)?"[17] Chiang's diary as well as his other writings reveal that he found the Christian emphasis on moral thought and action consistent with the Neo-Confucian teachings he had learned as a child, particularly its emphasis on shame, atonement, and perseverance in face of suffering. His practices were also shaped by other indigenous traditions such as keeping ledgers of merit and demerit (*gongguoge* 功過格).[18]

One final example of modern Chinese elite religiosity, which also sheds light on the convoluted interaction between Buddhism and spirit writing that also shaped the life of Wang Yiting, involves the renowned boxing instructor Chen Weiming 陳微明 (1881–1958), who built a successful career in Shanghai after moving there as a small boy with his family in 1889. In 1944, Chen penned a touching biography about his first and only son, Bangwu 邦武, as well as records of the spirit-writing exchanges between father and son that were published from 1944 to 1945.[19] Bangwu arrived relatively late in Chen's married life, being born in 1918 when Chen was in his late thirties. His wife found the labor to be excruciating and gave the baby boy the infant name Man 滿 ("sufficient") as a means of proclaiming her intention to stop having children. Bangwu was a sensitive and caring boy, kneeling by his mother's bedside when she fell ill and offering prayers for her speedy recovery, as well as insisting on giving money to every beggar the family passed on the street. Chen Weiming made sure that his son received a traditional Chinese education, including in the martial arts, but did not want him to pursue a career in officialdom, instead encouraging him to study Western medicine, English, and accounting. Bangwu also got married and was blessed with the birth of a daughter, but the family's days of peace and plenty came to an end with the outbreak of the Second Sino-Japanese War. Father and son struggled to make ends meet, but hardship and malnutrition proved too much for Bangwu, who succumbed to an illness at age twenty-six.

In trying to cope with every parent's nightmare, Chen chose to recount in moving detail how Bangwu cried for his mother while on his deathbed, trying to kiss her and clearly feeling distraught about not being able to perform his filial duties for his parents. Chen felt intense sorrow, which could be assuaged only by the performance of Buddhist chanting, which provided succor for father and son alike. At one point a small bird flew into the sickroom, which was viewed as a visit by the Bodhisattva Guanyin (Guanshiyin pusa 觀世音菩薩). When Bangwu finally died, the family was visited by a stream of mourners who had fond memories of what he had been able to accomplish during his short time on earth, but this was of little solace to Chen, who lamented, "When we returned from the burial, the house felt empty at his loss, while I wandered as if in a daze and could not sleep, thinking of how [Bangwu's] twenty-six years [of life] had been just a dream." Chen was sixty-two years old at the time of Bangwu's death and had hoped that his son would take charge of the household so that he could practice eremitism in a mountain monastery and prepare for the end of his own life. Death had changed everything. Chen then proceeded to list a series of other recent family tragedies, including those of a younger brother and two nephews, exclaiming in anguish that, "I have studied Buddhism for over twenty years and am profoundly aware of the impermanence of life as well as its suffering and emptiness. But now, when father and son have been separated, how could my heart not be moved?" Chen did conclude the biography on a hopeful note, stating that Bangwu's wife was pregnant; she eventually gave birth to a son, so the family line could continue.

But for father and son death was not the end. Chen was adept in spirit writing, and one day Bangwu descended to the planchette and wrote a message of greeting, stating that he had chosen not to be reborn in order to practice Esoteric Buddhist self-cultivation centering on the worship of Guanyin. He was now working to cultivate an indestructible *vajra* body (*jingangshen* 金剛身) and hoped to be a truly filial son by passing on to his parents the merit that he had accumulated during such practices. Records of spirit-writing messages exchanged between father and son continued to appear in print for the next few months, before the journal publishing these texts decided to cease doing so because of objections by some of its readers. Chen was hardly the sole elite to turn to spirit writing as a means of coping with the death of a child, with the Shanghai literatus Gao Chuiwan 高吹萬 (1879–1958) attempting to use spirit writing to contact the soul of his teenage daughter following her tragic death just prior to marriage.[20]

These accounts admittedly represent a very small sample, and more data will be required to determine how representative such beliefs and practices truly were among modern Chinese elites. Nonetheless, this evidence does suggest that for many such individuals religion retained its role in providing a source of individual faith, a means of coping with personal or family crises, and a motivation for taking action to improve oneself or assist others during troubled times. All of these elements can be seen in the religious life of Wang Yiting.

WANG YITING: A BRIEF BIOGRAPHY

My interest in Wang Yiting began while doing research on how Taizhou 台州 (Zhejiang) elites living in Shanghai organized disaster relief (*zhenzai* 賑災) during the 1920s.[21] In the course of working on this topic, I discovered that while previous scholars had discussed Wang's achievements in the realms of commerce, politics, and art, few had taken adequate account of his intense commitment to philanthropy and (with the exception of Buddhism) his profound religious faith. Despite his many accomplishments, Wang also experienced his share of tragedy, including the demise of his father, the loss of his first wife less than one year into their marriage, the death of his third daughter in infancy, and witnessing the brutal assassination of his comrade-in-arms Song Jiaoren 宋教仁 (1882–1913). Such adversity seems to have attuned Wang to the suffering of others, prompting him to serve in leadership positions on organizations such as the Chinese Red Cross (Zhongguo hongshizihui 中國紅十字會) and the International Relief Association (Huayang yizhenhui 華洋義賑會; founded in 1920). Furthermore, the subjects of his paintings (which he often sold in order to raise the funds necessary to provide aid to those in need) included not only landscapes, flora, and fauna, but also the victims of natural disasters as well as Buddhist deities. Some of Wang's charitable work was linked to his Buddhist faith, as he served on the Charity Committee (Cishan weiyuanhui 慈善委員會) of the Chinese Buddhist Association (Zhongguo Fojiaohui 中國佛教會; founded in Shanghai in 1929). Wang also participated in the philanthropic activities of other religious movements, serving as founder and head of the

China Rescuing Life Association (Zhongguo jishenghui 中國濟生會), a charitable organization whose members practiced spirit-writing rituals.

A sizeable body of secondary scholarship exists about Wang Yiting's life and deeds,[22] and numerous primary sources are available as well.[23] Some of the most detailed information about Wang may be found in lengthy biographies and necrologies composed by his contemporaries. For example, one account written on the occasion of his seventieth birthday provides details of his family life and personal tragedies, as well as links to Buddhism and spirit-writing groups.[24] Based on these sources, the highlights of Wang Yiting's life appear to have been as follows. Wang's family home was in Wuxing 吳興 (Huzhou 湖州; Zhejiang), and he maintained close ties with his hometown, but Wang was born in Shanghai because his father had fled their home during the 1860s (most likely as a result of the Taiping Rebellion). Wang's father died when he was a boy, and he ended up being raised in relative poverty[25] by his mother (née Jiang 蔣) and maternal grandmother. Perhaps his sense of filial duty prompted his love of the *Classic of Filial Piety* (*Xiaojing* 孝經), the illustrations of which are said to have inspired his early painting and calligraphy (some accounts also state that his love of painting came from his maternal grandmother).[26]

In 1872 one of Wang's uncles noticed his aptitude for art and book learning, and the uncle helped subsidize his education in a private school where he was also a tutor. Eight years later, Wang was apprenticed to a famous picture-mounting shop known as the Yichun Tang 怡春堂, where he met and studied under renowned modern artists such as Ren Bonian 任伯年 (1840–1896) and Li Ruiqing 李瑞清 (1867–1920).[27] Wang's first recorded painting, "Two Old Men inside a Tangerine," was completed in 1884. During the early 1880s Wang also became acquainted with the renowned Ningbo 寧波 merchant and collector Li Weizhuang 李薇莊 (1873–1913),[28] who helped him find a job at a local banking house that he managed along with Weizhuang's brother Li Yunshu 李雲書 (1867–?), who was also a lay Buddhist. Wang also met Li Pingshu 李平書 (1854–1927), a businessman who later served as the first elected "mayor" of the Chinese section of Shanghai. In addition to working at the banking house, he began to devote his evenings to learning English and Japanese at Shanghai's School for the Diffusion of Languages (Guang fangyanguan 廣方言館; founded by Li Hongzhang 李鴻章 (1823–1901)), although apparently he was not fluent in either language.[29]

During the remaining decades of the nineteenth century and the first years of the twentieth century, Wang devoted his efforts to making his fortune in the world and starting a family. He made his first trip to Japan (Yokohama 橫濱) in 1886, and in the same year married his first wife (née Xi 奚). She died of consumption less than one year later, and in 1888 Wang married his second wife (née Cao 曹). Their first child, a daughter, was born in 1889, followed two years later by a son, Mengnan 孟南. Additional children entered the world at regular two-year intervals, although the couple's third daughter (born in 1897) died young. In the year 1902, Wang started working as a comprador (*maiban* 買辦) for the Osaka Shipping Corporation, and he earned a considerable income because of his hard work and knowledge of Shanghai's commercial realm. His rising status became apparent in 1904 when he was chosen as one of the directors (*dongshi* 董事) of the Shanghai General Chamber of Commerce (Shanghai shangwu zonghui 上海商務總會). His experiences as a self-made man instilled in Wang a strong sense of the value of thrift, which can be seen in a set of family instructions (*jiaxun* 家訓) published in 1931:

> If a poor man earns one coin but spends less, he is wealthy despite being impoverished. If a rich man earns one thousand coins but spends more, he is impoverished despite being wealthy.

> If one were to save for one hundred days but fail to do so for just one of them, the loss of that one day would be no different from the loss for one hundred days. If one were to be frugal for one hundred affairs but fail to be so for just one of them, the waste incurred for that one matter would be no different from failing to be frugal for all one hundred.
>
> Those who start a family are devoted to its establishment. Their food, clothing, and utensils are all of the simplest. Their income exceeds their expenditures, so there is a surplus. Sons who inherit [as head of] a family tend to preside over its fall. The scale of their living expenses is huge, many times those of their forebears. How can a family support such wasteful expenditures?[30]

In 1906, Wang spent a year living at White Dragon Mountain (Bailong shan 白龍山) near the family home in Wuxing, which is also when he started to use the style name (*hao* 號) Bailong shanren 白龍山人. Just one year later, however, he took a position at the Nisshin Steamship Corporation, working alongside Gu Xinyi 顧馨一 and Li Pingshu. The next year witnessed Wang's establishment of his first bank, the Tongtai Bank. By 1910 he had founded the Lida Flour Factory while also working at Mitsubishi, earning over $100,000 in commissions a year. He was also active in Shanghai's artistic community, helping to establish the Yu Garden Calligraphy and Painting Charitable Society (Yuyuan shuhua shanhui 豫園書畫善會) in 1909 and the Shanghai Association for Research on Painting and Calligraphy (Shanghai shuhua yanjiuhui 上海書畫研究會) in 1910. His friendship with the famed artist Wu Changshuo 吳昌碩 (1844–1927) dates to this period. He was also involved in the Celestial Horse Association (Tianma hui 天馬會), which worked to encourage the interaction between Chinese and Western art, and in 1927 helped found the Shanghai Girls Aesthetic School (Shanghai nüzi meishu xuexiao 上海女子美術學校).[31]

In a more tranquil era, Wang might have spent the rest of his life as a prosperous and contented businessman, artist, and family patriarch, but he found himself unable to remain aloof from the tumultuous events of the early twentieth century. Thus, he joined the Chinese Revolutionary Alliance (Zhongguo tongmenghui 中國同盟會), supported Chen Qimei 陳其美 (1878–1915; like Wang, also a Wuxing native) during the 1911 Xinhai 辛亥 Revolution, and even helped lead a suicide squad (*gansi dui* 敢死隊) during an attack on the Jiangnan Arsenal along with his eldest son, Wang Mengnan.[32] Chiang Kai-shek also is said to have fought in this attack, and Wang's connections with Chiang proved invaluable when he was working to support the cause of Chinese Buddhism. In 1912 Wang was elected to the A Roll of Shanghai City Assembly, and during that same year he also served the new Republican government as minister of communications and later minister of commerce, while also helping to underwrite the revolution by borrowing $350,000 and buying $400,000 of government bonds. Wang's concern with philanthropy also appears to have begun during this time, as he is listed as one of the founders of the Chinese Society for the Rescue of Women and Children (Zhongguo jiuji furu zonghui 中國救濟婦孺總會), which was formed in 1912.[33]

Wang's conversion to Buddhism appears to be linked directly to the events of these years. I shall present more details on these aspects of his life; for now, suffice it to say that after 1913 Wang abandoned the world of revolutionary politics and began to devote himself to philanthropy, painting, and self-cultivation. Wang did not take part in the May Fourth Movement of 1919, but continued to be an active member of Shanghai elite society, inviting Albert Einstein and his wife to his home for dinner on November 13, 1922,[34] and being elected as director of the Shanghai General Chamber of Commerce (Shanghai zongshanghui 上海總商會). However, his greatest concern appears to have been providing assistance for others less fortunate than himself. For example, he served as one of the managers of the Shanghai Orphanage (Shanghai gu'eryuan 上海孤兒院), which he had helped found back in 1906 along with Li Pingshu.[35] In 1917 Wang worked with the renowned businessman and philanthropist Zhu Baosan 朱葆三 (1848–1926) to found a hospital for the practice of Chinese medicine (the Shanghai guangyi zhongyiyuan 上海廣益中醫院), and in 1919 he helped establish an institute for the handicapped (the Shanghai canfeiyuan 上海殘廢院). He was also an active member of the city's leading philanthropic organizations, including the International Relief Association and the Shanghai Union of Charitable Associations (Shanghai cishan tuanti lianhehui 上海慈善團體聯合會; founded in 1919, with Wang serving as its first chairperson).[36] In 1921, he helped found the Shanghai China Red Cross Epidemic Hospital (Shanghai Zhongguo Hongshizihui shiyi yiyuan 上海中國紅十字會時疫醫院). In addition, one 1924 record of charitable activities organized by Shanghai elites[37] provides detailed information about Wang Yiting's leadership role and also contains photos of Wang, Huang Hanzhi, and a third leading lay Buddhist elite named Guan Jiongzhi 關絅之 (also written as Guan Jiongzhi 關炯之; 1879–1942).[38] In some ways, the devotion of Wang and other elites to philanthropic activities appears to represent a continuation of patterns many scholars have observed for the late imperial era.[39]

It may be no coincidence that this time period is marked by a change in Wang's artistic style. According to an article in *Shenbao* 申報, Wang had sold paintings of flora and fauna in order to raise money for charity as early as the spring of 1887,[40] but the year 1916 was marked by his completion of a horizontal scroll entitled "Blind Men's Enjoyment" (Xiaqu tu 瞎趣圖), which bears a long colophon by Wu Changshuo about the need to show compassion toward the disabled. The next year Wang completed a painting about floods entitled "Hongshui hengliu" 洪水橫流, and in 1919 he joined with Wu to paint the plight of refugees (the "Liumin tu" 流民圖). It also seems significant that a painting by

Wang exhorting people to provide aid for disaster victims cited the venerable morality book entitled *Wenchang dijun yinzhiwen* 文昌帝君陰騭文, as this may in part reflect his interest in spirit writing.[41]

Another activity Wang engaged in during these years that may have links to his religious life was practicing the martial arts (*wushu* 武術). A series of August 1920 newspaper articles list Wang and his former Chinese Revolutionary Alliance comrade Ye Huijun 葉惠鈞 (1862–1932) as co-chairmen of Shanghai's Martial Arts Association (Wushu hui 武術會), which, like some of the redemptive societies, took as its founding principle the ideal of preserving China's national essence (*baoyou guocui wei zongzhi* 保佑國粹為宗旨).[42] Wang also worked as an "outside instructor" (*chuwai jiaoshou* 出外教授) for the Society of Gentle Fists (Zhirou quanshe 致柔拳社), a Taiji boxing (Taiji quan 太極拳) association that flourished during the late 1920s founded by none other than the Shanghai elite Chen Weiming, who stayed in contact with his deceased son via spirit writing.[43] Wang's friend and fellow lay Buddhist Guan Jiongzhi was also active in this group, serving as its honorary chairman (*mingyu huizhang* 名譽社長). In a preface written for the work entitled *Taiji Boxing Techniques* (*Taiji quanshu* 太極拳術) in 1925, Guan documents his and Wang's participation in the Society and notes that both joined because of the health benefits that could be gained from practicing these techniques.[44] Another work entitled *Questions and Answers about Taiji* (*Taiji dawen* 太極答問) also emphasizes the links between Taiji boxing and good health (especially for women), and notes that those who boxed could also continue practicing meditation (also referred to as *jingzuo* 靜坐), something attractive to men such as Guan and Wang who are known to have meditated.[45] Such interest and involvement in self-cultivation (literally "cultivating life" or *yangsheng* 養生) and even inner alchemy (*neidan* 內丹) techniques was commonplace among many urban elites (including those residing in Shanghai), one such notable personage being Chen Yingning 陳攖寧 (1880–1969), whose life and career have been studied by Liu Xun 劉迅.[46]

In recognition of Wang Yiting's long years of service, the Shanghai City Government planned to name a street after him in honor of his seventieth birthday, but these plans never came to fruition because of the outbreak of the Second Sino-Japanese War. Wang fled to Hong Kong following the Japanese attack on Shanghai that commenced on August 13, 1937, but he continued to be active in philanthropic efforts on behalf of the many refugees who flocked to the city, helping to found the Shanghai Union of Charitable Associations for Disaster Relief (Shanghai cishan tuanti jiuzai lianhehui 上海慈善團體聯合救災會). However, he fell seriously ill while in Hong Kong and decided to return to Shanghai to wait for the end. He arrived in the city he loved on November 12, 1938, and passed away the very next day. His funeral was held on January 22, 1939, at the Huzhou Society (Hushe 湖社). Over 1,800 people attended, including representatives of over 150 organizations as well as two of Wang's closest Buddhist companions, Guan Jiongzhi and Huang Hanzhi. Wang's contributions to the welfare of others were of such magnitude that, according to an obituary published in *Shenbao* on November 15, 1938, "In Shanghai, there were no charities without Master [Wang]'s involvement."[47]

WANG YITING'S DEVOTION TO BUDDHISM

The data reveal that the life of a devout Buddhist such as Wang Yiting can best be understood in light of the challenges this religion faced and the innovations it undertook during a time of traumatic transformation. The Republican era was a time of rapid institutional growth for modern Chinese Buddhism, especially in terms of large-scale Buddhist associations run by the *sangha*.[48] These included the China Association of Buddhism (Zhonghua Fojiao zonghui 中華佛教總會; founded in 1912), the Shanghai Association for the Preservation of Buddhism (Shanghai Fojiao weichihui 上海佛教維持會; founded in 1926), the Chinese Buddhist Association (founded in 1929), the Shanghai City Buddhist Association (Shanghaishi Fojiaohui 上海市佛教會; also founded in 1929), the Shanghai Branch of the Chinese Association for Buddhist Studies (Zhongguo Foxuehui Shanghai fenhui 中國佛學會上海市分會; founded in 1935), and so forth.[49] With the exception of the first group, Wang was involved in all of these organizations.[50]

The Republican era also witnessed extensive elite support for various forms of lay Buddhism (literally "householder Buddhism" or jushi Fojiao 居士佛教). Shanghai was home to numerous lay Buddhist associations, in all of which Wang played a leading role.[51] These included the Shanghai Buddhist Householder Association (Shanghai Fojiao jushilin 上海佛教居士林), which was founded in 1918 and four years later grew into the better-known World Buddhist Householder Association (Shijie Fojiao jushilin 世界佛教居士林), the [Buddhist] Enlightenment Society (Jueshe 覺社; also founded in 1918), and the Shanghai Buddhist Pure Karma Society (Shanghai Fojiao jingyeshe 上海佛教淨業社; founded in 1922). Of these, the World Buddhist Householder Association gained renown for its sponsorship of lectures and philanthropic activities (including preaching the *dharma* at prisons), while the Shanghai Buddhist Pure Karma Society helped organize a wide range of Buddhist rituals, particularly ceremonies to protect the nation and ease calamities (*huguo xizai fahui* 護國息災法會).[52] Wang and other lay Buddhists also were extremely active in numerous charities, ranging from establishing institutions for the unfortunate such as the Shanghai Buddhist Orphanage (Shanghai Fojiao ciyouyuan 上海佛教慈幼院; founded in 1933) to participating in the provision of disaster relief.[53]

One key aspect of modern Chinese Buddhism was its highly public nature, with believers using various forms of the mass media to transmit their views (see chapter 2). Wang and his fellow elites helped sponsor the city's numerous Buddhist publishing houses, most notably the Society for Propagating the Dharma and Shanghai Buddhist Books. Their efforts bore considerable fruit, and it hardly seems a coincidence that so many elite accounts of converting to Buddhism mention the importance of reading widely circulating texts such as the *Mahayana Awakening of Faith* (*Dasheng qixinlun* 大乘起信論). Wang also joined other leading Buddhist figures to sponsor the reprinting of the *Anshi quanshu* 安士全書, whose author Zhou Anshi 周安士 (Zhou Siren 周思仁; 1656–1739) was a devout lay Buddhist. Over three million copies of this text are said to have been printed during the Republican era, and elites such as Lu Xun 魯迅 (1881–1936) sung its praises.[54]

The lay Buddhist activism just described occasionally resulted from state attempts to limit Buddhism's growth, particularly on the part of leaders such as Yuan Shikai and Duan Qirui, who attempted to convert monasteries into schools (see chapter 1).[55] In other instances, however, Buddhist activism was less a response to state pressures and more an expression of deeply personal religious devotion. For Wang Yiting, who was also a leading member of modern Shanghai's elite, Buddhist faith involved a complex combination of motivations, including self-cultivation, concern for the welfare of others, and a commitment to helping this religious movement find its place in modern Chinese culture, including resisting temple destruction campaigns.

Wang Yiting's devotion to Buddhism is movingly described in a key primary source composed just after his death in 1938, the *Brief Account of the Deeds [Performed by] Householder Wang Yiting* (*Wang Yiting jushi shilue* 王一亭居士事略; note the use of the term "householder" or *jushi* 居士 in the work's title). According to this work's necrology, Wang first learned of Buddhism from his mother and maternal grandmother, and he set aside a portion of the family garden for the construction of a Buddhist hall (Foge 佛閣) where his mother could practice daily devotions in her old age.[56] However, Wang's conversion to Buddhism appears to be linked directly to the tumultuous events of the early twentieth century. Wang continued to work on behalf of the second revolution, and his name was placed on a wanted list by then-President Yuan Shikai. He was also an eyewitness to one of the most shocking events of the early twentieth century, the assassination of Song Jiaoren. Wang was standing beside Song when he was gunned down, and he helped prepare Song's tombstone.[57] Believing that he had escaped from harm because he had chanted the name of the Bodhisattva Guanyin, Wang began to undertake an annual pilgrimage to Mount Putuo (Putuo shan 普陀山) beginning that same year, and also devoted much of his time to painting Buddhist deities, particularly Guanyin and the Amitabha Buddha (Amituofo 阿彌陀佛).[58]

While Wang's devotion to Buddhism appears to have intensified after 1913, he did not formally become a Buddhist (*guiyi* 皈依) until 1916. In March of that year, during his annual pilgrimage to Mount Putuo, he engaged in a series of fervent conversations with the eminent monks Great Master Taixu (Taixu dashi 太虛大師; 1887–1947) and Dharma Master Yinguang, which resulted in his taking the Three Refuges (*sangui* 三皈).[59] Subsequently, Wang began to devote an increasing amount of his time to Buddhist causes, working alongside renowned members of the *sangha* such as Taixu, Yinguang, Hongyi, and Dharma Master Yuanying (Yuanying fashi 圓瑛法師; 1878–1953), as well as leading lay Buddhists such as Guan Jiongzhi, Huang Qinglan, Shi Xingzhi, Li Yunshu (1867–?), Ding Fubao, Di Baoxian 狄葆賢 (Chuqing 楚青; 1872–1941; also the publisher of the Shanghai newspaper *Shibao* 時報), Gao Henian 高鶴年 (1872–1962), and Zhu Ziqian 朱子謙 (n.d.; also a native of Wuxing).[60]

One of Wang's first acts in support of Buddhism was working with Kang Youwei 康有為 (1858–1927) to establish the Huayan Institute (Huayan daxue 華嚴大學), which from 1913 to 1915 was located in Hardoon Gardens (Hatong huayuan 哈同花園). The largest garden in Shanghai (covering more than twenty acres), its history clearly reflects the cosmopolitan nature of this city's modern history, being built in 1909 by Sir Silas Hardoon (d. 1931), a wealthy Jewish merchant from Great Britain. His wife, a Chinese woman named Luo Jialing 羅迦陵 (1864–1941), was a devout Buddhist, and allowed the Huayan Institute to operate on the garden's grounds. However, following a dispute between Luo and the Buddhists, the Institute moved to Hangzhou in 1915. A few years later the Cangsheng mingzhi daxue 倉聖明智大學 was founded in the garden, with renowned elites such as Wang Guowei 王國維 (1877–1927) and Xu Beihong 徐悲鴻 (1895–1953) serving as instructors. Hardoon Gardens also served as a site for meetings and other charitable events linked to the provision of disaster relief, many of which featured Wang Yiting and his comrades from the China Rescuing Life Association.[61] Sadly, all came to naught following the death of Hardoon in 1931, a big fire in the 1930s, and the death of Luo in 1941.[62]

During this time period Wang's Buddhist art appears to have been shaped by his friendship with the eminent monk Hongyi. This can be seen in a set of couplets (*lian* 聯) that Wang wrote in 1925 after reading Hongyi's handwritten copy of the Vinaya text known as the *Brahma Net Sutra* (*Fanwang jing* 梵網經), which extol the virtues of Buddhist precepts and discipline.[63] It seems significant that Wang and Hongyi shared an interest in this scripture, as its fifty-eight bodhisattva precepts had proven inspirational to prominent Ming-dynasty monks such as Yunqi Zhuhong 雲棲袾宏 (1535–1615).[64] Moreover, the *Brahma Net Sutra* is also well known for its emphasis on the ideal of nonkilling (*jiesha* 戒殺), which motivated the vegetarianism of elites such as Wang Yiting and Feng Zikai 豐子愷 (1898–1975)[65] and also featured prominently in morality books, including those published by the Illuminating Goodness Publishing House that were discussed in chapter 2. I should also note that apart from their artistic and religious penchants, Wang Yiting and Hongyi shared a number of other common experiences, including the death of their fathers when they were young, the tragic loss of young children, and failure in revolutionary politics.[66]

Wang appears to have been especially active in the Enlightenment Society and the World Buddhist Householder Association, serving as deputy head of the latter group in 1924 and head for three consecutive terms beginning in 1927.[67] However, his participation in the institutional side of Buddhism appears to have declined significantly following his entanglement in a schism between Taixu and Yuanying in 1931. Wang was close to both of these eminent monks, using his connections in Japan to arrange for Taixu to attend the East Asian Buddhist Conference in Tokyo in November 1925,[68] while also working with Yuanying to prevent the confiscation of Buddhist monasteries and their property during the 1920s and 1930s. However, the Buddhist reform movement in modern China had suffered intense differences of opinion since its beginnings in the 1910s, and things came to a head when Taixu and Yuanying struggled to gain control of the Chinese Buddhist Association in 1931. Taixu resigned from its standing committee in April, following which he launched an attack on the Association and its record. Shortly afterward, Taixu and his allies were elected to the Association's executive committee, but were unable to run the Association effectively because of opposition by more conservative Buddhists and their constituencies, leaving Taixu with no alternative but to resign in June. Wang tried to mediate the impasse and offered to help Yuanying manage the Association's affairs, but to no avail.[69]

Following this debacle, Wang continued to be involved with some aspects of Buddhist philanthropy, and in 1932 issued a strongly worded appeal for his fellow Buddhists to become more active in providing assistance to others.[70] In general, however, Wang appears to have devoted the remainder of his life to the meditational side of Buddhism (see Figure 3.1),[71] leaving its institutional affairs for others to handle.[72] Wang's Buddhist faith appears to have remained steadfast despite personal suffering and

FIGURE 3.1: *Wang Yiting with His Rosary Practicing Buddhist Meditation*

disillusionment with monastic infighting, and he took the time to help host the Ninth Panchen Lama (Banchan Lama 班禪喇嘛), Thubten Chökyi Nyima (1883–1937), during his visit to Shanghai in 1934.[73] That same year, one of Wang's grandsons was married during a vegetarian banquet, an event that attracted a veritable "Who's Who" of Shanghai notables and also provided a public occasion for extolling the merits of vegetarianism.[74] An even later account, from the October 2, 1936, issue of the *Zhe-Ou ribao* 浙甌日報, describes Wang presiding over a Buddhist-style vegetarian wedding ceremony for lay members of this religion.[75] Wang's devotion also was recognized in the primary sources of that era. For example, Taixu's necrology aptly summarizes Wang's religious life with the following couplets (*lian* 聯): "Saving others through philanthropy, protecting the dharma and the Buddhist faith, his paintings and calligraphy are transmitted through the ages, [his reputation] soars across the oceans" (*cishan jiuren, Fomen hufa, shuhua chuanhi, haiguo feisheng* 慈善救人，佛門護法，書畫傳世，海國飛聲).

BUDDHISM AND WANG'S LINKS TO JAPAN

Buddhism also shaped Wang Yiting's interaction with the many Japanese who visited Shanghai. Walter B. Davis's research shows that Wang often bestowed paintings and calligraphy on his Japanese guests, while he also hosted banquets at his residence's Catalpa Garden (Ziyuan 梓園) and a restaurant he managed known as the Bodhi Grove (Juelin 覺林). The fare was invariably vegetarian and was said to have been popular among both the Japanese and Chinese residents of Shanghai.[76] Wang's friends included not only leading industrialists such as Shibusawa Eiichi 澀澤榮一 (1840–1931), but also the renowned Buddhologist Omura Seigai 大村西崖 (1867–1927) as well as Otani Kozui 大谷光瑞 (1876–1948), who served as abbot of the Nishi Honganji 西本願寺. Another Japanese Buddhist, Shigahara Ryōsai 信々原良哉 (n.d.), who visited the Catalpa Garden in the spring of 1936 and enjoyed a vegetarian meal there, referred glowingly to Wang as "China's foremost Buddhist layman."[77]

Wang's commitment to Buddhist philanthropy blended neatly into his links to Japan. His crowning achievement may have been the massive relief effort that he helped organize following the Great Kantō 關東 Earthquake of September 1, 1923. This disaster and the fires that ensued (most people were cooking their lunch when the earthquake struck at 11:58 AM) caused 91,344 deaths, with an additional 13,275 people listed as missing. Over 550,000 homes were partially or totally destroyed. Wang sprang into action as soon as he heard the news of this horrible tragedy, helping to form the Buddhist Relief Association for the Japanese Calamity (Fojiao puji Rizai hui 佛教普濟日災會), as well as raising over 185,000 Japanese yen by means of front-page announcements in newspapers such as *Shenbao* and charitable auctions of artworks, including his own. He then arranged for the purchase of tons of supplies (most notably rice and flour), with the first shipment of relief aid leaving Shanghai on September 8 aboard the steamship Xinminglun 新銘輪 and arriving in the port of Kobe 神戶 on September 12. Wang's efforts involved far more than material aid, however; he was profoundly concerned for the spiritual condition of the survivors and the souls of the loved ones they had lost. Accordingly, he devoted unstinting efforts to sponsoring Buddhist services to pray for the souls of the dead. These rites, designed to achieve the "transfer of merit" to the earthquake's victims, were held on a massive scale, starting with forty-nine-day Land and Water Masses (Shuilu puli daochang da fashi 水陸普利道場大法事) held at the four sacred mountains of Chinese Buddhism: Emei 峨嵋, Jiuhua 九華, Wutai 五台, and Putuo 普陀. Subsequently, a second series of these rites were held at two leading sacred sites that Wang and his fellow Buddhists had the closest links to: the Monastery for Attracting Worthies (Zhaoxiansi 招賢寺) at West Lake (Xihu 西

湖) in Hangzhou (also a key sacred site for Hongyi) and the Jade Buddha Monastery (Yufosi 玉佛寺) in Shanghai.[78]

Apart from undertaking ritual remedies, Wang drew on his influence as head of the Chinese Buddhist Association to arrange for the casting of a ghost bell (youming zhong 幽冥鐘) to commemorate the victims of this tragic event. On November 7, 1923, Wang contacted Japan's foreign minister, Izyūin Hikokichi 伊集院彥吉 (1864–1924), as well as the United Buddhist Association of Japan (Nihon Bukkyō rengōkokai 日本佛教聯合會), to express his intent to undertake this task. The bell was cast in Hangzhou, completed in 1925, and shipped to Tokyo via Shanghai and Yokohama 横濱 in 1926. Four years later, in September 1930, it was moved to the newly constructed Tokyo Earthquake Memorial Hall (Tōkyō shinsai kinendō 東京震災紀念堂), which was later renamed the Tokyo Hall for the Comfort of Souls (Tōkyōto ireidō 東京都慰靈堂) after being expanded to commemorate the victims of the Tokyo Firebombings of 1945. A mammoth instrument, the bell weighed in at 1.56 tons, standing 1.69 meters in height and having a diameter at its mouth of 1.21 meters. On its side are carved the words, "For the benefit of all who hear the bell's sound, be they dead or living" (*puwen zhongsheng, mingyang liang li* 普聞鐘聲，冥陽兩利), along with the date the earthquake struck (1923) and Wang's name (see Figure 3.2). It is rung every year on the anniversary of the earthquake, a ceremony that Wang's descendents also have attended. In addition, the Hall contains four paintings that Wang donated on the occasion of its inauguration, the contents of which encompass both Buddhist and Daoist themes. There are also records of the relief efforts he helped to organize, his photograph, and a second inscription commemorating his accomplishments.[79]

The grateful Japanese referred to Wang as a "bodhisattva" (*pusa* 菩薩), and he was granted an audience with the Shōwa 昭和 Emperor, with the emperor's third son visiting Wang in

FIGURE 3.2: *The Ghost Bell*

Shanghai in 1927. The goodwill from Wang's deeds soon was reciprocated during the 1930s, when Shibusawa Eiichi and other friends of Wang formed the Association of Sympathetic Support for the Republic of China's Flood Calamity (Chūka Mingoku suisai dōjōkai 中華民國水災同情會) to aid the Chinese people when they were suffering in the aftermath of their own natural disasters.[80] In 1983 the head of the Japan-China Friendship Association (Nitchū yūkō kyōkai 日中友好協會), Utsunomiya Tokuma 宇都宮德馬 (1906–2000), presented China with a stele reading, "Mr. Wang Yiting, your benevolence and righteousness will never be forgotten" (*Wang Yiting xiansheng, en'yi yongyuan bu wangji* 王一亭先生，恩義永遠不忘記). The extent to which Wang may have been influenced by Japanese religious traditions is not clear, but his connections may have become a liability for him by the 1930s and after his death as well. Despite the fact that some biographers emphasize Wang's patriotism,[81] there is little evidence that he attempted to blend Buddhism and nationalism like other contemporary elites,[82] while the powerful nationalistic and anti-Japanese sentiments that have swept through China in recent decades appear to have inhibited scholarly initiative in examining his life and career, which have only begun to attract attention in these past few years.

BUDDHISM AND WANG YITING'S RELATIONSHIP WITH CHIANG KAI-SHEK

One especially instructive episode in Wang Yiting's religious life involves the way he used his friendship with Chiang Kai-shek to obtain government approval for the registration (*li'an* 立案) of the Chinese Buddhist Association. While Chinese Buddhism experienced considerable growth during the Republican era, it often proved difficult for Buddhists to gain state approval for their efforts, especially when Buddhism became caught up in the temple destruction campaigns (see chapter 1). Things came to a head in August and September 1928, when both the Ministry of Education and the Ministry of the Interior were on the verge of enacting a series of strict policies to further regulate temples, including Buddhist ones. It was at this time that Wang visited Chiang and persuaded him to protect the interests of legitimate Buddhist practitioners and their sacred sites. Chiang responded by stating that he was generally supportive of modern Buddhists' reform efforts, so long as they met the state's needs for maintaining social order.[83]

What factors may have contributed to Chiang's support of Buddhism, which in effect ended up at least partially overruling some of the state's planned policies? I consider this problem in light of Chiang's long-term friendship with Wang, as well as their common devotion to a wide range of religious traditions, including Buddhism. The bonds between Chiang Kai-shek and Wang Yiting appear to have been forged during the tumultuous years of the early twentieth century, and they also may have spent time together in Japan, all of which has led to the transmission of numerous seemingly apocryphal stories. Some accounts claim that Chiang addressed Wang as "senior uncle" (*bobo* 伯伯), while others state that Chiang was a regular visitor to Wang's home and even accompanied Wang to the burial rites for his wife in Huzhou. While the truth of these stories is difficult to ascertain,[84] we do know that Wang produced a painting for Chiang and Soong to celebrate the occasion of their wedding and also coauthored a 1929 book about Chiang entitled *General Chiang Kai-shek: The Builder of New China*. This work, published shortly after the encounter between Wang and Chiang described previously, also featured an introduction by the renowned diplomat (and lifelong Methodist Christian) Dr. Chenting T. Wang (Wang Zhengting 王正廷; 1882–1961) as well as a preface by Dr. Wang Chung-hui.[85]

Another factor that can help explain Chiang's receptiveness to Wang's appeals may be the importance of Buddhism as a part of Chiang's spiritual makeup. Chiang's life has been expertly documented, but most of the work on the religious aspects of his life has tended to focus on Christianity. Only in recent years have scholars begun to fully appreciate the role Buddhism played in shaping his worldview. One early example of this trend may be found in a book-length study by Chen Tiejian 陳鐵健, which documents the impact of indigenous cultural elements such as Confucianism, Buddhism, and even geomancy (*fengshui* 風水) on Chiang. Chiang's home in Fenghua 奉化 County (Zhejiang) boasted a sizeable number of sacred sites, most notably the Hole in the Snow Monastery (Xuedou Si 雪竇寺), which had long benefited from the patronage of the Chiang family, including Chiang himself. Many of Chiang's forbears had been devout Buddhists. His grandfather (Chiang Ssu-nien 蔣斯年; 1814–1894) took Chiang to Buddhist temples as a child, while a Five Dynasties (907–960) ancestor named Chiang Tsung-pa 蔣宗霸 even had ended up being venerated as a Buddhist deity. Chiang also is said to have worshipped his ancestors in both 1931 and even 1949, well after his conversion to Christianity.[86]

However, as was the case with Wang Yiting, the most important individual to shape Chiang's respect for Buddhism appears to have been his mother (née Wang 王; maiden name Wang Caiyu 王采玉; 1864–1921). Like Wang Yiting, Chiang suffered the death of his father when he was a child (age nine), so Chiang's mother had a huge influence on his life and proved responsible for inculcating many of his core values. A strong-willed woman who had suffered her share of hardship, she had been widowed from a previous marriage, following which she practiced Buddhist self-cultivation at a temple near her natal home. Following her marriage to Chiang's father (and subsequent second widowhood), she persisted in her devotions, which included numerous pilgrimages to Mount Putuo and lengthy periods of self-cultivation in local Buddhist temples. She also was a devoted philanthropist. Chiang expressed his appreciation of his mother's religious guidance in her necrology, which states that she would patiently explain the contents of Buddhist scriptures to him whenever he came home, and that any understanding he had attained of that religion's doctrines was because of her unstinting efforts.[87]

Chiang's Buddhist faith also flourished because of his extensive contacts with eminent monks such as Taixu, with Wang Yiting playing a role in the cultivation of such friendships.[88] Chiang's encounters with these monks were similar to the interactions between traditional literati and elite religious specialists, particularly in terms of spending time together on special occasions and exchanging poems, with these specialists often attempting to provide advice, comfort, and inspiration to leaders as they struggled to overcome adversity. One of Chiang's most renowned meetings with Taixu occurred at the Hole in the Snow Monastery in September 1927, following a KMT dispute over relocating the capital and a military defeat at Xuzhou 徐州 (Jiangsu). Chiang invited Taixu to lecture on Buddhist sutras (*jiangjing* 講經), with the resulting lecture series including an exposition on the *Heart Sutra* (*Xinjing* 心經) for Chiang Ching-kuo 蔣經國's (1910–1988) mother, Mao Fumei 毛福梅 (1882–1939), on the date of the Mid-Autumn Festival.[89] Other accounts claim that Taixu (or the monastery's Abbot Langqing 郎清) told Chiang's fortune, based either on his Eight Birth Characters (*bazi* 八字) or astrology (*xingxiangshu* 星相術), while still others maintain that Chiang went to the monastery to seek advice pertaining to the geomancy of his tomb.[90]

Chiang's pursuit of Buddhist practice continued even after his conversion to Christianity. For example, in December 1931 he sought out the peace and quiet of the Hole in the Snow Monastery, where he engaged in the close reading of the renowned tenth-century Zen Buddhist text known as the *Mirror of the Mind* (*Zongjing lu* 宗鏡錄),[91] which he continued to study until his flight to Taiwan in 1949. Chiang visited the Monastery and other Buddhist sites in Fenghua in 1947 (see Figure 3.3). During these

FIGURE 3.3: *Chiang Kai-shek at the Ancient Consecration Monastery (Gu Guanding Si* 古灌定寺*), 1947. This photo was taken on April 15, just over one week following the Easter Sunday of that year (April 6, 1947). Courtesy of Academia Historica, Republic of China.*

trying years of his life, Chiang journeyed to numerous renowned Buddhist sacred sites throughout Zhejiang, including those he had visited with his grandfather as a boy, and his devout Christian wife Soong May-ling is said to have accompanied him on at least one of these occasions.

Indigenous Chinese religious traditions also may have contributed to Chiang's promotion of the 1934 New Life Movement (see chapter 1). Conventional wisdom has given primacy to Christianity, and certainly there is strong evidence of Christian missionaries assisting the enactment of the New Life Movement.[92] This argument also makes sense in light of the tendency of leading Christian organizations to publicize progressive social ideals (including opposition to opium, cigarette smoking, alcohol use, prostitution, foot binding, the selling of daughters, and many other "social ills"), all of which prompted many non-Christian elites (including Wang) to work with Christians to achieve these goals.[93] Nonetheless, one cannot help wondering if the current fixation on Chiang's Christianity has obscured the importance of other factors. For example, some scholars have noted Chiang's emphasis on the revival of virtues taught by the sages, not to mention the Neo-Confucian ideals of frugality, self-discipline, honesty, and social harmony, all of which figure prominently in his diary yet also lay at the heart of the New Life Movement.[94] Finally, it is essential to remember that some of this movement's main ideals, most notably *liyi* 禮義 (propriety and righteousness), and *lianchi* 廉恥 (honesty and shame), lay at the core of the belief systems such as the Eight Virtues so actively promoted by redemptive societies (see chapter 2). These religious groups also played a key role in Wang's religious life.

WANG YITING'S PARTICIPATION IN REDEMPTIVE SOCIETIES

As we saw in the previous two chapters, during the Republican era redemptive societies gained considerable notoriety for their emphasis on proper moral conduct, engagement in philanthropic activities, and practice of spirit-writing rituals. They also developed into an integral component of Republican China's cultural life, which included networks of prominent elites such as Wang Yiting and other individuals who were businessmen, officials, intellectuals, and religious specialists. Their doctrines and practices were transmitted by itinerant leaders and specialists (including refugees) who roamed China's urban networks, while the socioeconomic changes that influenced urban life (in both positive and negative ways) were one factor prompting people to join these groups.[95] David Palmer's research reveals that, while many redemptive societies began in rural areas, they quickly found a niche in urban settings and proved able to develop forms of organization more suitable for urban life.[96] Similarly, David Ownby notes that redemptive societies were largely urban phenomena that appealed to China's rising middle class.[97] Some urban elites were attracted by these societies' cosmopolitan and eclectic doctrines, while others participated in order to engage in self-cultivation or practice philanthropy. The result, as one saying from Tianjin 天津 aptly put it, was that "the poor do not join the Li [Sect]; the rich do not join the [Green] Gang" (*qiong buzai Li, fu buzai bang* 窮不在理，富不在幫).[98]

Wang joined a number of redemptive societies during the 1920s and 1930s,[99] the most notable being the Teachings of Celestial Virtue (Tiande jiao 天德教), which was founded by Xiao Changming 蕭昌明 (1895–1943).[100] Wang was a prominent donor and guardian (*hufa* 護法) of this group, having been inaugurated as one of its eighteen Perfected Lords (*zhenjun* 真君) in 1934.[101] He also participated in the activities of the World Red Swastika Society, with one set of reports about its charitable works in the year 1937 listing him as an honorary chairman (*mingyu huizhang* 名譽會長).[102] The date Wang joined this organization is not clear, but he probably became familiar with its activities in 1923, when it played a major role in organizing relief efforts following the Great Kantō Earthquake.[103] The Society also sent a delegation to

Japan and subsequently helped found a Japanese branch affiliated with the Great Root Teachings (Ōmoto-kyō 大本教).[104]

WANG YITING'S INTEREST IN SPIRIT-WRITING ASSOCIATIONS

Wang's participation in redemptive societies seems to have been linked to his interest in one of their main practices, namely spirit-writing rituals such as those that Chen Weiming used to make contact with his deceased son. Spirit-writing rituals had long attracted the support of Chinese elites, especially examination candidates who asked deities such as the Purple Maiden (Zigu 紫姑) for help with their essays.[105] Spirit writing thrived during the late imperial era and was especially important in shaping the growth of contemporary sectarian and Daoist movements.[106] During the nineteenth and twentieth centuries, Westerners who visited China often were struck by the prevalence of such rites, with the diplomat and sociologist Herbert A. Giles (1845–1935) composing a vibrant account of spirit-writing rituals in Amoy. According to Giles, such rites were noteworthy for their high-quality poetry, but their goals tended to center not on the propagation of moral values but on winning the local lottery.[107]

Many Republican-era Chinese elites practiced spirit writing for a wide range of motivations, including contacting the dead, composing morality books, and so forth. For example, Fan Chunwu's research treats the religious activities of Zheng Guanying 鄭觀應 (1842–1922) in Shanghai and Guangzhou, noting how Zheng's spirit writing and Daoist self-cultivation helped shape his profound commitment to charity and reform.[108] Other elites, such as Xu Dishan 許地山 (1893–1941), may not have believed in the efficacy of spirit writing, but tacitly acceded that its importance merited historical studies.[109] Spirit-writing altars also served as public arenas in urban cultural life. One such instance may be found in a brief 1935 essay by Zheng Zhenduo 鄭振鐸 (1898–1958), which notes the immense popularity of such groups and their skill in raising large sums of money. Another account, appended to the World Bookstore (Shijie shuju 世界書局) edition of the *Zuben Jigong quanzhuan* 足本濟公全傳, further confirms the prevalence of spirit-writing rituals and associations in modern Chinese urban life.[110] The newspaper *Shenbao* contains numerous colorful articles about spirit-writing rituals, with the deities who were invited to descend into the planchette including not only Buddhist and Daoist figures but even former President Sun Yat-sen.[111]

Such rites also were popular among modern elite lay Buddhists, including Wang Yiting. The overlap between Buddhism and spirit writing had attracted elite attention as early as the Kangxi 康熙 era (1661–1722)[112] and persisted well into the modern era, as may be seen in critical remarks by Liang Qichao 梁啟超 (1873–1929), who lamented that many leading scholars of his age had become enamored of such practices.[113] This did nothing to dissuade many modern Buddhist elites, however, with leading figures such as Ding Fubao advocating the use of spirit writing as a means of transmitting Buddhist doctrine.[114] Even Buddhist monastic leaders such as Yinguang were not unsympathetic to spirit writing, provided that such rites were used to further the cause of philanthropy, not serve as an aid to Buddhist self-cultivation.[115]

Wang appears to have become an active participant in spirit-writing groups during the early and mid 1910s, at roughly the same time that he converted to Buddhism. For Wang, spirit writing readily overlapped with Buddhist practice, with him being mentioned as joining (and later leading) the China Rescuing Life Association (Zhongguo jishenghui 中國濟生會) in 1916. Scholars such as Tao Shuimu 陶水木 (and until recently, myself) consistently have assumed that the Association was merely a philanthropic organization, with Tao's recent article providing a great deal of information on Wang's efforts in this and other philanthropic groups.[116] However, the term "*ji*" 濟 in the Association's name also stands for Jigong 濟公, an eccentric Song-dynasty

Buddhist monk who ended up being worshipped as a popular deity. Jigong was the leading figure of the Association's spirit-writing rituals, and during such rites he regularly exhorted Association members to make ever-larger contributions to the welfare of others.[117] Wang Jianchuan 王見川 has convincingly demonstrated that the China Rescuing Life Association's own history was intimately linked to spirit writing, having been founded during the late nineteenth century as a spirit-writing altar known as the Gathering Clouds Studio (Jiyunxuan 集雲軒), which joined other such groups in providing famine relief for North China victims of the Boxer Rebellion.[118] The Association developed into the group's charitable branch, with the two groups constituting a form of dual identity (religious association combined with philanthropic group). The Association's philanthropic activities included famine and flood relief, providing medicines during outbreaks of epidemics, constructing hospitals, and so forth, with branch groups founded in other urban centers such as Beijing and Tianjin.[119] As for Gathering Clouds Studio, apart from the worship of Jigong it also produced Daoist poetry books and played an active role in hosting the Panchen Lama during his visit to Shanghai in 1934.[120] Both groups coexisted with and complemented each other, with the Association promoting its charitable aspects and serving as a means to register with the authorities and the Studio embodying its religious practices.[121] Similar pairings marked the development of Chinese redemptive societies, one example being the Society of the Way (religious activities) and Red Swastika Society (philanthropy).[122] News of the Association and its manifold activities spread to Taiwan as early as 1918, with one newspaper article noting the importance of Buddhist doctrine to the Association's members, as well as stressing their emphasis on keeping male and female worshippers separated.[123]

A number of sources claim that Wang joined the Association after undergoing a second conversion to Buddhism via

Jigong (*guiyi Jigong huofo* 皈依濟公活佛) and taking the *dharma* name Jueqi 覺器 while performing a spirit-writing ritual at the Studio.[124] Wang proved to be an active participant in both philanthropic and religious activities sponsored by the Association, becoming its leader in 1919 following the death of its prior head Chen Runfu 陳潤夫 (Chen Zuolin 陳作霖; 1841–1919) and working to build numerous charitable schools and hospitals. His interest in spirit writing also continued unabated. One account from the year 1924 describes large numbers of worshippers (including Wang Yiting) taking part in spirit-writing rites held on the premises of the China Rescuing Life Association, and is especially significant for indicating the roles played by elite women in this group, as well as the enforced segregation of the sexes, characteristics that were highly common among other spirit-writing groups as well.[125] It is important to note that Buddhist leaders such as Taixu openly describe Wang's involvement in spirit-writing associations in great detail, which seems to indicate that few objections were raised to lay Buddhists taking part in such groups.[126] Moreover, Buddhist elites such as Yinguang, Ding Fubao, and Ye Erkai did not hesitate to become involved in the Association's religious activities.[127]

Apart from worshipping Jigong at the Association, Wang also was an active patron of many of this deity's sacred sites.[128] One example features the modern history of a famed Jigong temple located at Mount Tiantai (Tiantai shan 天台山) in Zhejiang, the Hall of the Buddha Ji[gong] at the Cave of Auspicious Mists (Ruixiadong Jifoyuan 瑞霞洞濟佛院), which was originally founded on Mount Chicheng (Chicheng shan 赤城山) in 1209. Wang provided financial support for a temple reconstruction project organized by a local spirit-writing group in 1927, and also composed a calligraphic inscription reading "the ancient monument again shines with light" (*guji chongguang* 古跡重光).[129] In addition, in 1929 he wrote an article using his pen name "Master of the Plum Flower Hall" (Meihua guanzhu 梅花館主), which described how a Shanghai theatre decided to stage a Jigong play following a medium's intervention.[130] Wang's faith in Jigong also was vividly expressed in a painting of this deity that he completed in 1926 (see Figure 3.4).[131]

WANG YITING'S PARTICIPATION IN DAOIST MOVEMENTS

Spirit writing also appears to have shaped Wang Yiting's involvement in some of the leading Daoist movements of his era. This phenomenon might best be understood in the context of the history of modern Daoism, as seen in Vincent Goossaert's innovative analysis of the complex interaction and competition between Daoism, spirit-writing groups, and redemptive societies, which contributes immensely to our understanding of the extensive diffusion of Daoist beliefs and practices in modern China. Many Daoist lay organizations were constituted around spirit-writing cults, with such groups being extremely widespread throughout China during the late nineteenth and early twentieth centuries. Devout believers could be formally accepted as disciples by the immortal Lü Dongbin 呂洞賓 and other deities during spirit-writing rituals, with some also practicing various forms of "cultivating life" (*yangsheng*) and internal alchemy (*neidan*).[132] Daoist spirit-writing groups also were prominent in Guangdong 廣東 and Hong Kong, where they contributed significantly to the growth of the Wong Tai Sin (Huang Daxian 黃大仙) cult, which featured elites such as Feng Qizhuo 馮其焯 (?–1953) and Huang Yuntian 黃允畋 (1920–1997) as well as sacred sites such as the Puqing Tan 普慶壇 and the Sik Sik Yuen 嗇色園.[133]

Daoist spirit-writing associations proved to be extremely popular in the Jiangnan 江南 region, where they interacted extensively with Buddhist and sectarian groups. These associations tended to be organized around altars (*tan* 壇) dedicated to the worship of Lü Dongbin, yet also included deities such as Jigong.[134] Many of these movements appear to have originated atop Daoist mountains, with one key sacred site being

FIGURE 3.4: *Wang Yiting Painting of Jigong*

the Venerable Plum Flower Temple (Gu Meihuaguan 古梅花觀; also known as the Hall of Purified Yang or Chunyang Gong 純陽宮), located on Mount Jingai (Jingai shan 金蓋山) in Wang Yiting's native home of Huzhou. This temple was home to one of the most renowned Qing-dynasty figures of the Longmen 龍門 branch of Quanzhen 全真 Daoism, Min Yide 閔一得 (1758–1836), and under the leadership of Min and his disciples branch altars soon covered much of the region, including Shanghai.[135]

One source suggests a possible link between the Venerable Plum Flower Temple and Shanghai's Gathering Clouds Studio, while also clearly demonstrating Wang Yiting's role in Daoist spirit-writing groups.[136] Recent research by Vincent Goossaert confirms that the Venerable Plum Flower Temple spawned a network of seventy-two branch altars, the largest being Shanghai's Cloud Enlightenment Altar (Jueyun tan 覺雲壇), which was founded in 1888 and had clear links to Longmen Daoism, as can be seen in the name of its genealogy, the *Longmen zhengzong Jueyun benzhi daotong xinchuan* 龍門正宗覺雲本支道統薪傳 (published in 1927). Wang was a leading member of this altar, where he assumed the religious name Benzhen 本真. Apart from noting that Wang was a Buddhist, as well as a renowned philanthropic leader, the previously mentioned genealogy stated that Wang had become a member of Shanghai's Cloud Enlightenment Altar in 1920 and that his disciples were already playing active roles in other Daoist altars throughout the city.[137] Wang is also listed under the religious name Wanchan 完禪 in another source about these Daoist groups, the *Daotong yuanliuzhi* 道統源流志, which lists both his Daoist and Buddhist names (Benzhen and Jueqi), while also mentioning his artistic skills and devotion to a Buddhist vegetarian lifestyle, concluding that he was one of the most admired senior religious figures in Shanghai.[138] In short, there is little doubt that joining a Daoist altar (as well as initiating disciples in others) fit neatly into Wang's Buddhist practice.

The network of Daoist spirit-writing altars that encompassed Shanghai and other nearby metropolises constantly evolved during the late nineteenth and early twentieth centuries, with some branch altars blending with groups that worshipped Jigong, meaning that both deities could be featured on the same altar. In other words, while these networks had different origins, they shared similar models of practice and many of the same members, often becoming close allies. This meant that people who took part in both groups (such as Wang Yiting) could have both a Daoist name given by Lü Dongbin (in Wang's case Benzhen) and a Buddhist name given by Jigong (in Wang's case Jueqi).[139] Thus, it hardly seems surprising that Wang would choose to lead members of China Rescuing Life Association in the restoration of a prominent Daoist sacred site in Nanjing 南京, the Monastery of the Jade Void (Yuxuguan 玉虛觀), also composing an inscription to commemorate its completion.[140]

WANG YITING'S UNIVERSALIST PERSPECTIVE

Wang's commitment to both embracing and transmitting the doctrines and values of the many different religious organizations with which he was affiliated may be seen in his publishing a mammoth collection of morality books in 1936, entitled *A Treasury of Blessings and Longevity* (see chapter 2). Wang's preface to this work of 151 volumes (*ce* 冊) containing 140 separate texts (*zhong* 種) is notable for embodying some redemptive society ideals, particularly the willingness to embrace both science and religion:

> In this age, when people vie with each other in their admiration of new knowledge and engage in the study of science and evolution, the Populace Publishing House [Dazhong shuju 大眾書局] has striven to collect writings that admonish goodness [*quanshan* 勸善], blending them into this huge compi-

> lation. Its contents are profound indeed, revealing that the establishment of the individual self [*lishen zhi ben* 立身之本] derives primarily from mastering oneself and reviving ritual propriety [*keji fuli* 克己復禮; the term *ke* also appears in the title of Chiang Kai-shek's diary discussed earlier in this chapter]. All things have their origins: the tree its roots, the river its source. There are no distinctions between ancient and modern, just as none exist between China and the foreign.[141]

A statement attributed to Wang by one of his biographers expresses sentiments quite similar to the universalist values propagated by the redemptive societies of his era, specifically in terms of mentioning the Five Teachings (*wujiao* 五教: Buddhism, Daoism, Confucianism, Christianity, and Islam) and their links to preserving moral values.[142] These ideas also are reflected in the fact that the *Jueshe congshu* 覺社叢書, a journal published by the Enlightenment Society that Wang helped to run, expanded its definition of "religion" to encompass not only Confucianism, Daoism, Christianity, and Islam, but also Hinduism (*ru, dao, ye, hui, fan* 儒、道、耶、回、梵).[143]

Wang's open attitude toward all religious traditions was also manifested in his attending events at the International Institute of China (Shangxian Tang 尚賢堂), established by the American Presbyterian missionary Gilbert Reid (Li Jiabai 李佳白; 1857–1927). Reid journeyed to China in 1882, and in order to achieve his goal of preaching the gospel to members of the Chinese elite, founded the International Institute in Beijing in 1894 (it was formally established with state approval in 1897). After the Institute was destroyed during the Boxer Uprising, Reid moved its operations to Shanghai in 1903, where it became a site for a wide range of cultural and religious events that attracted many members of Shanghai's upper classes, including Wang Yiting. In 1912, Reid also joined forces with the British Baptist missionary Timothy Richard (1845–1819) to found the Shanghai Society of World Religions (Shanghai shijie zongjiaohui 上海世界宗教會). Reid also proved willing to take part in some redemptive society activities, including serving as an honorary president of the Universal Morality Society and being involved in the Society of the Way.[144]

Despite it ostensibly being a Christian organization, the International Institute of China resembled redemptive societies in its use of the term "hall" (*tang* 堂) for sacred space, its emphasis on the ideals of "rescuing the world" (*jishi* 濟世) and "saving the people" (*jiuren* 救人), and especially in terms of its universalist goal of encouraging the union of all Chinese and Western religions. This ideal was expressed both in words, with slogans such as "Confucius plus Jesus" (*Kongzi jia Yesu* 孔子加耶穌) and "Confucianism plus Christianity" (*Kongjiao jia Jidu* 孔教加基督), and in actions, for example, inviting eminent Buddhist monks such as Taixu as well as the 62nd Heavenly Master Zhang Yuanxu 張元旭 (1862–1925) to give lectures.[145] One undated Institute publication entitled *Religion and Revolution*, which is preserved at the Oriental Library (Tōyō bunkō 東洋文庫) in Japan, presents a series of ten Sunday lectures on many of the world's major religious traditions, including Confucianism, Daoism, Buddhism, Shinto, Islam, Hinduism, Judaism, and Christianity. Another letter, dated January 1, 1912, states that "Representatives of every Faith are welcome, that the interchange of ideas between men with widely differing view-points may promote tolerance and brotherliness, remove friction, and emphasize the supremacy of the ethical and the spiritual . . . we ask for the cooperation of the leaders of religious and philanthropic movements among the Chinese." These shared values apparently caused the relationship between Wang and Reid to become quite close, as can be seen in the touching memorial couplet (*wanlian* 輓聯) that Wang composed for Reid's funeral. The first line stresses their long-term friendship, as well as their common concern for universal religious values, while the second expresses Wang's profound sorrow at Reid's untimely departure from this world.[146]

■ The evidence presented in this chapter reveals the vibrant diversity of religious traditions that influenced the lives of China's elites. We have seen that urban elites such as Wang Yiting lived in a world that defies easy labeling by current academic categories: a world where "religion" and "science," or for that matter "tradition" and "modernity," coexisted and interacted; where one worked to make profits yet also donated one's savings to aiding others; where one could have dinner with Albert Einstein and his wife one night, and receive revelations from Jigong via spirit writing the next. Wang's life is especially striking in terms of its diversity, including his religious experiences. This man, who has so often been lauded as a modern and secular Chinese elite for his political and commercial activities, also possessed a sense of faith that inspired many of his words and deeds yet did not seem to be in conflict with his "modern" existence in the eyes of his contemporaries or himself. Thus, the religious life of Wang Yiting might be understood best in terms of what Paul Cohen calls the "lived or experienced past,"[147] a seemingly inextricable knot of information that defies easy exegesis.

Wang was hardly alone or unique. Numerous Chinese urban elites belonged to a closely knit cultural world featuring a wide range of personal and organizational connections. They circulated in and out of each other's networks and were kindred spirits in their emphasis on morality, their pursuit of self-cultivation, and their commitment to philanthropy. These men lived in a new world largely unimaginable to their forefathers, yet they did more than simply respond to or cope with change; they created new organizations for their own self-cultivation while also contributing to the well-being of those less fortunate than themselves. Cities provided an ideal setting for their activities, with their cosmopolitan environment providing inspiration in the form of Christian charity and modern Japanese culture. In addition, these elites were able to access a range of material resources and social connections that were largely unavailable in smaller towns, all of which enabled them not only to engage in acts of philanthropy but also to practice many diverse forms of religious self-cultivation.

Admittedly, a number of unanswered questions still remain about Wang's religious life, beginning with the conspicuous lack of his own published writings about Buddhism and the other religions that shaped his life. (There are numerous paintings, however, and their calligraphic colophons merit close study in future research efforts.) This seems to be because Wang's approach to religion was not as "philosophical" or intellectual as other religious leaders of his day, such as Hongyi, Yinguang, Taixu, Ding Fubao, or Huang Hanzhi. Instead, he was a man of action who gained respect for his skill in managing philanthropic and religious organizations, as well as sponsoring mammoth relief efforts and rituals such as those undertaken in the wake of the Great Kantō Earthquake. Thus, the impact Wang exerted on the religious organizations he joined or led appears to have been less one of providing inspiration and more that of exerting the perspiration necessary for such groups to run relatively smoothly. While much scholarship has focused on charisma as a key factor in religious leadership,[148] Wang's career reveals that organizational skills and managerial competence could be of equal importance, which in turn suggests a need to devote more effort to studying the roles that organizers such as Wang played in the development of modern Chinese religious traditions.

The final question about Wang's religious life concerns an issue raised at the beginning of this chapter, namely, that of Chinese religious modernity.[149] This term is clearly problematic and immediately inspires queries about whether religious modernity is something other than modernized religion, as well as the elements that make such modernity uniquely "Chinese." I would respond by pointing out that, until recently, the religious lives of modern Chinese elites have been overlooked largely because of a bias in the field that has been shaped by concepts of secularization and Weberian models of modernity.[150] As a result, classical typologies of modern Chinese elites have classified them according to categories such as political, economic, educational, military, and so on, or according to some ideology (revolutionary, reformist, traditional . . .), without taking religion fully into account. In contrast, the data presented here and in previous chapters indicate the clear presence of a "modern" religious culture in urban China that flourished in the form of the diverse religious groups that Wang Yiting and other elites chose to join, including lay Buddhist and Daoist associations, redemptive societies, spirit-writing groups, urban Christian organizations, and so on. While these various associations did not advocate the cessation of traditional beliefs and practices, they did work to remold them into forms that proved more viable in modern urban settings, while also providing a path toward self-cultivation and enlightenment for those men and women who felt disillusioned with the disruptive and at times even amoral features of capitalism.[151] The cases of elites such as Wang Yiting and Chiang Kaishek, which illustrate how Chinese elites attempted to negotiate the seeming contradictions between secularization and religion, suggest that urban modernity in China encompassed a wide range of meanings and possibilities. These included not only standard features such as capitalism, consumerism, and scientism, but also the beliefs and practices that helped shape elite religious lives.

CONCLUSION

This book has endeavored to shed new light on the fate of Chinese religions during the fifty years extending from the antireligion policies enacted during the 1898 reforms to the devastation wrought on Chinese religious life by years of natural disasters, warfare, and civil strife culminating in the CCP's rule over China. Its main agenda has been to comprehend more fully how the Chinese religious traditions and the diverse resources associated with their practice either survived or ended up being reconfigured during this critical era. In chapter 1, we considered how communal religious traditions were affected by a range of campaigns launched against temples and festivals. Chapter 2 examined how new printing technologies sparked the growth of religious publishing enterprises that contributed to the spread of innovative forms of knowledge, while chapter 3 portrayed the ways in which religiosity shaped the lives of modern Chinese elites. Based on the data presented in these chapters, it would seem that communal religious traditions experienced processes of adaptation and negotiation, while religious publishing witnessed both adaptation and innovation, and elite religiosity negotiation and innovation. In the pages that follow, I will assess how the phenomena discussed in these chapters continue to influence Chinese religious life today.

In the case of modern Taiwan, some scholars maintain that state-society interactions have contributed to the formation of a "civil religion" that has links to Western ideas of modern democracy without conforming fully to secularization models. As in the West, religious affiliation does seem to have some impact on political behavior, with believers who identify themselves as Presbyterians, Dharma Drum Mountain (Fagushan 法鼓山) Buddhists, Daoists, and members of redemptive societies such as the Way of Pervading Unity (Yiguandao) tending to be more pan-Green, while other Christians and members of the Buddhist Compassion Relief Tzu Chi Foundation (Ciji gongdehui 慈濟功德會) seem more likely to be pan-Blue.[1] The interplay between religion and the state continues in China as well, albeit with some new wrinkles. Chinese temple cults and the ritual events they organize flourish as hotbeds of cultural innovation and negotiation, with local elites working to expand the space for religious activities while also legitimizing them.[2] China also is experiencing a "Confucian revival," especially in the realm of ritual,[3] and the authorities even have been exploring the possibility of allowing the legalization of the Yiguandao, partly because its popularity and emphasis on Chinese values might serve as a counterweight to the rise of Christianity, particularly in the form of Protestant underground churches.[4] Christianity itself remains a cause for state concern because of the power that outside forces such as the Vatican exert on Chinese Catholics and because of the mixed results of state attempts to regulate Protestant pastors in the Three Self Patriotic Movement (TSPM; Zhongguo Jidujiao Sanzi aiguo yundong 中國基督教三自愛國運動), which have ended up inadvertently benefiting underground churches. The growth of Chinese Christianity also is being molded by indigenous Protestant groups, a trend that merits further comparison to the history of Taiwanese Christianity during the postwar era.[5]

Other contemporary catalysts for change come in the form of tourism and new categories such as intangible cultural heritage. Recent research has identified tourism as a crucial arena for understanding state attempts to effectively manage and standardize the local forces shaping China's religious revival, particularly in terms of promoting religious tourism as a healthy form of consumption that can contribute to exemplary modern behavior and nationalist sentiments, as well as the various forms of resistance that such projects encounter. Another central theme is the impact of tourism on non-Han communities, with state attempts to reframe sacred sites as tourist centers providing local authorities with opportunities to transform beliefs and practices formerly labeled as "superstition" (*mixin* 迷信) into "customs" (*fengsu* 風俗) or "intangible cultural heritage" (*fei wuzhi wenhua yichan* 非物質文化遺產) that possess intrinsic value.[6]

Overall, the data coming out of China make it clear that modernization has not led to the decline of religiosity, which is in fact booming.[7] Now we are witnessing a religious revival in China, but it is an odd revival indeed because of the lack of direct state participation. As we saw in chapter 1, throughout the imperial era the legitimacy of the Chinese state depended in part on its ability both to control and to practice religion. Many forms of religious practice featured active interaction between local society and the imperial state, which legitimated while also striving to regulate those practices it felt able to tolerate, either explicitly or implicitly.[8] Today, however, China is experiencing a religious revival without the state, which seems largely unable to respond to it. For example, City God temples are being rebuilt (see Figures C.1 and C.2), but no party official is able to perform sacrifices there like his late imperial counterpart would have done. Such a revival represents a huge challenge, and now the state is trying to adapt by formulating new categories such as intangible cultural heritage. In addition, the term *minjian xinyang* 民間信仰 for popular religion and local cults is gradually becoming established in state discourse as a legitimate category. Another new concept is that of religious ecology (*zongjiao shengtai* 宗教生態),[9] which is seen as a key factor in achieving the goal of a harmonious society (*hexie shehui* 和諧社會), especially to counter the influence of Christianity. In effect, the state is pushing a hidden agenda,

FIGURE C.1: *Guangzhou City God Temple, November 2006. This photo, taken by Poon Shuk-wah, shows a shell of a shrine with a security guard sitting outside. (The temple had been turned into a Native Goods Exhibition Hall in 1932 and was used as a nightclub and a factory, respectively, during the 1980s and 1990s.)*

FIGURE C.2: *Guangzhou City God Temple, May 2012. This photo, also taken by Poon Shuk-wah, shows a newly renovated temple now under the management of the Guangzhou Daoist Association.*

which is not so hidden now, to encourage the revival of indigenous religious traditions so that Christianity doesn't fill the gap that in Republican times had been occupied largely by redemptive societies. However, this hardly means that things will spin out of control. It is clear that if a new temple arises featuring some sort of animal deity with an ecstatic medium, the state will generally shut it down, unless it has very strong elite support or else remolds itself into something more palatable by asking the medium to practice at home instead of on its premises.

Another fascinating problem is how religion might provide a means for the state to legitimize itself, because this was one of the essential ways the state did so in the past (consider, for example, the Mandate of Heaven or Tianming 天命). Now that Communism's luster has faded, getting rich quick is no longer satisfying, and nationalism can turn into a powder keg, what will China's new leaders rely on to enhance their legitimacy? As the Chinese state continues to evolve, will it try to revive religion as a form of legitimacy, and will it be the sort of Christian ideal that Sun Yat-sen, Chiang Kai-shek, and so many Republican-era elites advocated? The answer is still unknown, but it is interesting to note that Confucian ceremonies are being revived throughout China, and not only in the north but also in such places as Quzhou 衢州 (Zhejiang). One striking aspect of these ceremonies is that students, who used to be at the vanguard of temple destruction campaigns, are now drafted to help carry offerings to Confucius, suggesting that we have come full circle.[10] There is also the use of Confucius Institutes (Kongzi xueyuan 孔子學院) and the tolerance of classes for reading Confucian scriptures (*dujing ban* 讀經班; some of which are managed by redemptive societies), all of which suggest that the state is trying at least indirectly to promote Confucianism, perhaps along the lines of the Singapore model of a "benevolent autocracy." Such phenomena will merit our close attention as China's new leadership consolidates its power.

Modern technologies continue to mold the development of Chinese religious movements as well. In Taiwan, the ability of Dharma Master Hsing Yun (星雲法師; b. 1927) to use slide projectors to illustrate his lectures, as well as his skill in broadcasting his messages via radio and T.V., may have been influenced by some of the practices described in chapter 2. Similarly, since the 1960s, Taiwanese spirit-writing organizations such as the Hall of Sages and Worthies (Shengxian Tang 聖賢堂) in Taizhong have resembled the Illuminating Goodness Bookstore in publishing religious books and periodicals with the help of a full-time staff.[11] However, few religious websites have used the full communicative potential of the Internet to stimulate new forms of religious action, in part because of traditional notions of authentic religious experience plus the tendency to quantify merit based on the numbers of printed books that one sponsors.[12] Throughout China, new forms of media are assuming increasing importance in its religious revival, with temples and religious bookstores selling or giving away DVDs and CDs that can be used for sutra chanting or listening to liturgical music. Moreover, many temples use computers on a regular basis for tasks such as printing stele inscriptions, temple histories, ritual texts, and even menus for vegetarian meals. Computers also provide some religious specialists with a means of resisting government policies, as can be seen in the case of the Dai 傣 monks of Xishuangbanna 西雙版納 (southern Yunnan), who used computers brought in by compatriots in Thailand to reintroduce the traditional script in monastic education and sutra publication enterprises.[13] In both China and Taiwan, the growing availability of religious texts in both print form and online is reshaping relationships between clerical elites and lay devotees in new and unexpected ways, particularly in terms of decreasing laypeople's dependence on religious leaders for face-to-face interaction in the quest for religious knowledge and enlightenment.[14]

When we turn our attention to religious elites and individual forms of religious life in contemporary China, we discover similar patterns of change and continuity. One of the most noteworthy aspects of Wang Yiting's religious life as described in chapter 3 was that all the groups he took part in were voluntary associations, not ascriptive communities. Moreover, while Wang Yiting may have resembled many late imperial elites in terms of taking refuge in religion following personal crises, the voluntary associations he took part in were very different from their imperial-era counterparts in terms of being organizations consciously modeled on Christianity. In China today, while there is an effervescence of both ascriptive and voluntary forms of religious life, the latter now seems increasingly important. This is especially true for urban areas, where rapacious realtors and dynamo developers have effectively given the *coup-de-grâce* to most of the sacred sites that had survived the temple destruction campaigns of the twentieth century. Beliefs and practices do survive, however, but in a more diversified fashion, especially those practices involving healing and body cultivation that center on small-scale shrines, bookstores, and vegetarian restaurants. Even in Taiwan, where religion has continued to thrive, cities have witnessed the rapid growth of "divine altars" (*shentan* 神壇) located in stores and apartments. It is also noteworthy that some surveys recently undertaken in urban China show that many people retain a positive perspective on religious practice. While only 5 percent of the respondents interviewed in 2005 would admit to any formal religious affiliation, with 33 percent claiming to be atheists and 26 percent viewing religion as "cheating and nonsense," most people stated that they would burn incense for the gods or their ancestors, with 15 percent worshipping deity statues in their homes and over three-quarters believing in divine retribution.[15]

In addition, throughout Chinese communities worldwide, one sees a growing emphasis on individualism, with people increasingly pursuing their own forms of spiritual practice, especially those who live far away from their hometowns.[16] Many of these individuals are women. Elder women have been vital players in preserving and transmitting traditional concepts and cosmologies, especially within the family, as well as leading temple reconstruction projects, while a new generation of younger women practitioners are taking the lead in many religious groups and using their status in the fight against gender inequality. As Kang Xiaofei eloquently observes, in today's China, "women are neither victims of superstition nor obstacles of modernity. They ingeniously construct female religiosity with both traditional and modern resources at their own disposal."[17]

All in all, if one takes a close look at Chinese religious life today, one cannot help but be struck by the extent of continuity amidst so much dramatic change. One striking facet of religion in Taiwan is that economic growth and technological development have not resulted in the decline of religious life; on the contrary, many educated men and women who surf the web on a daily basis apparently feel no qualms about practicing religion (in fact, most large religious organizations and temples now have their own websites). Religion continues to play an integral role in individual, family, and community life, with temples retaining their importance as sites for daily worship, community service, and massive festivals.[18] In China as well, temples retain the potential to serve as "living cultural centers" able to negotiate the forces of capitalism and nationalism while celebrating the importance of local cultural difference.[19] In contrast, one cannot help but notice that the Chinese lineage appears to be on its last legs, the reasons for which have yet to be clearly understood.[20]

Another major force transforming Chinese religious life is globalization, with thriving transnational religious networks (including those consisting of spirit-medium cults) effectively challenging conventional wisdom on the insularity of Chinese society.[21] Transnational links also have influenced religion's role in environmental resistance movements, with trends in postwar Taiwan now beginning to have an impact on China.[22] Globalization, burgeoning religiosity, and the assertive nature of many religious associations pose unprecedented challenges for China's new leaders, as can be seen in the role of Falungong among overseas Chinese, the impact of Christianity on China's underground churches, the influence of Islam in Xinjiang, and the crisis involving Tibetan Buddhism in China.[23]

I conclude by returning to the theme that has served as the underlying motivation for the volume, that of cross-cultural comparison.[24] Perhaps the most important lesson I have learned in the course of giving the Jerusalem Lectures is the distinction between the communally enforced piety of the Abrahamic religions (Judaism, Christianity, and Islam) and the individually enforced piety of the Chinese religions. One striking facet of Chinese religious culture, and also one of the most moving conclusions of Meir's first book on Jigong, is the idea of humor: When a worshipper asks the gods a question by using woodblock divination, they can respond by laughing; in Western religions, the thought of any god or saint chuckling about such an issue would be unimaginable.[25] Why is this? I would hypothesize that, while the practice of religion is a central part of Chinese life, it is never dependent on a great sense of piety. Even in temples, one often sees children running around making noise, people coming in wearing sandals and shorts, and so on. It's true that there are exceptions when a Daoist *jiao* festival is going on, but in the daily life of a temple all sorts of behavior occurs that would seem absolutely outrageous in a Jewish, Christian, or Muslim sacred site. In short, in China the practice of religion is central, but the idea of piety is not. This is not to deny that piety does play a role in individual self-cultivation and the voluntary associations that promote it, but overall it seems that piety is enforced on a communal level in Abrahamic religions, whereas piety in China is a voluntary decision at the individual level. I would never have come up with this analysis had I not been given the chance to come to Israel and interact with the intellectual community there. Such comparisons clearly need further refinement, but their very presence may give credence to Levenson's observation quoted in the preface: "If we can make this kind of sense, perhaps we can help to make this kind of world."

NOTES

FOREWORD

1. See respectively Paul Katz, *Images of the Immortal: The Cult of Lü Dongbin at the Palace of Eternal Joy* (Honolulu: University of Hawaii Press, 1999); Paul Katz, *When Valleys Turned Blood-Red: The Ta-ba-ni Incident in Colonial Taiwan* (Honolulu: University of Hawaii Press, 2005); Paul Katz, *Divine Justice: Religion and the Development of Chinese Legal Culture* (London: Routledge, 2009); and Paul Katz, *Demon Hordes and Burning Boats: The Cult of Marshal Wen in Late Imperial Chekiang* (Albany: State University of New York Press, 1995).

2. See, among others, Vincent Goossaert, "1898: The Beginning of the End for Chinese Religions?" *Journal of Asian Studies*, 65.2 (2006): pp. 307–336; and Rebecca A. Nedostup, *Superstitious Regimes: Religion and the Politics of Chinese Modernity* (Cambridge: Harvard University Press, 2009).

PREFACE

1. Joseph Richmond Levenson, "The Genesis of Confucian China and Its Modern Fate" in *The Historian's Workshop: Original Essays by Sixteen Historians*, ed. L. P. Curtis, Jr. (New York: Alfred A. Knopf, 1970), pp. 283–284.

2. Berkeley: University of California Press, 1958–1965.

3. The project has focused on achieving the following goals: 1) collect data on temple destruction campaigns in Wenzhou (Zhejiang), 2) locate information about religious publishing in Shanghai, and, 3) systematically examine the religious lives of modern Chinese elites, especially those from Huzhou (Zhejiang), many of whom had close connections to or even resided in Shanghai. For more information, see the project website: http://www.mh.sinica.edu.tw/PGGroupStudyPlan_Page.aspx?groupStudyPlanID=8.

INTRODUCTION

1. See, for example, Peter Zarrow, *China in War and Revolution, 1895–1949* (London and New York: Routledge, 2005); Peter Zarrow, *After Empire: The Conceptual Transformation of the Chinese State, 1885–1924* (Stanford: Stanford University Press, 2012).

2. Among the most important works are Mayfair Mei-hui Yang, ed., *Chinese Religiosities: Afflictions of Modernity and State Formation* (Berkeley: University of California Press, 2008); Yoshiko Ashiwa and David Wank, eds., *Making Religion, Making the State: The Politics of Religion in Contemporary China* (Stanford: Stanford University Press, 2009); Rebecca A. Nedostup, *Superstitious Regimes: Religion and the Politics of Chinese Modernity* (Cambridge: Harvard University Press, 2009); Poon Shuk-wah, *Negotiating Religion in Modern China: State and Common People in Guangzhou, 1900–1937* (Hong Kong: Chinese University Press, 2010); John Lagerwey, *China: A Religious State* (Hong Kong: Hong Kong University Press, 2010); Adam Yuet Chau, ed., *Religion in Contemporary China: Revitalization and Innovation* (London: Routledge, 2011); Yang Fenggang, *Religion in China: Survival and Revival under Communist Rule* (New York: Oxford University Press, 2011); David A. Palmer, Glenn Shive, and Philip L. Wickeri, eds., *Chinese Religious Life* (Oxford: Oxford University Press, 2011); and Vincent Goossaert and David A. Palmer, *The Religious Question in Modern China* (Chicago: University of Chicago Press, 2011).

3. Arthur P. Wolf, ed., *Religion and Ritual in Chinese Society* (Stanford: Stanford University Press, 1974).

4. Cynthia J. Brokaw, *The Ledgers of Merit and Demerit: Social Change and Moral Order in Late Imperial China* (Princeton: Princeton University Press, 1991); Paul R. Katz, *Divine Justice—Religion and the Development of Chinese Legal Culture* (London and New York: Routledge, 2009), esp. pp. 1–46.

5. David K. Jordan, *Gods, Ghosts, & Ancestors: Folk Religion in a Taiwanese Village* (Stanford: Stanford University Press, 1972).

6. For more on these issues, see Kenneth Dean and Zheng Zhenman, *Ritual Alliances of the Putian Plain*, vol. 1: *Historical Introduction to the*

Return of the Gods and vol. 2: *A Survey of the Village Temples and Ritual Activities* (Leiden and Boston: Brill, 2010); see also Barend ter Haar, "Local Society and the Organization of Cults in Early Modern China: A Preliminary Study," *Studies in Central & East Asian Religions*, 8 (1995): 1–43.

7. Goossaert and Palmer, *Religious Question*, pp. 24–27.

8. For an overview of these developments, see Catherine Bell, "Religion and Chinese Culture: Toward an Assessment of 'Popular Religion,'" *History of Religions*, 29.1 (1989): 35–57.

9. Mary B. Rankin, *Elite Activism and Political Transformation in China, Zhejiang Province, 1865–1911* (Stanford: Stanford University Press, 1986); see also Marie-Claire Bergère, *The Golden Age of the Chinese Bourgeoisie, 1911–1937*, trans. Janet Lloyd (Cambridge: Cambridge University Press, 1989); R. Keith Schoppa, *Chinese Elites and Political Change: Zhejiang Province in the Early Twentieth Century* (Cambridge: Harvard University Press, 1982).

10. William T. Rowe, "The Public Sphere in Modern China," *Modern China*, 16.3 (1990): 309–326; William T. Rowe, "The Problem of 'Civil Society' in Late Imperial China," *Modern China*, 19.2 (1993): 143–153; Philip C.C. Huang, "'Public Sphere'/'Civil Society' in China? The Third Realm between State and Society," *Modern China* 19.2 (1993): 216–240.

11. David Strand, *Rickshaw Beijing: City People and Politics in 1920s China* (Berkeley: University of California Press, 1989); Wang Di, *Street Culture in Chengdu: Public Space, Urban Commoners, and Local Politics, 1870–1930* (Stanford: Stanford University Press, 2003).

12. For more on these issues, see Timothy Brook, *Praying for Power: Buddhism and the Formation of Gentry Society in Late-Ming China* (Cambridge: Harvard University Press, 1993), pp. 13–15, 23–29, 54–126, 316–321; Kenneth Dean, "China's Second Government: Regional Ritual Systems in Southeast China," in *Shehui, minzu yu wenhua zhanyan guoji yantaohui lunwenji* 社會、民族與文化展演國際研討會論文集, eds. Wang Ch'iu-kuei 王秋桂, Chuang Ying-chang 莊英章, and Chen Chung-min 陳中民 (Taipei: Center for Chinese Studies, 2001), pp. 77–109; Paul R. Katz, *Demon Hordes and Burning Boats: The Cult of Marshal Wen in Late Imperial Chekiang* (Albany: State University of New York Press,

1995), pp. 6–7, 180–189; ter Haar, "Local Society and the Organization of Cults in Early Modern China," pp. 30–36.

13. Prasenjit Duara, *Culture, Power, and the State: Rural North China, 1900–1942* (Stanford: Stanford University Press, 1988), pp. 5, 15–16, 26–38, 118–157.

14. Detailed studies of pilgrimage networks may be found in Brian R. Dott, *Identity Reflections: Pilgrimages to Mount Tai in Late Imperial China* (Cambridge: Harvard University Press, 2004); Susan Naquin and Yü Chün-fang, eds., *Pilgrims and Sacred Sites in China* (Berkeley: University of California Press, 1992). For more on the division of incense (*fenxiang* 分香) networks and their links to pilgrimages, see Kristofer M. Schipper, "The Cult of Pao-sheng ta-ti 保生大帝 and Its Spreading to Taiwan—A Case Study of *fen-hsiang*," in *Development and Decline of Fukien Province in the 17th and 18th Centuries*, ed. E. B. Vermeer (Leiden: E. J. Brill, 1990), pp. 397–416.

15. David G. Johnson, ed., *Ritual Opera, Operatic Ritual: "Mu-lien Rescues His Mother" in Chinese Popular Culture*, Publications of the Chinese Popular Culture Project, vol. 1 (Berkeley: University of California Press, 1989). See also Meir Shahar, "Vernacular Fiction and the Transmission of Gods' Cults in Late Imperial China," in *Unruly Gods: Divinity and Society in China*, eds. Meir Shahar and Robert Weller (Honolulu: University of Hawai'i Press, 1996), pp. 184–211).

16. Paul R. Katz, *Images of the Immortal: The Cult of Lü Dongbin at the Palace of Eternal Joy* (Honolulu: University of Hawai'i Press, 1999), pp. 131–176.

17. Katz, *Divine Justice*, pp. 47–104.

18. Other resources included material wealth (land, money, and weapons), social connections (personal networks), and what has been defined as "symbolic capital" (status or "face"); see Pierre Bourdieu, *Outline of a Theory in Practice*, trans. R. Nice (Cambridge: Cambridge University Press, 1977), pp. 171–183; Joseph W. Esherick and Mary Backus Rankin, eds., *Chinese Local Elites and Patterns of Dominance* (Berkeley: University of California Press, 1990), pp. 10–13, 326–328; David Faure, *The Structure of Chinese Rural Society: Lineage and Village in the East-*

ern New Territories (Hong Kong and New York: Oxford University Press, 1986); David Faure and Helen F. Siu, eds., *Down to Earth: The Territorial Bond in South China* (Stanford: Stanford University Press, 1995); Michael Szonyi, "Local Cult, *Lijia* 里甲, and Lineage: Religious and Social Organization in the Fuzhou Region in the Ming and Qing," *Journal of Chinese Religions*, 28 (2000): 97, 105–106, 111–115; Michael Szonyi, *Practicing Kinship: Lineage and Descent in Late Imperial China* (Stanford: Stanford University Press, 2002); Wang Mingming, "Place, Administration, and Territorial Cults in Late Imperial China," *Late Imperial China*, 16.1 (1995): 33–78.

19. Susan Naquin, *Peking: Temples and City Life, 1400–1900* (Berkeley: University of California Press, 2000).

20. Richard Belsky, *Localities at the Center: Native-Place, Space, and Power in Late Imperial Beijing* (Cambridge and London: Harvard University Press, 2005). For a discussion of similar phenomena in Shanghai, see Bryna Goodman, *Native Place, City, and Nation: Regional Networks and Identities in Shanghai, 1853–1937* (Berkeley: University of California Press, 1995).

21. Many of the results have been published in the journal *Sanjiao wenxian* 三教文獻*: Matériaux pour l'étude de la religion chinoise* (4 vols.: 1997, 1998, 1999, 2005). See also Vincent Goossaert, *The Daoists of Peking, 1800–1949: A Social History of Urban Clerics*, Harvard East Asian Monographs, no. 284 (Cambridge: Harvard University Press. 2007). For more on the history of Beijing during the Republican era, see Madeline Yue Dong, *Republican Beijing: The City and Its Histories* (Berkeley: University of California Press, 2003).

22. Bujard recently has completed a Chiang Ching-kuo Foundation research project entitled, "The Temples of Peking: Epigraphy and Oral Sources—The Social History of an Imperial Capital" (RG002-U-03). One important result of this project is Lü Min 呂敏 (Marianne Bujard) and Dong Xiaoping 董曉萍, eds., *Beijing neicheng simiao beike* 北京內城寺廟碑刻志 (*Temples et stèles de pékin*) (Beijing: Guojia tushuguan chubanshe, 2011).

23. Paul R. Katz, "Orthopraxy and Heteropraxy Beyond the State:

Standardizing Ritual in Chinese Society," *Modern China*, 33.1 (January 2007), pp. 72–90. See also Vincent Goossaert, "The Social Organization of Religious Communities in the Twentieth Century," in *Chinese Religious Life*, eds. David A. Palmer, Glenn Shive, and Philip L. Wickeri (Oxford: Oxford University Press, 2011), Palmer, Shive, and Wickeri, eds., *Chinese Religious Life*, pp. 172–190.

24. Michael Szonyi, "The Illusion of Standardizing the Gods: The Cult of the Five Emperors in Late Imperial China," *The Journal of Asian Studies*, 56.1 (1997): 113–135; Richard von Glahn, *The Sinister Way: The Divine and the Demonic in Chinese Religious Culture* (Berkeley: University of California Press, 2004); Wu Cheng-han, "The Temple Fairs in Late Imperial China" (Ph.D. diss., Princeton University, 1988), pp. 66–157.

25. James Flath, "Temple Fairs and the Republican State in North China," *Twentieth-Century China*, 30.1 (2004): 39–63.

26. Poon Shuk-wah, "Refashioning Festivals in Republican Guangzhou," *Modern China*, 30.2 (2004): 199–227.

27. Ann S. Anagnost, "The Politics of Ritual Displacement," in *Asian Visions of Authority: Religions and the Modern States of East and Southeast Asia*, eds. Charles F. Keyes, Laurel Kendall, and Helen Hardacre (Honolulu: University of Hawai'i Press, 1994), pp. 221–254; John M. Flower, "A Road Is Made: Roads, Temples, and Historical Memory in Ya'an County, Sichuan," *The Journal of Asian Studies*, 63.3 (2004): 649–685; Mayfair Mei-hui Yang, "Putting Global Capitalism in Its Place: Economic Hybridity, Bataille, and Ritual Expenditure," *Current Anthropology*, 41.4 (2000): 477–510; Mayfair Mei-hui Yang, "Spatial Struggles: Postcolonial Complex, State Disenchantment, and Popular Reappropriation of Space in Rural Southeast China," *The Journal of Asian Studies*, 63.3 (2004): 719–755.

28. Fiorella Allio, "Spatial Organization in a Ritual Context: A Preliminary Analysis of the *Koah-hiun* Processional System of the Taiwan Region and Its Social Significance," in *Xinyang, yishi, yu shehui: Disanjie guoji Hanxue huiyi lunwenji—Renleixue zu* 信仰、儀式與社會：第三屆國際漢學會議論文集—人類學組, ed. Lin Mei-rong 林美容 (Nankang: Institute of Ethnology, Academia Sinica, 2003), pp. 131–177.

29. Katz, *Demon Hordes*, pp. 169–170; Katz, *Divine Justice*, pp. 107–115.

30. Excellent overviews of Christianity in modern China may be found in Daniel H. Bays, ed., *Christianity in China: From the Eighteenth Century to the Present* (Stanford: Stanford University Press, 1996); Daniel H. Bays, *A New History of Christianity in China* (West Sussex, UK: Wiley-Blackwell, 2012). See also Eugenio Menegon, *Ancestors, Virgins, and Friars: Christianity as a Local Religion in Late Imperial China* (Cambridge: Harvard University Press, 2010).

31. Goossaert and Palmer, *Religious Question*, pp. 68–73; see also Kuo Cheng-tian, *Religion and Democracy in Taiwan* (Albany: State University of New York Press, 2008), p. 44.

32. Goossaert and Palmer, *Religious Question*, pp. 73–83; Ashiwa and Wank, *Making Religion, Making the State*, pp. 44–55, 66–67, 137–146.

33. For more on the Japanese experience, see Jason Ānanda, *The Invention of Religion in Japan* (Chicago: University of Chicago Press, 2012). See also the papers by Elisabetta Porcu, John K. Nelson, Mark R. Mullins, and Ian Reader in the *Journal of Religion in Japan*, 1.1 (2012): 3–106.

34. Karel Dobbelaere, *Secularization: An Analysis at Three Levels* (Brussels: P.I.E.-Peter Lang, 2002).

35. Talal Asad, *Formations of the Secular: Christianity, Islam, Modernity* (Stanford: Stanford University Press, 2003); José Casanova, "Secularization Revisited: A Reply to Talal Asad," in *Powers of the Secular Modern: Talal Asad and His Interlocutors*, eds. David Scott and Charles Hirschkind (Stanford: Stanford University Press, 2006), pp. 12–30.

36. Roy Wallis and Steve Bruce, "Secularization: The Orthodox Model," in *Religion and Modernization: Sociologists and Historians Debate the Secularization Thesis*, ed. Steve Bruce (Oxford and New York: Oxford University Press, 1992), pp. 8–22.

37. Michael Szonyi, "Secularization Theories and the Study of Chinese Religions," *Social Compass*, 56.3 (2009): 312–327.

38. Goossaert and Palmer, *Religious Question*, pp. 68, 73–75, 83, 89.

39. Vincent Goossaert, "1898: The Beginning of the End for Chinese Religion?" *Journal of Asian Studies*, 65.2 (2006): 307–336; Vincent Goossaert, "Détruire les temples pour construire les écoles: reconstitution d'un objet historique," *Extrême-Orient Extrême-Occident*, 33 (2011):

35–51. See also Nedostup, *Superstitious Regimes*, pp. 11–16, 39–43, 143–145; Kuo Ya-pei, "Redeploying Confucius: The Imperial State Dreams of the Nation, 1902–1911," in *Chinese Religiosities: Afflictions of Modernity and State Formation*, ed. Mayfair Mei-hui Yang (Berkeley: University of California Press, 2008), pp. 65–84; David Ownby, "The Politics of Redemption: Redemptive Societies and the Chinese State in Modern and Contemporary Chinese History," in *Belief, Practice and Cultural Adaptation: Papers from the Religion Section of the Fourth International Conference on Sinology*, eds. Paul R. Katz and Shufen Liu (Nankang: Academia Sinica Press, 2013), pp. 677–735. For more on how the term "superstition" was initially adopted by Chinese Christian elites, see Chu Ping-yi 祝平一, "'Mixin': Shiqi shiji ruHua Tianzhujiao de zaidi zongjiao dijing" 「迷信」：十七世紀入華天主教的在地宗教地景, paper presented at the Third Session of the 2013 Institute of History and Philology Seminar Series, Academia Sinica, Taipei, Taiwan, February 4, 2013.

40. Robert P. Weller, "Taiwan and Global Religious Trends," paper presented at the First World Congress of Taiwan Studies, Academia Sinica, Taipei, Taiwan, April 26–28, 2012. See also Robert P. Weller, *Alternate Civilities: Democracy and Culture in China and Taiwan* (Boulder, CO: Westview Press, 1999).

41. Hu Shih 胡適, "Lun huichu shenfo" 論毀除神佛, *Jingye xunbao* 競業旬報, 28 (September 1, 1908); reprinted in *Hu Shih zaonian wencun* 胡適早年文存, ed. Chou Chih-ping 周質平 (Taipei: Yuanliu chuban shiye gufen youxian gongsi, 1995), pp. 164–167.

42. For more on the role of modern religious organizations during this era, see Vincent Goossaert, "Republican Church Engineering: The National Religious Associations in 1912 China," in *Chinese Religiosities: Afflictions of Modernity and State Formation*, ed. Mayfair Mei-hui Yang (Berkeley: University of California Press, 2008), pp. 209–232. See also Ji Zhe, "Secularization as Religious Restructuring: Statist Institutionalization of Chinese Buddhism and Its Paradoxes," in *Chinese Religiosities: Afflictions of Modernity and State Formation*, ed. Mayfair Mei-hui Yang (Berkeley: University of California Press, 2008), pp. 233–260.

43. Goossaert and Palmer, *Religious Question*, pp. 393–404.

1. STATE VERSUS SOCIETY: TEMPLE DESTRUCTION CAMPAIGNS

1. Pitman B. Potter, "Belief in Control: Regulation of Religion in China," in *Religion in China Today*, ed. Daniel L. Overmyer (Cambridge: The China Quarterly and Cambridge University Press, 2003), pp. 11–31.

2. Hsiao Kung-ch'üan, *Rural China: Imperial Control in the Nineteenth Century* (Seattle and London: University of Washington Press, 1960).

3. The term *yin* (淫) has been variously translated as "excessive," "licentious," "illicit," "improper," "perverse," "profane," and "profligate." I believe that the way one chooses to translate this term depends on its context. For example, I would argue that the term *yin* as found in official documents and elite writings adhering to an official point of view should be translated as "illicit," as the authors thereof mainly objected to the fact that such cults were not included in the register of sacrifices. However, the term *yin* as found in the writings of Daoist priests and other members of the elite may be translated as "licentious" or "excessive" in order to reflect the fact that such individuals were clearly offended by what they considered to be heterodox or improper practices, especially the prominence of spirit mediums (*wu* 巫) and offerings of bloody sacrifices (*xueshi* 血食). For more on this problem, see Paul R. Katz, "Daoism and Local Cults—A Case Study of the Cult of Marshal Wen," in *Heterodoxy in Late Imperial China*, eds. Kwang-ching Liu and Richard Shek (Honolulu: University of Hawai'i Press, 2004), pp. 172–208.

4. Modified translation based on Daniel L. Overmyer, "Attitudes toward Popular Religion in the Ritual Texts of the Chinese State: The Collected Statutes of the Great Ming," *Cahiers d'Extrême Asie*, 5 (1989–1990): 191–221, esp. p. 201. Overmyer's version was based on the translation by the renowned Scottish sinologist and missionary James Legge (1815–1897). For more on Legge's life and career, see Lauren F. Pfister, *James Legge and the Scottish Protestant Encounter with China* (Frankfurt and New York: Peter Lang, 2004); Norman J. Girardot, *The Victorian Translation of China: James Legge's Oriental Pilgrimage* (Berkeley and London: University of California Press, 2002).

5. Overmyer, "Attitudes toward Popular Religion in the Ritual Texts of the Chinese State," pp. 205–206.

6. Vincent Goossaert, "Counting the Monks: The 1736–1739 Census of the Chinese Clergy," *Late Imperial China*, 21.2 (2000): 40–85.

7. Barend ter Haar, *The White Lotus Teachings in Chinese Religious History* (Leiden: E. J. Brill, 1992); ter Haar, *Ritual and Mythology of the Chinese Triads: Creating an Identity* (Leiden: E. J. Brill, 1998).

8. Prasenjit Duara, *Culture, Power, and the State: Rural North China, 1900–1942* (Stanford: Stanford University Press, 1988); James L. Watson, "Standardizing the Gods: The Promotion of T'ien-hou 天后 ('Empress of Heaven') Along the South China Coast, 960–1960," in *Popular Culture in Late Imperial China*, eds. David G. Johnson, Andrew J. Nathan, and Evelyn S. Rawski (Berkeley: University of California Press, 1985), pp. 292–324. See also Terry Kleeman, "Licentious Cults and Bloody Victuals: Sacrifice, Reciprocity, and Violence in Traditional China," *Asia Major*, 7.1 (1997): 185–211.

9. Timothy Brook, "The Policies of Religion: Late-Imperial Origins of the Regulatory State," in *Making Religion, Making the State: The Politics of Religion in Contemporary China*, eds. Yoshiko Ashiwa and David Wank (Stanford: Stanford University Press, 2009), pp. 22–42.

10. Fu Haiyan 付海晏, "Geming, falü yu miaochan—Minguo Beiping Tianshansi an yanjiu 革命, 法律與廟產—民國北平鐵山寺案研究, *Lishi yanjiu* 歷史研究, 3 (2003): 105–120, as well as personal communications in February 2012. See also Makita Tairyō 枚田諦亮, "Seimotsu irai ni okeru byōsan kōgaku" 清末以來に於ける廟產興學, in *Chūgoku bukkyōshi kenkyū* 中國佛教史研究, vol. 2 (Tokyo: Taito shuppansha, 1984), pp. 290–318.

11. Chen Jinlong 陳金龍, "Cong miaochan xingxue fengbo kan Minguo shiqi de Zhenjiao guanxi—Yi 1927 zhi 1937 nian wei zhongxin de kaocha" 從廟產興學風波看民國時期的政教關系—以1927至1937年為中心的考察, *Guangdong shehui kexue* 廣東社會科學, 1 (2006): 114–121. See also his recently published book, *Nanjing Guomin zhengfu shiqi de zhengjiao guanxi: Yi Fojiao wei zhongxin de kaocha* 南京國民政府時期的

政教關係：以佛教為中心的考察 (Beijing: Zhongguo shehui kexue chubanshe, 2011). For background information on Republican-era education movements, see Paul J. Bailey, *Reform the People: Changing Attitudes Towards Popular Education in Early Twentieth-Century China* (Edinburgh: Edinburgh University Press, 1990) and Helen Chauncey, *Schoolhouse Politicians: Localities and State During the Chinese Republic* (Honolulu: University of Hawai'i Press, 1992).

12. Fu Haiyan 付海晏, "1940 niandai Edong simiao caichanquan chutan" 1940 年代鄂東寺廟財產權初探, *Guizhou shifan daxue xuebao (Shehui kexueban)* 貴州師范大學學報(社會科學版), 5 (2005): 6–10.

13. Ai Ping 艾萍, "Minguo jinzhi yingshen saihui lunxi—Yi Shanghai wei ge'an" 民國禁止迎神賽會論析－以上海為個案, *Jiangsu shehui kexue* 江蘇社會科學, 5 (2010): 216–221.

14. Goossaert and Palmer, *Religious Question*, pp. 62–63, 125.

15. Nedostup, *Superstitious Regimes*, pp. 39–43, 79–97, 108, 295–300; Poon, *Negotiating Religion in Modern China*, pp. 49, 73, 118. See also Rebecca Nedostup, "Ritual Competition and the Modernizing Nation-State," in *Chinese Religiosities: Afflictions of Modernity and State Formation*, ed. Mayfair Mei-hui Yang (Berkeley: University of California Press, 2008), pp. 87–112.

16. Many of these documents may be found in Chiu Hei-yuan 瞿海源, "Zhonghua minguo youguan zongjiao faling ji falü cao'an huibian" 中華民國有關宗教法令及法律草案彙編, *Zhongyang yanjiuyuan Minzuxue yanjiusuo ziliao huibian* 中央研究院民族學研究所資料彙編, 2 (1990): 113–139. See also *Zhonghua minguoshi dang'an ziliao huibian, ser. 5, pt. 1, Wenhua* (1) 中華民國史檔案資料彙編，第5輯，第一編，文化 (1) (Nanjing: Jiangsu guji chubanshe, 1994), pp. 490–513, 1017–1029, 1075–1082.

17. Zhongxuan 中宣, "Pochu mixian zhi yiyi he banfa" 破除迷信之意義和辦法, *Shidai* 時代, 1.3 (1929): 13–17. Zhongxuan 中宣 apparently was the pseudonym used by a Nationalist elite deeply concerned with religious affairs. See also Hu Qiaomu 胡喬木, "Fan mixin tigang" 反迷信提綱, *Zhongguo qingnian* 中國青年, 2.11 (1940), reprinted in *Zhonggong dangshi yanjiu* 中共黨史研究 1.5 (1999): 1–4.

18. "Shishi xinwen: Gailiang menshen: Pochu mixin: Minshengfu bandao sanxiang faban" 時事新聞：改良門神：破除迷信，閩省府頒到三項辦法, *Gongjiao zhoukan* 公教周刊, 7.1 (1935): 9.

19. For historical background, see Parks M. Coble, *Facing Japan: Chinese Politics and Japanese Imperialism, 1931–1937* (Cambridge: Harvard University Press, 1991) and Diana Lary, *The Chinese People at War: Human Suffering and Social Transformation, 1937–1945* (New York: Cambridge University Press, 2010).

20. Lo Shih-chieh 羅士傑, "The Order of Local Things: Popular Politics and Religion in Modern Wenzhou 溫州 (1840–1940)" (Ph.D. diss., Brown University, 2010). See also his "Investiture and Local Politics: Yang fujun 楊府君 (Lord Yang) in Late Qing Wenzhou (1840–1867)," *Late Imperial China*, 33.1 (June 2012): 89–121. See also Nedostup, *Superstitious Regimes*, p. 97.

21. For more on the intellectual ideals of that era, see John Fitzgerald, *Awakening China: Politics, Culture, and Class in the Nationalist Revolution* (Stanford: Stanford University Press, 1996); Henrietta Harrison, *The Making of the Republic Citizen: Political Ceremonies and Symbols in China, 1911–1929* (Oxford: Oxford University Press, 2000); Kuo Yapei, *Debating "Culture" in Interwar China*, Leiden Series in Modern East Asian Politics and History (London and New York: Routledge, 2010). See also Paul A. Cohen, *History in Three Keys: The Boxers as Event, Experience, and Myth* (New York: Columbia University Press, 1997), pp. 223–237.

22. Li Xuexhang 李學昌 and Dong Jianbo 董建波, "20 shiji shangbanye Hangxian yingshen saihui shuailuo yinsu qianxi" 20 世紀上半葉杭縣迎神賽會衰落因素淺析, *Huadong shifan daxue xuabao (Zhexue shehui kexue ban)* 華東師範大學學報(哲學社會科學版), 39.5 (2007): 49–53; Liu Chengyou 劉成有, "Luelun miaochan xingxue ji qi dui Daojiao de yingxiang—cong 1928 nian de yiduan difanfzhi ziliao tongji shuoqi" 略論廟產興學及其對道教的影響－從1928年的一段地方志資料統計說起, *Zhongguo Daojiao* 中國道教, 1 (2004): 50–52; Zheng Guo 鄭國, "Minguo qianqi mixin wenti yanjiu (1912–1928)" 民國前期迷信問題研究 (1912–1928), (master's thesis, Shandong University, 2003). Nedostup, *Superstitious Regimes*, pp. 11–16.

23. Goossaert and Palmer, *Religious Question*, pp. 62–63, 125; Nedostup, *Superstitious Regimes*, pp. 79–87. See also Zhao Mingjuan 趙明娟, "20 shiji shangbanye Zhejiang Daojiaoshi yanjiu" 20世紀上半葉浙江道教史研究 (master's thesis, Zhejiang University, 2011), pp. 5–6.

24. Xu Xiaozheng 許效正, "Qingmo Minchu miaochan wenti yanjiu (1895–1916)" 清末民初廟產問題研究 (1895–1916) (Ph.D. diss., Shaanxi Normal University, 2010), 120–137.

25. Poon, *Negotiating Religion in Modern China*, pp. 42–49. For more on Guangzhou's history during this era, see Michael Tsin, *Nation, Governance, and Modernity in China: Canton, 1900–1927* (Stanford: Stanford University Press, 1999).

26. Ai Ping, "Minguo jinzhi yingshen saihui lunxi."

27. Vincent Goossaert, "The Local Politics of Festivals: Hangzhou, 1850–1950" (paper presented at the conference "Past and Present in China: The Influence of History from Empire to Republic," New York University, December 2–3, 2011).

28. *Zhonghua minguoshi dang'an ziliao huibian, ser. 5, pt. 1*, pp. 492–495.

29. Goossaert and Palmer, *Religious Question*, pp. 44–49.

30. Xu Xiaozheng, "Qingmo Minchu miaochan wenti yanjiu," pp. 120–123. One notable exception is the late Qing political novel *The Broom to Sweep Away Superstition* (*Saomizhou* 掃迷帚), which was published in 1905; see Nedostup, *Superstitious Regimes*, p. 13.

31. Li Ganchen 李幹忱, ed. and comp., *Pochu mixin quanzhu* 破除迷信全書, in *Zhongguo minjian xinyang ziliao huibian* 中國民間信仰資料彙編, ser. 1, vol. 30 (Taipei: Xuesheng shuju, 1989). For more on the use of such labels, see David. A. Palmer, "Heretical Doctrines, Reactionary Secret Societies, Evil Cults: Labeling Heterodoxy in Twentieth-Century China," in *Chinese Religiosities: Afflictions of Modernity and State Formation*, ed. Mayfair Mei-hui Yang (Berkeley: University of California Press, 2008), pp. 113–134. Examples of antisuperstition stories may be found in part 3 of *One Day in China: May 21, 1936*, trans., ed., and intro. Sherman Cochran, Andrew C.K. Hsieh, and Janis Cochran (New Haven, CT: Yale University Press, 1983).

32. Poon, *Negotiating Religion in Modern China*, pp. 74, 86. See also Zheng Guo, "Mingui qinaqi mixin wenti yanjiu." For more on the Chinese folklore movement, see Hung Chang-tai 洪長泰, *Going to the People: Chinese Intellectuals and Folk Literature, 1918–1937* (Cambridge: Harvard University Press, 1985).

33. Nedostup, *Superstitious Regimes*, pp. 105, 123–133.

34. See the nearly 150 pages of data in *Zhonghua minguoshi dang'an ziliao huibian, ser. 5, pt. 1*, pp. 580–726.

35. "Zhonghua minguo miaochan xingxue cujinhui xuanyan" 中華民國廟產興學促進會宣言, *Jiaoyu jikan* 教育季刊, 1.2 (1930): 156–159.

36. Sarah Schneewind, *Community Schools and the State in Ming China* (Stanford: Stanford University Press, 2006), p. 73.

37. Schneewind, *Community Schools and the State in Ming China*, pp. 73–86, 146–150. See also Wu Jen-shu 巫仁恕, "Jieqing, xinyang yu kangzheng—Ming-Qing Chenghuang xinyang yu chengshi qunzhong de jiti kangyi xingwei" 節慶，信仰與抗爭明清城隍信仰與城市群眾的集體抗議行為, *Bulletin of the Institute of Modern History, Academia Sinica*, 34 (2000): 145–210; Vincent Goossaert, "The Destruction of Immoral Temples in Qing China," in *ICS Visiting Professor Lectures Series*, 2 (*Journal of Chinese Studies*, Special Issue) (Hong Kong: Chinese University Press, 2009), pp. 131–153.

38. *Zhonghua minguoshi dang'an ziliao huibian, ser. 5, pt. 1*, pp. 496–497, 504–513; Nedostup, *Superstitious Regimes*, pp. 84–85.

39. Vincent Goossaert, "A Question of Control: Licensing Local Ritual Specialists, 1850–1950," in *Belief, Practice and Cultural Adaptation: Papers from the Religion Section of the Fourth International Conference on Sinology*, eds. Paul R. Katz and Shufen Liu (Nankang: Academia Sinica Press, 2013), pp. 563–598.

40. Nedostup, *Superstitious Regimes*, pp. 104; Poon, *Negotiating Religion in Modern China*, pp. 81–83.

41. Nedostup, "Ritual Competition and the Modernizing Nation-State," pp. 96–97.

42. Chen Jinlong 陳金龍, "Minguo 'Simiao guanli tiaoli' de banbu

yu feizhi" 民國《寺廟管理條例》的頒布與廢止, *Fayin* 法音, 4 (2008): 54–59.

43. "Zhonghua minguo miaochan xingxue cujinhui xuanyan," pp. 156–157.

44. He Zhiming 何志明, "Minguo qi'an—Cong 'Da Chenghuang' dao 'Da dangbu'" 民國奇案—從「打城隍」到「打黨部」, *Wenshi tiandi* 文史天地, 11 (2010): 41–45. For more on this province's elites during this time period, see Bradley Kent Geisert, *Radicalism and Its Demise: The Chinese Nationalist Party, Factionalism, and Local Elites in Jiangsu Province, 1924–1931* (Ann Arbor: Center for Chinese Studies Publications, University of Michigan, 2001).

45. "Pochu mixin—Baoying xian feichu ouxiang yundong" 破除迷信—寶應縣廢除偶像運動, *Zhenguang zazhi* 真光雜誌, 28.2 (1929): 84–85. See also Vincent Goossaert, "The Shifting Balance of Power in the City God Temples, 1800–1937" (paper presented at the Association for Asian Studies Annual Meeting, Honolulu, Hawaii, March 30-April 3, 2011).

46. *Zhonghua minguoshi dang'an ziliao huibian, ser. 5, pt. 1*, pp. 490–491.

47. See especially Nedostup, *Superstitious Regimes*, pp. 79–87, 103, 113, 148–149; Poon, *Negotiating Religion in Modern China*, pp. 45–47.

48. Xu Xiaozheng, "Qingmo Minchu miaochan wenti yanjiu," pp. 101–114, 137. See also Shen Jie 沈潔, "Xiandaihua jianzhi due xinyang kongjian de zhengyong—Yi ershi shiji chunian de miaochan xingxue yundong wei li" 現代化建制對信仰空間的徵用—以二十世紀初年的廟產興學運動為例, *Lishi jiaoxue wenti* 歷史教學問題, 2 (2008): 56–59, as well as Goossaert and Palmer, *Religious Question*, p. 49. For more on late-Qing local resistance movements, see Roxann Prazniak, *Of Camel Kings and Other Things: Rural Rebels against Modernity in Late Imperial China* (New York: Rowman and Littlefield, 1999).

49. Goossaert and Palmer, *Religious Question*, pp. 46–47; Nedostup, *Superstitious Regimes*, pp. 76–77. See also Vera Schwarcz, *The Chinese Enlightenment: Intellectuals and the Legacy of the May Fourth Movement of 1919* (Berkeley: University of California Press, 1986).

50. Tai Shuangqiu 郃爽秋, *Miaochan xingxue wenti* 廟產興學問題 (Shanghai: Zhonghua shubao liutongchu, 1929), pp. 11–15.

51. "Pochu mixin—Xiaoshan xuesheng daohui Chenghuang" 破除迷信一蕭山學生搗毀城隍, *Zhenguang zazhi* 真光雜誌, 28.2 (1929): 84–85.

52. See Nedostup, *Superstitious Regimes*, p. 68. For more on how Christianity (and especially Catholicism) interacted with communal religious traditions, see Joseph Tse-Hei Lee, *The Bible and the Gun: Christianity in South China, 1860–1900* (New York: Routledge, 2003); Eugenio Menegon, *Ancestors, Virgins, & Friars: Christianity as a Local Religion in Late Imperial China* (Cambridge: Harvard University Press, 2009); Henrietta Harrison, "Rethinking Missionaries and Medicine in China: The Miracles of Assunta Pallotta, 1905–2005," *The Journal of Asian Studies*, 71.1 (2012): 127–148.

53. Feng Yuxiang 馮玉祥, "Mixin shi minzu luohou de xiangzheng, mixin shi wangguo miezhong de genyuan, geming de minzhong yao pochu mixin" 迷信是民族落後的象徵，迷信是亡國滅種的根源，革命的民眾要破除迷信, *Xinghua* 興華, 25.16 (1928): 10–17.

54. Yan Yutang 嚴玉堂, "Zhengfu pochu mixin yu Zhongguo jidujiao de qiantu" 政府破除迷信與中國基督教的前途," Xinghua 興華, 25.35 (1928): 13–14.

55. Important historical background may be found in Ryan Dunch, *Fuzhou Protestants and the Making of Modern China, 1857–1927* (New Haven, CT: Yale University Press, 2001).

56. *Haichaoyin* 海潮音, 10.1 (1929): 80–82.

57. Vincent Goossaert, "Irrepressible Female Piety: Late Imperial Bans on Women Visiting Temples," *Nan Nü. Men, Women and Gender in China*, 10.2 (2008): 212–241. See also Julia C. Huang, Elena Valussi, and David A. Palmer, "Gender and Sexuality," in *Chinese Religious Life*, eds. David A. Palmer, Glenn Shive, and Philip L. Wickeri (Oxford: Oxford University Press, 2011), pp. 107–123. Accounts of some incidents may be found in the following issues of *Shenbao* 申報: 1872.05.30, 1877.04.27, 1877.07.03, 1878.11.26, and 1878.12.03. I am profoundly grateful to Vincent Goossaert for sharing these materials.

58. Nedostup, *Superstitious Regimes*, p. 112; Poon, *Negotiating Reli-*

gion in Modern China, pp. 53, 63, 139–140. See also Kang Xiaofei, "The Changing Place of Women in Religion and Society in Twentieth-Century and Contemporary China" (paper presented at the international conference on "Modern Chinese Religion: Value Systems in Transformation, Part 2: 1850–present," Chinese University of Hong Kong, December 12–15, 2012).

59. Fu Haiyan, "Geming, falü, yu miaochan," p. 117.

60. Ai Ping, "Minguo jinzhi yingshen saihui lunxi."

61. He Zhiming, "Minguo qi'an."

62. Sha Qingging 沙青青, "Xinyang yu quanzheng—1931 nian Gaoyou 'Da Chenghuang' fengchao zhi yanjiu" 信仰與權爭—1931年高郵「打城隍」風潮之研究, *Jindaishi yanjiu* 近代史研究, 1 (2010): 115–127.

63. Goossaert and Palmer, *Religious Question*, pp. 54–55, 124–125, 131. See also Xu Xiaozheng, "Qingmo Minchu miaochan wenti yanjiu," pp. 92–114; Zheng Guo, "Minguo qianqi mixin wenti yanjiu"; Li Xuechang and Dong Jianpo, "20 shiji shangbanye Hangxian yingshen saihui shuailuo yuanyin qianxi."

64. Nedostup, *Superstitious Regimes*, pp. 104, 144–147.

65. Poon, "Thriving under an Anti-superstition Regime: The Cult of Dragon Mother in Yuecheng 悅城, Guangdong during the 1930s" (paper presented at the Association for Asian Studies Annual Meeting, Honolulu, Hawaii, March 30–April 3, 2011).

66. Nedostup, *Superstitious Regimes*, pp. 40–41, 50. See also Shen Kuuyi, "Wang Yiting in the Social Networks of 1910s–1930s Shanghai," in *At the Crossroads of Empires: Middlemen, Social Networks, and State-building in Republican China*, eds. Nara Dillon and Jean C. Oi (Stanford: Stanford University Press, 2008), pp. 45–64, esp. pp. 56, 64. For more on Wang's life and career, see chapter 3 and Kang Bao 康豹 (Paul R. Katz), "Yige zhuming Shanghai shangren yu cishanjia de zongjiao shenghuo—Wang Yiting" 一個著名上海商人與慈善家的宗教生活—王一亭, in *Cong chengshi kan Zhongguo de xiandaixing* 從城市看中國的現代性, eds. Wu Jen-shu 巫仁恕, Lin May-li 林美莉, and Kang Bao 康豹 (Nankang: Institute of Modern History, Academia Sinica, 2010), pp. 275–296. I am especially grateful to Ma Jun 馬軍 for giving me a list of articles published in

the *China Buddhist Association News* (*Zhongguo Fojiaohui bao* 中國佛教會報) from 1931–1933, which document the work by Wang Yiting in protecting Buddhist monastic properties (*huchi sichan* 護持寺產).

67. *Zhonghua minguoshi dang'an ziliao huibian, ser. 5, pt. 1*, pp. 15–16. See also Beverly Foulks McGuire, "Bringing Buddhism into the Classroom: Jiang Qian's 江謙 (1876–1942) Vision for Education in Republican China," *Journal of Chinese Religions*, 39 (2011): 33–54.

68. *Haichaoyin* 海潮音, 10.1 (1929): 77–78; "Gedi miaochan zhi chuli" 各地廟產之處理, *Shenbao* 申報 (1929.02.19).

69. Fu Haiyan, "Geming, falü yu miaochan"; see also Tai Shuangqiu, *Miaochan xingxue wenti*.

70. Goossaert, "The Local Politics of Festivals: Hangzhou"; see also Shen Jie 沈潔, "Fanmixin yu shequ xinyang kongjian de xiandai licheng—Yi 1934 nian Suzhou de qiuyu yishi wei li" 反迷信與社區信仰空間的現代歷程－以1934年蘇州的求雨儀式為例, *Shilin* 史林, 2 (2007): 44–63, esp. pp. 54–59, 62.

71. "Lunshuo: Jizu pochu mixin bian" 論說：濟祖破除迷信辯, *Daode zazhi* 道德雜誌, 2.8 (1922): 48. For more on the historical development of Jigong's cult, see Meir Shahar, *Crazy Ji: Chinese Religion and Popular Literature* (Cambridge: Harvard University Press, 1998).

72. The use of the term "redemptive societies" is not without its drawbacks. At times it is used rather broadly to cover an extremely wide range of religious associations (see, for example, Goossaert and Palmer, *Religious Question*, pp. 292–297). In addition, it overlooks the fact that many other religious groups, such as lay Buddhist associations, also stressed a discourse of redemption, including the expression *jiushi* 救世. Thus, the term "redemptive societies" runs the risk of creating a false distinction between different religious groups that shared similar values and practices. I am thankful to J. Brooks Jessup for his thoughtful guidance on these matters.

73. For more on these phenomena, see the special double issue entitled "Redemptive Societies and New Religious Movements in Modern China," recently published in vols. 172 (June 2011) and 173 (September 2011) of *Minsu quyi* 民俗曲藝 (*Journal of Chinese Ritual, Theatre, and*

Folklore). See also Goossaert and Palmer, *Religious Question*, pp. 135–137; David Ownby, "Redemptive Societies in China's Long Twentieth Century" (paper presented at the international conference on "Modern Chinese Religion: Value Systems in Transformation, Part 2: 1850-present," Chinese University of Hong Kong, December 12–15, 2012); David Ownby, *Falun Gong and the Future of China* (New York and Oxford: Oxford University Press, 2008).

74. Huang Ko-wu 黃克武, "Minguo chunian Shanghai Lingxue yanjiu: Yi 'Shanghai Lingxuehui' wei li" 民國初年上海的靈學研究：以「上海靈學會」為例, *Bulletin of the Institute of Modern History Academia Sinica*, 55 (2007): 99–136; Takai Sadao 酒井忠夫, "Minguo chuqi zhi xinxing zongjiao yundong yu xinshibdai chaoliu" 民國初期之新興宗教運動與新時代潮流, trans. Chang Shu-e 張淑娥, *Minjian zongjiao* 民間宗教, 1 (1995): 1–36; Sun Jiang 孫江, *Kindai Chūgoku no kakumei to himitsu kessha: Chūgoku kakumei no shakaishi kenkyū (1895–1955)* 近代中國の革命と秘密結社：中國革命の社會史的研究（一八九五-一九五五）(Tokyo: Kyūko sho-in, 2007).

75. For the histories of specific groups, see Prasenjit Duara, *Sovereignty and Authenticity: Manchukuo and the East Asian Modern* (Lanham, MD: Rowman and Littlefield, 2003), pp. 103–122, 139–140, 154–162; Thomas David DuBois, *The Sacred Village: Social Change and Religious Life in Rural North China* (Honolulu: University of Hawai'i Press, 2005), pp. 107–120; Lu Zhongwei, "Huidaomen in the Republican Period," trans. David Ownby, *Chinese Studies in History*, 44.1–2 (Fall 2010/Winter 2011): 10–37; Shao Yong 邵雍, *Zhongguo huidaomen* 中國會道門 (Shanghai: Shanghai renmin chubanshe, 1997); Sakai Tadao 酒井忠夫, *Kingendai Chūgoku ni okeru shūkyō kessha no kenkyū* 近、現代中國における宗教結社の研究 (Tokyo: Tokyo kabushiki kaishi kokusho kankōkai, 2002). A useful overview of Chinese-language works may be found in David Ownby, "Recent Chinese Scholarship on the History of 'Redemptive Societies': Guest Editor's Introduction," *Chinese Studies in History* 44.1–2 (Fall 2010/Winter 2011): 3–9.

76. Sakai Tadao, "Minguo chuqu zhi xinxing zongjiao ynudong yu xinshidai chaoliu," pp. 23, 28.

77. Ownby, "The Politics of Redemption."

78. Goossaert and Palmer, *Religious Question*, pp. 44–45.

79. Fu Haiyan, "Geming, falü yu miaochan."

80. Xu Xiaozheng, "Qingmo Minchu miaochan wenti yanjiu," p. 117.

81. Goossaert and Palmer, *Religious Question*, pp. 126–127.

82. Poon, *Negotiating Religion in Modern China*, p. 48.

83. *Zhonghua minguoshi dang'an ziliao huibian, ser. 5, pt. 1*, pp. 509–513.

84. See Zhang Gang 張棡, *Zhang Gang riji* 張棡日記, ed. Yu Xiong 俞雄 (Shanghai: Shanghai shehui kexue chubanshe, 2003), pp. 411–412. Lo Shih-chieh adeptly uses this source in his doctoral dissertation, "The Order of Local Things."

85. Zhongxuan, "Pochu mixin zhi yiyi he banfa."

86. Xu Xiaozheng, "Qingmo Minchu miaochan wenti yanjiu," pp. 92–101.

87. One notable exception may be found in Shen Jie, "Fanmixin yu shequ xinyang kongjian de xiandai licheng."

88. Goossaert and Palmer, *Religious Question*, p. 126.

89. Liu Xun 劉迅 and Mei Li 梅莉, "Constructing Modern Daoism" (paper presented at the international conference on "Modern Chinese Religion: Value Systems in Transformation, Part 2: 1850-present," Chinese University of Hong Kong, December 12–15, 2012).

90. Liu Chengyou, "Luelun miaochan xingcu ji qi dui Daojiao de yingxiang," p. 51.

91. Xu Xiaozheng, "Qingmo Minchu miaochan wenti yanjiu," pp. 92–117.

92. Willem A. Grootaers, *The Sanctuaries in a North-China City: A Complete Survey of the Cultic Buildings in the City of Hsüan-hua 宣化 (Chahar 察哈爾)* (Bruxelles: Institut Belge des Hautes Études Chinoises, 1995); Sidney D. Gamble, *North China Villages: Social, Political, and Economic Activities before 1933* (Berkeley: University of California Press, 1963), p. 119; DuBois, *The Sacred Village*, pp. 30–33, 49–51, 56–59. Recent studies of North China religion include David G. Johnson, *Spectacle and Sacrifice: The Ritual Foundations of Village Life in North China*

(Cambridge: Harvard University Press, 2009); Daniel L. Overmyer, *Local Religion in North China in the Twentieth Century: The Structure and Organization of Community Rituals and Beliefs* (Leiden and Boston: Brill, 2009); and Stephen Jones, *In Search of the Daoists of North China* (Aldershot, UK: Ashgate, 2010). See also Vincent Goossaert, "Is There a North China Religion? A Review Essay," *Journal of Chinese Religions*, 39 (2011): 83–93.

93. Xu Xiaozheng, "Qingmo Minchu miaochan wenti yanjiu," pp. 92–117.

94. Xu Yao 徐躍, "Qingmo Sicuan miaochan xingxue ji you ci chansheng de sengsu jiufen" 清末四川廟產興學及由此產生的僧俗糾紛, *Jindaishi yanjiu* 近代史研究, 5 (2008): 73–88. See also Liang Yong 梁勇, "Qingmo 'Miaochan xingxue' yu xiangcun quanshi de zhuanyi—Yi Baxian wei zhongxin" 清末'廟產興學'與鄉村權勢的轉移—以巴縣為中心, *Shehuixue yanjiu* 社會學研究, 1 (2008): 102–119, 244.

95. Xu Xiaoming 許曉明, "Zongjiao wenhua da shiyi—Qingmo Minchu Guangxi 'Miaochan xingxue' yundong" 宗教文化大失憶—清末民初廣西「廟產興學」運動, *Nanfang luntan* 南方論壇, 12 (2007): 94–95.

96. Fu Haiyan, "1940 niandai Edong simiao caichanquan chutan," p. 7.

97. Goossaert and Palmer, *Religious Question*, pp. 125, 128, 130; Goossaert, "The Local Politics of Festivals: Hangzhou."

98. Wan Jianzhong 萬建中, "Minchu de fengsu biange yu biange fengsu" 民國的風俗變革與變革風俗, *Liaoxibei minzu yanjiu* 遼西北民族研究, 33 (2002): 119–128.

99. Goossaert and Palmer, *Religious Question*, pp. 62–63.

100. Lo Shih-chieh's Ph.D. thesis, "The Order of Local Things," represents a fine start.

101. For more on these issues, see Nedostup, *Superstitious Regimes*, pp. 103, 126, 142.

102. Qi Gang, personal communication, February 3, 2012.

103. Joseph W. Esherick, "Modernity and Nation in the Chinese City," in *Remaking the Chinese City: Modernity and National Identity, 1900–1950*, ed. idem (Honolulu: University of Hawai'i Press, 2000), pp. 1–16.

See also Li Guannan, "Reviving China: Urban Reconstruction in Nanchang (南昌) and the Guomindang National Revival Movement, 1932–1937," *Frontiers of History in China*, 7.1 (2012): 106–113; Kristin Stapleton, *Civilizing Chengdu: Chinese Urban Reform, 1895–1937* (Cambridge: Harvard University Press, 2000).

104. Poon, "Thriving under an Anti-superstition Regime"; Poon, *Negotiating Religion in Modern China*, p. 59.

105. Chen Jinlong, "Cong miaochan xingxue fengbo kan Minguo shiqi de zhengjiao guanxi."

106. Zhao Mingjuan, "20 shiji shangbanye Zhejiang Daojiaoshi yanjiu," pp. 5, 10–12.

107. Goossaert and Palmer, *Religious Question*, p. 131; Fu Haiyan, "1940 niandai Edong simiao caichanquan chutan." For more on the wartime era, see Diana Lary, *The Chinese People at War: Human Suffering and Social Transformation, 1937–1945*, as well as Stephen R. MacKinnon, Diana Lary and Ezra F. Vogel, eds., *China at War: Regions of China, 1937–1945* (Stanford: Stanford University Press, 2007); Hans J. van de Ven, *War and Nationalism in China, 1925–1945* (London and New York: RoutledgeCurzon, 2003).

108. Xue Yu 學愚, *Buddhism, War, and Nationalism: Chinese Monks in the Struggle against Japanese Aggressions, 1931–1945* (New York: Routledge, 2005), as well as J. Brooks Jessup, "The Householder Elite: Buddhist Activism in Shanghai, 1920–1956" (Ph.D. diss., University of California, Berkeley, 2010).

109. See, for example, Duara, *Culture, Power, and the State* and Naquin, *Peking: Temples and City Life*.

110. Xiao Tian 小田, "Jindai Jiangnan miaohui yu nongjia jingji shenghuo" 近代江南廟會與農家經濟生活, *Zhongguo nongshi* 中國農史, 21.2 (2002): 79–86. See also Shen Jie, "Fanmixin yu shequ xinyang kongjian de xiandai licheng."

111. Poon, *Negotiating Religion in Modern China*, pp. 43–44, 48–60, 85; Goossaert and Palmer, *Religious Question*, pp. 128–130.

112. Goossaert, "The Local Politics of Festivals: Hangzhou"; Li Xue-

chang and Dong Jianbo, "20 shiji shangbanye Hangxian yingshen saihui shuailuo yinsu qianxi."

113. Nedostup, *Superstitious Regimes*, pp. 118–119, 142.

114. Shen Jie 沈潔, "Xiandaihua jianzhi dui xinyang kongjian de zhengyong—Yi ershi shiji chunian miaochan xingxue yundong wei li"; Nedostup, *Superstitious Regimes*, pp. 103–120.

115. Xiao Tian 小田, "Shequ chuantong de xiandai mingyun—Yi Suzhou Qionglong laohui wei duixiang de li'an yanjiu" 社區傳統的近代命運—以蘇州穹窿老會為對象的例案研究, *Jiangsu shehui kexue* 江蘇社會科學, 6 (2002): 141–147.

116. Goossaert, "Détruire les temples pour construire les écoles."

117. Zhang Hua 張化, et. al., ed. and comp., *Shanghai zongjiao tonglan* 上海宗教通覽 (Shanghai: Shanghai guji chubanshe, 2004), pp. 11–12, 223–224. Shanghai's religious life is also discussed in Ruan Renze 阮仁澤 and Gao Zhennong 高振農, eds., *Shanghai zongjiaoshi* 上海宗教史 (Shanghai: Shanghai renmin chubanshe, 1992); Ge Zhuang 葛壯, *Zongjiao yu jindai Shanghai shehui de bianqian* 宗教與近代上海社會的變遷 (Shanghai: Shanghai shudian chubanshe, 1999); Bryna Goodman, *Native Place, City, and Nation: Regional Networks and Identities in Shanghai, 1853–1937* (Berkeley: University of California Press, 1995).

118. Only 23 of the supposedly 1,135 Buddhist temples housed resident monks (*seng* 僧), while just 27 had nuns (*ni* 尼). A total of 72 had lay Buddhist householders (*jushi* 居士) in residence.

119. Zhang Hua, *Shanghai zongjiao tonglan*, pp. 6–183, 217–330. The historical development of Daoism in modern China has been expertly examined in Vincent Goossaert, *The Daoists of Peking, 1800–1949*; David A. Palmer and Liu Xu 劉迅, eds., *Daoism in the Twentieth Century: Between Eternity and Modernity* (Berkeley: University of California Press, 2012). See also Liu Xun's pioneering study of Daoism in Shanghai, *Daoist Modern: Innovation, Lay Practice, and the Community of Inner Alchemy in Republican Shanghai* (Cambridge: Harvard University Asia Center, 2009).

120. Goossaert, "Détruire les temples pour construire les écoles," as well as personal communication via e-mail on March 21, 2012.

121. There were also five instances of such sites being converted into charitable schools (*yishu* 義塾).

122. The total of sixty-one also includes three instances of temples being turned into schools during the Republican era, but without a specific date being provided.

123. As noted, many of these sacred sites were in fact communal temples (or even temples that had once been part of the state cult, including twenty City God temples, sixteen Guandi 關帝 temples, and six Tianhou 天后 (Mazu 媽祖) temples.

124. The total of 103 also includes two instances of temples being abandoned during the Republican era, but without a specific date being provided.

125. *Shenbao*, 1929.02.04. See also Huzhou Archives, ed., *Shenbao Huzhou lüHu tongxiang tuanti shiliao* 申報湖州旅滬同鄉團體史料 (Huzhou: Huzhou Archives, 2011), pp. 119–120, 133–134, 137, 140–141, 150–151, 152–154. Liu Wenxing 劉文星 is currently undertaking a study of these events.

126. *Zhonghua minguoshi dang'an ziliao huibian, ser. 5, pt. 1*, pp. 509–513.

127. Ai Ping's work on this topic is especially important.

128. "Pochu mixin—Shanghaixian Gong'anju chajin Chenghuang quqi" 破除迷信－上海縣公安局查禁城隍娶妾. *Zhenguang zazhi* 真光雜誌, 28.2 (1929): 84–85. Like Wang, Qin was not only a Buddhist practitioner but also an avid philanthropist, and the close ties between these two men can be seen in the fact that Qin composed Wang's necrology; see Kang Bao, "Yige zhuming Shanghai shangren yu cishanjia de zongjiao shenghuo."

129. *Shenbao*, 1935.03.24.

130. For more on such terminology, see Adam Chau, "Superstition Specialist Households? The Household Idiom in Chinese Religious Practices," *Minsu quyi*, 153 (2006): 157–202.

131. *Shenbao*, 1930.09.25.

132. *Haichaoyin* 海潮音, 10.1 (1929): 78, 80.

133. Wang Liping, "Tourism and Spatial Changes in Hangzhou,

1900–1927," in *Remaking the Chinese City: Modernity and National Identity, 1900–1950*, ed. Joseph W. Esherick (Honolulu: University of Hawai'i Press, 2000), pp. 107–120; He Wangfang 何王芳, "Minguo sihqi Hangzhou chengshi shehui shenghuo yanjiu" 民國時期杭州城市社會生活研究 (Ph.D. diss., Zhejiang University, 2006), 167–196. See also Goossaert, "The Local Politics of Festivals: Hangzhou" and Zhao Mingjuan, "20 shiji shangbanye Zhejiang Daojiaoshi yanjiu," pp. 43–47.

134. Li Xuechang and Dong Jianpo, "20 shiji shangbanye Hangxian yingshen saihui shuailuo yinsu qianxi," p. 50.

135. *Haichaoyin*, 10.1 (1929): 81; "Pochu mixin—Shaoxing juban miaochan xingxue" 破除迷信—紹興舉辦廟產興學, *Zhenguang zazhi*, 28.2 (1929): 84–85.

136. Wan Jianzhong, "Minguo de fengsu biange yu biange fengsu."

137. Shen Jie, "Xiandaihui jianzhi dui xinyang kongjian de zhengyong."

138. *Shenbao*, 1922.10.27.

139. "Pochu mixin—Huishen zaji Shaoxing juban miaochan xingxue" 破除迷信—毀神雜記, *Zhenguang zazhi*, 28.2 (1929): 84–85; Yang Dehui 楊德惠, "Ningbo daohui ouxiang ji" 寧波搗毀偶像記, *Shenbao*, 1929.1.20.

140. *Haichaoyin*, 10.1 (1929): 78–79.

141. Zhang Weijing 張韋靜, "Dui pochu mixin yundong de shangque" 對破除迷信運動的商榷, *Ningbo Minguo ribao liu zhounian jinian ji ershi nian guoqing jinian hekan* 寧波民國日報六周年紀念暨二十年國慶紀念合刊 (1931): 90–92.

142. Huang Shiling 黄式陵, "Pochu mixin wenti: Cong Yuyao daohui Minjiaoguan an shuoqi" 破除迷信問題：從餘姚搗毀民教館案說起, *Chenguang zhoukan* 晨光周刊, 5.47 (1936): 6–10.

143. Zhang Chuanbao 張傳保, et. al., ed. and comp., *Yinxian tongzhi* 鄞縣通志 (1935), in *Zhongguo difangzhi jicheng, Zhejiang fuxianzhi ji* 中國地方志集成, 浙江府縣志輯, vols. 16–18 (Shanghai: Shanghai shudian chubanshe, 1993), vol. 17, pp. 725–793. The historical significance of this work is discussed in Barend ter Haar, "Local Society and the Organization of Cults in Early Modern China."

144. Lo Shih-chieh, "The Order of Local Things."

145. For more on the founding of Western-style schools in Wenzhou, see Hu Zhusheng 胡珠生, *Wenzhou jindaishi* 溫州近代史 (Shenyang: Liaoning renmin chubanshe, 2000), pp. 203–210. See also Li Shizhong 李世眾, *WanQing shishen yu difang zhengzhi: Yi Wenzhou wei zhongxin de kaocha* 晚清士紳與地方政治：以溫州為中心的考察 (Shanghai: Shanghai renmin chubanshe, 2006).

146. *Ruian wenshi ziliao* 瑞安文史資料, 5 (1987): 16.

147. *Zhang Gang riji*, p. 112.

148. Ibid., p. 386.

149. Lo Shih-chieh, "The Order of Local Things." See also Fang Zongbao 方宗苞, "Yuecheng daoshentuan" 樂成搗神團, *Yueqing wenshi ziliao* 樂清文史資料, 1 (1984): 116. These events are also mentioned in *Haichaoyin*, 10.1 (1929): 76.

150. Lo Shih-chieh, "The Order of Local Things"; *Zhang Gang riji*, p. 550.

151. In this case the Public Security Bureau (Gonganju 公安局), People's Political Consultative Conference (Renmin zhengxie 人民政協), Civil Affairs Department (Minzhengke 民政科), and United Front (Tongzhanbu 統戰部).

152. Perhaps an example of people taking advantage of chaotic times to assume control over valuable sacred sites (*chenhuo dajie* 趁火打劫)?

153. Many thanks to Qi Gang and Liu Wenxing for their invaluable assistance in compiling and analyzing this data.

154. Goossaert, "Détruire les temples pour construire les écoles."

155. Zheng Guo, "Minguo qianqi mixin wenti yanjou (1912–1928)," p. 11. See also Wan Jinazhong, "Minguo de fengsu biange yu biange fengsu"; Li Xuechang and Dong Jianpo, "20 shiji shangbanye Hangxian yingshen saihui shuailuo yinsu qianxi."

156. I am grateful to Fu Haiyan, Qi Gang, and Liu Wenxing for sharing their views on this topic.

157. Paul R. Katz, "The Tao among the Miao: The Transformation of Religious Traditions and Ethnic Identities in Western Hunan during the Modern Era," Academia Sinica Investigator Award, 2010–2014.

158. Liu Yangyang 劉泱泱, *Jindai Hunan shehui bianqian* 近代湖南社會變遷 (Changsha: Hunan renmin chubanshe, 1998), pp. 431–465.

159. See also Cui Rong 崔榕, "Guojia zaichang yu Xiangxi Miaozu wenhua de bianqian—Minguo zhengfu de wenhua tonghua celue zai Xiangxi Miaozu diqu de shijian" 國家在場與湘西苗族文化的變遷——民國政府的文化同化策略在湘西苗族地區的實踐, *Qinghai minzu yanjiu* 青海民族研究, 22.1 (2011): 69–74.

160. Zeng Jiwu 曾繼梧, *Hunan gexian diaocha biji* 湖南各縣調查筆記 (Hunan: Heji yinshuasuo, 1931), pp. 153–156. See also Wang Jinghuan 王靜寰, "Xiang-Qian bianqu Miaoren qingkuang shiling" 湘黔邊區苗人情況拾零, in *Minguo nianjian Miaozu lunwenji* 民國年間苗族論文集, eds. Zhang Yongguo 張永國, et. al. (Guiyang: Guizhou minzu yanjiusuo, 1983), pp. 45–46; Yang Lixing 楊力行, "Xiangxi Miaozu de xinyang" 湘西苗族的信仰, *Minguo nianjian Miaozu lunwenji*, eds. Zhang Yongguo 張永國, et. al. (Guiyang: Guizhou minzu yanjiusuo, 1983), pp. 293–297; Shen Zan 沈瓚 (fl. 1465–1487) and Chen Xinchuan 陳心傳 (fl. 1917–1937), ed. and comp., *Wuxi Mantuzhi* 五溪蠻圖志 (also known as *Wuxi Miaozu fengtuji* 五溪苗族風土記 or *Wuxi Miaozu gujin shenghuoji* 五溪苗族古今生活集) (Changsha: Yulu shushe, 2012). For more on the ways in which modern scholars and officials wrote about China's non-Han peoples, see Thomas S. Mullaney, James Leibold, Stéphane Gros, and Eric Vanden Bussche, eds., *Critical Han Studies: The History, Representation, and Identity of China's Majority* (Berkeley: University of California Press, 2012).

161. Colin Mackerras, *China's Minority Cultures: Identities and Integration since 1912* (Sydney, Australia: Longmans, 1995).

162. Ling Chunsheng 凌純聲 and Rui Yifu 芮逸夫, *Xiangxi Miaozu diaocha baogao* 湘西苗族調查報告 (1947; reprint, Taipei: Southern Materials Center, 1978), pp. 127–193; Shi Qigui 石啟貴, *Xiangxi Miaozu shidi diaocha baogao* 湘西苗族實地調查報告 (1986; reprint, Changsha: Hunan renmin chubanshe, 1999), pp. 520–525. See also Cheung Siu-woo 張兆和, "Miao Identity in Western Guizhou: Indigenism and the Politics of Appropriation in Southwest China during the Republican Period," in *Hmong/Miao in Asia*, eds. Nicholas Tapp, et. al. (Chiangmai: Silkworm, 2004), pp. 237–272.

163. Wu Xiyun 吳曦云, *HongMiao fengsu* 紅苗風俗 (Hong Kong: Tianma Publishing Company, 2006); Shi Jianhua 石建華 and Wu Xianyou 伍賢佑, eds., *Xiangxi Miaozu bainian shilu* 湘西苗族百年實錄, 2 vols. (Beijing: Fangzhi chubanshe, 2008).

164. Tim Oakes and Donald S. Sutton, eds., *Faiths on Display: Religion, Tourism, and the Chinese State* (Lanham, MD: Rowman and Littlefield, 2010); Louisa Schein, *Minority Rules: The Miao and the Feminine in China's Cultural Politics* (Durham, NC: Duke University Press, 2000); Goossaert and Palmer, *Religious Question*, p. 61.

165. Scholars are also beginning to study the impact of religious policies promulgated by the Japanese during the period when they ruled many areas of China. See, for example, Thomas D. DuBois, *Religion and the Making of Modern East Asia* (Cambridge: Cambridge University Press, 2011); Thomas D. DuBois, ed., *Casting Faiths: Imperialism and the Transformation of Religion in East and Southeast Asia* (New York: Palgrave Macmillan, 2009).

166. See, for example, Zheng Guo, "Minguo qianqi mixin wenti yanjiu (1912–1928)," pp. 93–98.

167. Steve A. Smith, "Local Cadres Confront the Supernatural: The Politics of Holy Water (*Shenshui* 神水) in the PRC, 1949–1966," in *The History of the PRC (1949–1976)*, ed. Julia Strauss (Cambridge and New York: Cambridge University Press, 2007), pp. 145–168.

168. Goossaert and Palmer, *Religious Question*, pp. 140–165. See also Steven A. Smith, "Talking Toads and Chinless Ghosts: The Politics of 'Superstitious' Rumors in the People's Republic of China," *The American Historical Review*, 111.2 (2006): 405–427.

169. See "Writing a Place for Rites—Visions of 'Old Customs' in Wenzhou during the Great Leap Forward" (paper presented at the Association for Asian Studies Annual Meeting, Honolulu, Hawaii, March 30-April 3, 2011).

170. For more on post-1949 developments in Chinese Buddhism, see Holmes Welch, *Buddhism Under Mao* (Cambridge: Harvard University Press, 1972). J. Brooks Jessup examines the fate of Buddhism in post-1949 Shanghai in his "Flipping the Script: Buddhist Youth in Commu-

nist Shanghai, 1949–1956" (paper presented at the American Academy of Religion Annual Meeting, San Francisco, November 21, 2011). See also J. Brooks Jessup, "Beyond Ideological Conflict: Incorporation of Buddhist Youth in the Early PRC," *Frontiers of History in China*, 7.4 (2012): 551–581.

171. There was also one temple listed as having been abandoned after the Republican era.

172. These figures only take into account the final fate of each temple. Some temples went through a number of changes, which cannot fully be taken into account for the purposes of this preliminary statistical analysis. I am planning to consider this issue more thoroughly in the future.

173. For more on these processes, see Julia Strauss, "Editor's Introduction: In Search of PRC History," in *The History of the PRC (1949–1976)*, ed. Julia Strauss (Cambridge and New York: Cambridge University Press, 2007), pp. 1–15. See also her "Morality, Coercion, and State Building by Campaign in the Early PRC: Regime Consolidation and After, 1949–1956," in *The History of the PRC (1949–1976)*, ed. Julia Strauss (Cambridge and New York: Cambridge University Press, 2007), pp. 37–58.

174. Paul R. Katz, "Festivals and the Recreation of Identity in South China: A Case Study of Processions and Expulsion Rites in Pucheng, Zhejiang," *Journal of Ritual Studies*, 19.1 (2005), pp. 57–86; reprinted in Pamela J. Stewart and Andrew Strathern, eds., *Asian Ritual Systems. Syncretisms and Ruptures* (Durham, NC: Carolina Academia Press, 2007), pp. 153–182.

175. Paul R. Katz, "Religion and the State in Postwar Taiwan," *The China Quarterly*, 174 (June 2003), pp. 395–412; reprinted in Overmyer, *Religion in China Today*, pp. 89–106. See also Kuo, *Religion and Democracy in Taiwan*; Richard Madsen, *Democracy's Dharma: Religious Renaissance and Political Development in Taiwan* (Berkeley and Los Angeles: University of California Press, 2007); Weller, *Alternate Civilities*.

176. Katz, *Divine Justice*, pp 142–178.

177. See the essays in Oakes and Sutton, *Faiths on Display: Religion, Tourism, and the Chinese State*.

178. Chau, *Religion in Contemporary China*, p. 6.

179. Dean and Zheng, *Ritual Alliances of the Putian Plain*, vol. 1, pp. 3–9, 280–281.

2. TIME AND A WORD: NEW FORMS OF RELIGIOUS PUBLISHING

1. See, for example, Barbara Mittler, *A Newspaper for China? Power, Identity, and Change in Shanghai's News Media, 1872–1912* (Cambridge: Harvard University Asia Center, 2004); Tsai Weipin, *Reading Shenbao: Nationalism, Consumerism and Individuality in China, 1919–37* (Basingstoke, U.K. and New York: Palgrave Macmillan, 2010); Rudolf G. Wagner, ed., *Word, Image, and City in Early Chinese Newspapers, 1870–1910* (Albany, NY: State University of New York Press, 2007). For more on the impact of new printing technologies, see Christopher Reed, *Gutenberg in Shanghai: Chinese Print Capitalism*, 1876–1937 (Vancouver, BC: UBC Press, 2004); Cynthia Brokaw and Christopher Reed, eds., *From Woodblocks to the Internet: Chinese Publishing and Print Culture in Transition, circa 1800 to 2008* (Leiden and Boston: Brill, 2010).

2. James Robson, "Brushes with Some 'Dirty Truths': Handwritten Manuscripts and Religion in China," *History of Religions*, 51.4 (2012): 317–343.

3. See T. H. Barrett, *The Woman Who Invented Printing* (New Haven, CT and London: Yale University Press, 2008); Frances Wood and Mark Barnard, *The Diamond Sutra: The Story of the World's Earliest Dated Printed Book* (London: British Library, 2010).

4. Excellent overviews of these trends may be found in Cynthia Brokaw and Kai-wing Chow, eds., *Printing and Book Culture in Late Imperial China* (Berkeley: University of California Press, 2005), as well as Lucille Chia and Hilde de Weerdt, eds., *Knowledge and Text Production in an Age of Print* (Leiden: Brill, 2011).

5. Li Shiyu 李世瑜, "*Baojuan* xinyan" 寶卷新研, *Wenxue yichan zengkan* 文學遺產增刊, 4 (1957): 165–181; reprinted in Li Shiyu, *Baojuan lun ji* 寶卷論集, *Zongjiao yu shehui congshu* 宗教與社會叢書, vol. 1 (Taipei: Lantai chubanshe, 2007).

6. Susan Naquin, "The Transmission of White Lotus Sectarianism in Late Imperial China," in *Popular Culture in Late Imperial China*, eds. David G. Johnson, Andrew J. Nathan, and Evelyn S. Rawski (Berkeley: University of California Press, 1985), pp. 255–291; Daniel L. Overmyer, "Values in Chinese Sectarian Literature: Ming and Ch'ing *pao-chüan* 寶卷," in Johnson, *Popular Culture in Late Imperial China*, pp. 219–254; Daniel J. Overmyer, *Precious Volumes: An Introduction to Chinese Sectarian Scriptures from the Sixteenth and Seventeenth Centuries* (Cambridge: Harvard University Press, 1999). See also Ma Xisha 馬西沙 and Han Bingfang 韓秉方, *Zhongguo minjian zongjiaoshi* 中國民間宗教史 (Shanghai: Shanghai renmin chubanshe, 1992), pp. 173–187.

7. Philip Clart, "Sacred Texts, Religious Publishing, and New Technologies in China & Taiwan, 19th to 21st centuries" (paper presented at the international conference on "Modern Chinese Religion: Value Systems in Transformation, Part 2: 1850-present," Chinese University of Hong Kong, December 12–15, 2012).

8. Clart, "Sacred Texts, Religious Publishing, and New Technologies in China & Taiwan." See also Gregory Adam Scott, "Classical Exegesis and the Dharma: Navigating the Sea of Scriptures with Ding Fubao 丁福保 (1874–1952)" (paper presented as part of the panel "New Perspectives on Religion in China: Publishing Religion, Negotiating the Party-State," American Academy of Religion Annual Meeting, San Francisco, November 21, 2011).

9. Adrian A. Bennett, *Missionary Journalist in China: Young J. Allen and His Magazines, 1860–1883* (Athens, GA: University of Georgia Press, 1983).

10. Zhang Xiantao, *The Origins of the Modern Chinese Press: The Influence of the Protestant Missionary Press in Late Qing China* (London: Routledge, 2007), pp. 34–50, 105–111.

11. Goossaert and Palmer, *Religious Question*, pp. 68–83.

12. For Islam, see Zhang Zhihua 張志華, *Zhongguo Isilan wenhua yaolue* 中國伊斯蘭文化要略 (Yinchuan: Ningxia renmin chubanshe, 2010). See also Wlodzimierz Cieciura, "In Defense of Religion and Its People: Hui Reactions to Anti-Muslim Publications in Republican-Era

Mass Media" (paper presented at the Association for Asian Studies Annual Conference, Toronto, March 15–18, 2012); Stephane A. Dudoignon, Komatsu Hisao, and Kosugi Yasushi, eds., *Intellectuals in the Modern Islamic World: Transmission, Transformation and Communication* (London and New York: Routledge, 2009); see especially the papers by Françoise Aubin and Matsumoto Masumi. For Judaism, see Jonathan Goldstein, ed. and intro., *The Jews of China*, con. Benjamin I. Schwartz, biblio. Frank Joseph Shulman (Armonk, NY: M. E. Sharpe, 1999).

13. Nancy Stalker, "Showing Faith: Exhibiting Ōmoto to Consumers in Early-Twentieth-Century Japan," in *Casting Faiths: Imperialism and the Transformation of Religion in East and Southeast Asia*, ed. Thomas D. DuBois (New York: Palgrave Macmillan, 2009), pp. 239–256.

14. Francesca Tarocco, *The Cultural Practices of Modern Chinese Buddhism: Attuning the Dharma* (New York and London: Routledge, 2007), pp. 16–20, 30, 46–49, 59–63; Jan Kiely, "Spreading the Dharma with the Mechanized Press: New Buddhist Print Cultures in the Modern Chinese Print Revolution, 1865–1949," in Reed and Brokaw, *From Woodblocks to the Internet*, pp. 185–210. See also Wu Ping 吳平, "Jindai Shanghai de Fojiao chuban jigou" 近代上海的佛教出版機構, *Huaxia wenhua* 華夏文化, 1 (2000): 41–42, 37.

15. J. Brooks Jessup, "The Householder Elite," 56–58; Ge Tao 葛濤, *Changpian yu jindai Shanghai shehui shenghuo* 唱片與近代上海社會生活 (Shanghai: Shanghai cishu chubanshe, 2009); Huang Weichu 黃維楚, *Huayan zimu ji qi changfa* 華嚴字母及其唱法 (Shanghai: Foxue shuju, 2009); Yung Sai-shing (Rong Shicheng) 容世誠, *Yueyun liusheng—Changpian gongye yu Guangdong quyi (1903–1953)* 粵韻留聲—唱片工業與廣東曲藝 (1903–1953) (Hong Kong: Tiandi tushu, 2006); Lee Tong Soon, "Technology and the Production of Islamic Space: The Call to Prayer in Singapore," *Ethnomusicology*, 43.1 (1999): 86–100.

16. J. Brooks Jessup, "Flipping the Script." See also Jan Kiely, "Shanghai Public Moralist Nie Qijie and Morality Book Publication Projects in Republican China," *Twentieth-Century China*, 36.1 (January 2011): 4–22.

17. Information on this thesis ("Conversion by the Book—Buddhist Print Culture in Republican China") may be found at http://www.bud

dhiststudies.net/print_culture_dissertation.html. For more on Scott's research, see http://www.buddhiststudies.net/gregoryadamscott.html. See also Scott, "Classical Exegesis and the Dharma."

18. Scott, "Conversion by the Book"; Scott, "Classical Exegesis and the Dharma."

19. Jessup, "The Householder Elite," pp. 54–55, 58–59.

20. This problem is discussed in Jessup, "The Householder Elite," pp. 54–59; Scott, "Classical Exegesis and the Dharma." One issue that I hope to address in future research is patterns of literacy in Republican China.

21. Liu Xun, *Daoist Modern: Innovation, Lay Practice, and the Community of Inner Alchemy in Republican Shanghai* (Cambridge: Harvard University Asia Center, 2009), esp. pp. 231–271. See also Liu Xun, "Body Cultivation" (paper presented at the international conference on "Modern Chinese Religion: Value Systems in Transformation, Part 2: 1850-present," Chinese University of Hong Kong, December 12–15, 2012); Wu Yakui 吳亞魁, *Jiangnan Quanzhen Daojiao* 江南全真道教 (Hong Kong: Zhonghua shuju, 2006).

22. Liu Xun, "Body Cultivation"; Liu Xun and Mei Li, "Constructing Modern Daoism." See also Goossaert, *The Daoists of Peking, 1800–1949*, pp. 308–319.

23. Wang Jianchuan 王見川, "Qingmo Minchu de Jigong xinyang yu fuji tuanti: Jian tan Zhongguo jishenghui de youlai" 清末民初中國的濟公信仰與扶乩團體：兼談中國濟生會的由來, *Minsu quyi*, 162 (2008): 139–169; Fan Chunwu 范純武, "Feiluan, xiuzhen yu banshan—Zheng Guanying yu Shanghai zongjiao shijie" 飛鸞、修真與辦善—鄭觀應與上海的宗教世界, in *Cong Chengshi kan Zhongguo de xiandaixing*, eds. Wu Jen-shu, Lin May-li, and Kang Bao (Paul R. Katz) (Nankang: Institute of Modern History, Academia Sinica, 2010), pp. 247–274; Yau Chi On (You Zi'an) 游子安, *Shan yu ren tong: Ming-Qing yilai de cishan yu jiaohua* 善與人同：明清以來的慈善與教化 (Beijing: Zhonghua shuju, 2005).

24. For more on these associations, see David K. Jordan and Daniel L. Overmyer, *The Flying Phoenix: Aspects of Chinese Sectarianism in Taiwan* (Princeton: Princeton University Press, 1986). See also Philip A. Clart,

"Chinese Tradition and Taiwanese Modernity: Morality Books as Social Commentary and Critique," in *Religion in Modern Taiwan: Tradition and Innovation in a Changing Society*, eds. Philip A. Clart and Charles B. Jones (Honolulu: University of Hawai'i Press, 2003), pp. 84–97; Paul R. Katz, "Spirit-Writing Halls and the Development of Local Communities—A Case Study of Puli (Nantou County)," *Minsu quyi*, 174 (2011): 103–184; Gary W. Seaman, *Temple Organization in a Chinese Village*, in *Asian Folklore and Social Life Monographs*, vol. 101, ed. Lou Tzu-k'uang 婁子匡 (Taipei: The Orient Cultural Service, 1978).

25. Rudolf Löwenthal, *The Religious Periodical Press in China* (Peking: The Synodal Commission in China, 1940; reprint, San Francisco: Chinese Materials Center, 1978), pp. 139–192, 282–292.

26. The confusion between Daoism and redemptive societies also may be seen in the claim that Yao Jicang 姚濟蒼 (fl. 1920), who gave Richard Wilhelm (1873–1930) the inner alchemy text *Taiyi jinhua zongzhi* 太乙金華宗旨 that he later translated as *The Secret of the Golden Flower*, was a Daoist. In fact, he was one of the founders of the Fellowship of Goodness (Tongshanshe 同善社) described later in this chapter. See Wang Jianchuan, "An Exploration of the Early History of the Tongshanshe (1912–1945)," trans. David Ownby, *Chinese Studies in History*, 44.1–2 (Fall 2010/Winter 2011): 121–131, esp. 121.

27. Thomas D. DuBois, "Japanese Print Media and Manchurian Cultural Community: Religion in the Pages of the *Shengjing Times*, 1906–1944," in *Casting Faiths: Imperialism and the Transformation of Religion in East and Southeast Asia*, ed. Thomas D. DuBois (New York: Palgrave Macmillan, 2009), pp. 217–238.

28. Liu, *Daoist Modern*, pp. 174, 186, 209–216, 240–260, 275.

29. These phenomena are examined in detail in the special double issue of *Minsu quyi* entitled "Redemptive Societies and New Religious Movements in Modern China"; see vols. 172 (June 2011) and 173 (September 2011).

30. Löwenthal, *The Religious Periodical Press in China*, pp. 177–178.

31. Rostislav Berezkin, "Lithographic Printing and the Development of the *Baojuan* 寶卷 Genre in Shanghai in the 1900–1920s: On the Ques-

tion of the Interaction between Print Technology and Popular Literature in China (Preliminary Observations)," *Zhongzheng dauxue Zhongwen xueshu niankan* 中正大學中文學術年刊, 17 (2011): 337–368.

32. This text originally had been composed in a spirit-writing hall known as the Gathering Clouds Studio (Jiyunxuan 集雲軒), which operated as the religious arm of the Shanghai branch of the China Rescuing Life Association (see chapter 3).

33. "Jixian lin Shanghai Jiyunxuan jiyu erze" 濟仙臨上海集雲軒乩諭二則, *Daode zazhi* 道德雜誌, 1.2 (1921): 87–95.

34. Clart, "Sacred Texts, Religious Publishing, and New Technologies in China & Taiwan."

35. Jessup, "The Householder Elite," pp. 49–59; Clart, "Sacred Texts, Religious Publishing, and New Technologies in China & Taiwan."

36. See, for example, Sawada, *Zōho hōkan no kenkyū*, pp. 70–75.

37. Berezkin, "Lithographic Printing and the Development of *Baojuan* Genre in Shanghai in the 1900–1920s."

38. Yau Chi On, *Shan yu ren tong*, pp. 82–86.

39. This road was named after M. Emile Kraetzer (1839–1887), a respected French judge and diplomat.

40. See Wang Jianchuan 王見川, "Mingshan shuju yu Tongshanshe—Jiantan *Xuanling Yuhuangjing* de liuchuan" 明善書局與同善社—兼談《玄靈玉皇經》的流傳, *Mazu yu minjian xinyang: Yanjiu tongxun* 媽祖與民間信仰: 研究通訊, 1 (2012): 1–13.

41. Examples of these reprints may be found at http://shanshu.im.tiit.edu.tw/blog/348. See also Wang Jianchuan 王見川 and Li Shiwei 李世偉, et. al., eds., *Minjian sicang Taiwan zongjiao ziliao huibian: Minjian xinyang, minjian wenhua* 民間私藏臺灣宗教資料彙編：民間信仰・民間文化, ser. 1, 34 vols. (Taipei: BoyYoung Publishing, 2009); ser. 2, 33 vols. (Taipei: BoyYoung Publishing, 2010).

42. http://www.kongfz.com/.

43. Note the use of the term "*shan* 善" (goodness) in the names of both the society and the bookstore.

44. Wang Jianchuan 王見川, "Tongshanshe zaoqi de tedian ji zai Yunnan de fazhan (1912–1937): Jian tan qi yu '*luantang*,' 'Rujiao' de

guanxi" 同善社早期的特點及在雲南的發展 (1912–1937)：兼談其與「鸞壇」、「儒教」的關係, *Minsu quyi*, 172 (2011): 127–159; Wang Jianchuan, "Tongshanshe de zaoqi lishi (1912–1945) chutan" 同善社的早期歷史(1912–1945)初探, *Minjian zongjiao* 民間宗教, 1 (1995): 57–82. See also Fan Chunwu 范純武, "Minchu Ruxue de zongjiaohua: Duan Zhengyuan yu Daode xueshe de jige lishi wenti" 民初儒學的宗教化：段正元與道德學社的幾個歷史問題, *Minsu quyi*, 172 (2011): 161–203; Suemitsu Takayoshi 末光高義, *Shina no himitsu kessha to jizen kessha* 支那の秘密結社と慈善結社 (1927; reprint, Taipei: Guting shuwu, 1974); Goossaert and Palmer, *Religious Question*, pp. 100–105.

45. Wang Jianchuan, "An Exploration of the Early History of the Tongshanshe (1912–1945)," p. 124.

46. Ibid., pp. 129–130.

47. Ibid., p. 127; Wang Jianchuan, "Mingshan shuju yu Tongshanshe."

48. Wang Jianchuan, "Mingshan shuju yu Tongshanshe."

49. This periodical is not discussed in Löwenthal's survey. Two versions survive, although both are incomplete. The first version may be found in the *Minguo Fojiao qikan wenxian jicheng* 民國佛教期刊文獻集成, vol. 79 (Beijing: Quanguo tushuguan wenxian suowei fuzhi zhongxin, 2006). The second version, which is much more extensive with better-quality images, may be found in the *Xijian Minguo Fojiao wenxian huibian* 稀見民國佛教文獻彙编, vols. 11 and 12 (Beijing: Zhongguo shudian, 2008). I am grateful to Poon Shuk-wah, Yau Chi On, and Liu Wenxing for their help in locating these editions.

50. Reports about this movement may be found in the following issues of *Shenbao*: 1932.07.20, 1933.08.31, 1934.02.23, 1934.08.14, 1932.10.03–10.05. Poon Shuk-wah is currently undertaking a study of the animal rights movement during the Republican era.

51. This periodical also is not discussed in Löwenthal's survey. The accuracy of these circulation figures remains unknown, but the August 7, 1935 issue of *Shenbao* lists the *Cishan huibao* as having been approved for publication inside the French Concession.

52. Articles describing Zhang's life and career, including his phil-

anthropic deeds, may be found in the following issues of *Shenbao*: 1921.10.17, 1922.11.11, 1922.11.27, 1922.12.08, 1923.01.09, 1923.04.06, 1923.09.07–09.08, 1926.03.13, 1929.12.20, and 1934.02.12. For his obituary, see 1945.12.23.

53. Wang Jianchuan, "Mingshan shuju yu Tongshanshe."

54. *Shenbao*, 1927.11.12. Articles describing Zhang's other religious activities (founding temples, participating in local festivals, and so forth) may be found in the following issues of *Shenbao*: 1933.10.15, 1933.12.10, 1934.04.29, 1934.05.17, and 1935.07.04.

55. See *Yinguang fashi wenchao* (Beijing: Zongjiao wenhua chubanshe, 2000) vol. 1, p. 585. Online versions include http://www.minlun.org.tw/haihui/data/56/index.asp?t1=2&t2=1&t3=44, as well as http://www.pureland.tw/pureland/master13/cczl/ygfswc/y3a/y3a01/y3a0180-0182.htm.

56. See the *Taixu dashi nianpu* 太虛大師年譜, in *Yinshun fashi Foxue zhuzuo quanji* 印順法師佛學著作全集, vol. 6 (Beijing: Zhonghua shuju, 2009), pp. 79–85.

57. *Shenbao*, 1924.04.08.

58. Lu Zhongwei 陸仲偉, *Tongshan she* 同善社 (Beijing: Shehui wenti yanjiu congshu bianji weiyuanhui, 2005). See also Wang Jianchuan, "Mingshan shuju yu Tongshanshe."

59. Wang Jianchuan, "Mingshan shuju yu Tongshanshe." As noted, Fellowship members often adopted such innocuous titles in order to disguise their religious activities after the movement had been forced underground.

60. *Minguo shiqi chuban shumu huibian* 民國時期出版書目彙編, vol. 20 (Beijing: Guojia tushuguan chubanshe, 2010), pp. 203, 205.

61. For more on the antisuperstition campaigns, see Nedostup, *Superstitious Regimes*; Palmer and Goossaert, *Religious Question*.

62. *Minguo shiqi chuban shumu huibian*, vol. 20, pp. 193–194.

63. Ibid., pp. 329–330.

64. Ibid., p. 231.

65. These issues are thoughtfully considered in Scott, "Conversion by the Book"; Scott, "Classical Exegesis and the Dharma."

66. Wang Jianchuan, "Mingshan shuju yu Tongshanshe."

67. These same categories also were used for the partially preserved 1930s catalogue.

68. For more on this practice, see Adam Chau, "Script Fundamentalism: The Practice of Cherishing Written Characters (Lettered Paper) (*xizizhi* 惜字紙) in the Age of Literati Decline and Commercial Revolution," in *New Approaches to Studying Chinese Popular Religion and Sectarianism*, ed. Philip Clart (Taipei: BoyYoung Publishers), pp. 129–167.

69. See Vincent Goossaert's pioneering study on the beef taboo (*niujie* 牛戒) in Chinese religious culture, *L'Interdit du boeuf en Chine: Agriculture, éthique et sacrifice* (Paris: Collège de France, Institut des Hautes Études Chinoises, 2005).

70. *Minguo shiqi chuban shumu huibian*, vol. 20, pp. 277–278.

71. One Daoist classification system may be found in Yau Chi On, *Shan yu ren tong*, p. 78.

72. Ibid., pp. 160–164, 332–333.

73. Bai Chun 白純, "Jiang Jieshi Ruhua Sanmin zhuyi zhi pingxi" 蔣介石儒化三民主義之評析, *Nanjing zhengzhi xueyuan xuebao* 南京政治學院學報, 1 (2003): 77–79. See also Wang Shou-nan, "Chiang Kai-shek and the Promotion of the Chinese Cultural Renaissance Movement," *Chinese Studies in History*, 21.2 (Winter 1987–1988), pp. 66–90; Fukamachi Hideo, "Prairie Fire or the Gimo's New Clothes? Chiang Kai-shek's New Life Movement," *The Chinese Historical Review*, 17.1 (2010): 68–84. See also Jay Taylor, *The Generalissimo: Chiang Kai-shek and the Struggle for Modern China* (Cambridge: The Belknap Press of Harvard Press, 2009), pp. 13–14, 108–109; Hollington Kong Tong, *Chiang Kai-shek, Soldier and Statesman; Authorized Biography by Hollington K. Tong*, 1st ed. (London: Hurst and Blackett, 1938), pp. 546, 547, 550, 552.

74. Yau Chi On, *Shan yu ren tong*, p. 85; Wang Jianchuan, "Mingshan shuju yu Tongshanshe."

75. Goossaert and Palmer, *Religious Question*, pp. 95–96.

76. *Minguo shiqi chuban shumu huibian*, vol. 20, pp. 193–194.

77. Ibid., pp. 232–236.

78. I am grateful to Rostislav Berezkin for helping to clarify this important point.

79. I am deeply indebted to Sun Huei-min 孫慧敏 for providing this information.

80. Many thanks to Li Kai-kuang 李鎧光 for his kind assistance.

81. *Minguo shiqi chuban shumu huibian*, vol. 20, pp. 330–331.

82. Ibid., p. 227.

83. Ibid., pp. 237–276, 318–322.

84. Ibid., pp. 230, 242, 254.

85. Wang Zongxiu 王中秀, et. al., ed., Jinxiandai *Jinshi shuhuajia runli* 近現代金石書畫家潤例 (Shanghai: Shanghai shuhua chubanshe, 2004), pp. 297–303. I am grateful to Lai Yu-chih 賴毓芝 for her help with this matter.

86. Yau Chi On, *Shan yu ren tong*, pp. 70–71.

87. See Rostislav Berezkin, "The Multiple Ways of Printing and Circulation of 'Precious Scrolls' in Early Twentieth-Century Shanghai and Its Vicinity: Towards the Assessment of Multifunctionality of the Genre." This paper, originally entitled "*Baojuan* Publishing by Shanghai and Ningbo Publishers (1911–1940) and Its Connection with the Expansion and Changes of the Genre," was first presented as part of the panel "New Perspectives on Religion in China: Publishing Religion, Negotiating the Party-State," American Academy of Religion Annual Meeting, San Francisco, November 21, 2011.

88. Patricia Ebrey, ed., *Women and the Family in Chinese History* (London and New York: Routledge, 2003); Dorothy Ko, *Teachers of the Inner Chambers: Women and Culture in Seventeenth-Century China* (Stanford: Stanford University Press, 1995); Susan Mann, *Precious Records: Women in China's Long Eighteenth-Century* (Stanford: Stanford University Press, 1997).

89. Paul J. Bailey, *Gender and Education in China: Gender Discourses and Women's Schooling in the Early Twentieth Century* (London and New York: Routledge, 2007).

90. Zhou Zuoren 周作人, "Gua dou ji" 瓜豆集, in *Zhou Zuoren quan ji* 周作人全集, vol. 4 (Taipei: Landeng wenhua shiye, 1992), p. 25.

91. Hu Shih 胡適, *Sishi zishu* 四十自述 (Taibei: Yuandong tushu gongsi, 1992), pp. 39–41.

92. Qijun 琦君, *San geng you meng shu dang zhen* 三更有夢書當枕 (Taibei: Erya chubanshe, 1975), pp. 42–43.

93. Löwenthal, *The Religious Periodical Press in China*, p. 287.

94. Paul R. Katz, "An Unbreakable Thread? Preliminary Observations on the Interaction between Chinese and Taiwanese Religious Traditions under Japanese Colonial Rule" (paper presented at the First World Congress of Taiwan Studies, Academia Sinica, Taipei, Taiwan, April 26–28, 2012), published in *Taiwan zongjiao yanjiu* 台灣宗教研究, 11.2 (2013): 39–70. See also Lai Ch'ung-jen 賴崇仁, "Taizhong Ruicheng shuju ji qi gezaice yanjiu" 台中瑞成書局及其歌仔冊研究 (master's thesis, Fengchia University, Taichung, Taiwan, 2004), as well as the Ruicheng Bookstore's own website (http://www.ruicheng.com.tw/initial.php).

95. Information on Huang's life and activities may be found in Wang Jianchuan 王見川, "Guomin zhengfu lai Tai (1949) qian liang'an de zongjiao wanglai yu cishan huodong chutan: Jian tan Lanji shuju Huang Maosheng de jiaose" 國民政府來台(1949)前兩岸的宗教往來與慈善活動初探：兼談蘭記書局黃茂盛的角色, *Mazu yu minjian xinyang: Yanjiu tongxun* 媽祖與民間信仰: 研究通訊, 1 (2012): 57–69, as well as Wang Jianchuan 王見川 and Li Shiwei 李世偉, *Taiwan de minjian zongjiao yu xinyang* 台灣的民間宗教與信仰 (Luzhou: BoyYoung Publishing, 2000), pp. 130–131. See also articles from the following editions of the *Taiwan nichi-nichi shimpō* 臺灣日日新報: 1924.04.14, 1934.04.07, 1937.03.31.

96. See Wang Jianchuan "Guomin zhengfu lai Tai (1949) qian liang'an de zongjiao wanglai." Data on the *Jingshenlu* may be found in the online version of the *Encyclopedia of Taiwan* (entry by Wang Jianchuan; http://taiwanpedia.culture.tw/web/content?ID=4188). For more on Wang Yiting, see chapter 3.

97. This account is based on research done by Fan Chun-wu 范純武 in *Jiayi shizhi* 嘉義市志, *juan* 卷 10 (*Zongjiao lisu zhi* 宗教禮俗志), ed. Yan Shang-wen 顏尚文 (Jiayi: Jiayi City Government, 2005).

98. Kiely, "Shanghai Public Moralist Nie Qijie."

99. Ownby, "The Politics of Redemption."

100. For more on this phenomenon, see Fan Chun-wu 范純武, "Jinxiandai Zhongguo Fojiao yu fuji" 近現代中國佛教與扶乩, *Yuanguang Foxue xuebao* 圓光佛學學報, 3 (1999): 261–292. See also Wang Jianchuan 王見川, "Jindai Zhongguo de fuji, cishan yu 'mixin'—Yi Yinguang wenchao wei kaocha xiansuo" 近代中國的扶乩、慈善與「迷信」—以印光文鈔為考查線索, in *Belief, Practice and Cultural Adaptation: Papers from the Religion Section of the Fourth International Conference on Sinology*, eds. Paul R. Katz and Shufen Liu (Nankang: Academia Sinica Press, 2013), pp. 525–562.

101. See http://udn.com/NEWS/OPINION/OPI4/5882209.shtml. I am grateful to Huang Ko-wu 黃克武 for calling my attention to this important essay.

3. SECULAR YET SACRED: THE RELIGIOUS LIVES OF MODERN CHINESE ELITES

1. Chang Hao, *Chinese Intellectuals in Crisis: Search for Order and Meaning (1890–1911)* (Berkeley: University of California Press, 1987); Benjamin Schwartz, *In Search of Wealth and Power: Yen Fu and the West* (Cambridge: The Belknap Press of Harvard University Press, 1964); Huang Ko-wu, *The Meaning of Freedom: Yan Fu and the Origins of Chinese Liberalism* (Hong Kong: The Chinese University Press, 2008). See also Levenson, *Confucian China and Its Modern Fate*.

2. For more on these issues, see Michael Saler, "Modernity and Enchantment: A Historiographic Review," *The American Historical Review*, 111.3 (June 2006), pp. 692–716. See also Dipesh Chakrabarty, *Provincializing Europe: Postcolonial Thought and Historical Difference* (Princeton: Princeton University Press, 2000), p. 89.

3. Peter Gay, *The Enlightenment: An Interpretation*, 2 vols. (London: Weidenfeld and Nicholson, 1967–1970).

4. Saler, "Modernity and Enchantment," pp. 699–700.

5. Lorraine Daston and Katherine Park, *Wonders and the Order of Nature* (New York: Zone Books, 1998); Paul Heelas, Paul Morris, and David Martin, eds., *Religion, Modernity and Postmodernity* (London: London School of Economics and Political Science, 1998); Raymond L.M. Lee

and Susan E. Ackerman, *The Challenge of Religion After Modernity: Beyond Disenchantment* (Aldershot, UK: Ashgate, 2002); Alex Owen, *The Place of Enchantment* (Chicago: University of Chicago Press, 2004).

6. Alison Winter, *Mesmerized: Powers of Mind in Victorian Britain* (Chicago: University of Chicago Press 1998).

7. Corinna Treitel, *A Science for the Soul: Occultism and the Genesis of the German Modern* (Baltimore, MD: Johns Hopkins University Press, 2004); Thomas Laqueur, "Why the Margins Matter: Occultism and the Making of Modernity," *Modern Intellectual History*, 3.1 (2006): 111–135.

8. Ryan Dunch, "Science, Religion, and the Classics in Christian Higher Education to 1920," in *China's Christian Colleges: Cross-Cultural Connections, 1900–1950*, eds. Daniel H. Bays and Ellen Widmer (Stanford: Stanford University Press, 2009), pp. 57–82; Huang Ko-wu 黃克武, "Minguo chunian Shanghai de lingxue yanjiu: Yi 'Shanghai lingxuehui' wei li" 民國初年上海的靈學研究：以「上海靈學會」為例, *Bulletin of the Institute of Modern History, Academia Sinica*, 55 (2007): 99–136; Erik J. Hammerstrom, "Science and Buddhist Modernism in Early 20th Century China: The Life and Works of Wang Xiaoxu 王小徐," *Journal of Chinese Religions*, 39 (2011): 1–32; Ori Sela, "Confucian Scientific Identity: Qian Daxin's (1728–1804) Ambivalence toward Western Learning and Its Adherents," *East Asian Science, Technology and Society: An International Journal*, 6.2 (2012): 147–166.

9. S. J. Barnett, *The Enlightenment and Religion. The Myths of Modernity* (Manchester, UK: Manchester University Press, 2003). A stimulating overview of the links between science and religion may be found in Michael Heyd, "Introduction," *Science in Context*, 15 (2002): 1–8.

10. See the following masterful studies by Raoul Birnbaum: "Master Hongyi Looks Back: A Modern Man Becomes a Monk in Twentieth-Century China," in *Buddhism in the Modern World*, eds. Steven Heine and Charles S. Prebish (Oxford: Oxford University Press, 2003), pp. 75–124; "The Deathbed Image of Master Hongyi," in *The Buddhist Dead: Practices, Discourses, Representations*, eds. Jacqueline Stone and Bryan Cuevas (Honolulu: University of Hawai'i Press, 2007), pp. 175–207.

11. Data about Huang's life and career may be found in the Buddhist

self-cultivation handbook he authored entitled *Chuji jingye zhinan* 初機淨業指南, which was first published in 1922 and has been reprinted regularly ever since. Online versions include http://www.ucchusma.net/samanta/pure_land/chr/5/chr5_21.htm and http://www.dizang.org/rm/jyzn/index.htm. This work contains an autobiographical preface by Huang, as well as a longer preface by Yinguang.

12. *Yinguang fashi wenchao* 印光法師文鈔, pp. 221–225. An online version of their correspondence may be found at http://www.xuefo.net/nr/article3/28592.html.

13. See for example Taylor, *The Generalissimo*; Tong, *Chiang Kai-shek*.

14. Slightly modified translation from Tong, *Chiang Kai-shek*, p. 597. Further evidence about Chiang's Christian faith may be found in a volume of translations of comments appended to his own Bible, which contains a long postscript by Chin Hsiao-yi 秦孝儀 (1921–2007) on Chiang's Christianity; see *Jiang Zhongzheng xiansheng shougai Shengjing Shengyong yigao* 蔣中正先生手改聖經聖詠譯稿, 6 vols., trans. Wu Ching-hsiung 吳經熊 (Taipei: Chung-kuo Kuo-min-tang tang-shih wei-yuan-hui, 1986).

15. For more on the importance of diaries and other autobiographical texts, see Wu Pei-yi, *The Confucian's Progress: Autobiographical Writings in Traditional China* (Princeton: Princeton University Press, 1990).

16. Huang Ko-wu 黃克武, "Xiushen yu zhiguo—Jiang Jieshi de xingke shenghuo 修身與治國—蔣介石的省克生活, *Bulletin of Academia Historica*, 34 (2012): 45–68.

17. This work is contained in Huang Tzu-chin 黃自進 and Pan Kwang-che 潘光哲, ed. and comp., *Jiang Zhongzheng zongtong wuji* 蔣中正總統五記 (Taipei: Academia Historica, 2011), p. 85.

18. See Taylor, *The Generalissimo*, pp. 27–28, 73–76, 91–92, 108–109, 259–260, 456; Tong, *Chiang Kai-shek*, pp. 595–599. See also Brokaw, *The Ledgers of Merit and Demerit*.

19. Chen Weiming 陳微明, "Wang'er Banwu xingshu" 亡兒邦武行述, *Jueyouqing* 覺有情, 123–124 (1944): 10–11; Chen Weiming, "Bangwu jiyu" 邦武乩語, *Jueyouqing*, 133–134 (1945): 2.

20. Zhou Yumin 周育民, "Minguo shiqi yige wentan juzi jibixia de

lingjie" 民國時期一個文壇巨子乩筆下的靈界, *Minjian zongjiao* 民間宗教, 1 (1995): 37–55. Tobie Meyer-Fong's new book on the cultural impact of the Taiping Rebellion reveals that late Qing elites such as the literatus and philanthropist Yu Zhi 余治 (1809–1874) often belonged to spirit-writing groups. See Tobie Meyer-Fong, *What Remains: Coming to Terms with Civil War in Nineteenth-Century China* (Stanford: Stanford University Press, 2013).

21. See my paper on this topic, "'It Is Difficult to Be Indifferent to One's Roots'—Taizhou 台州 Sojourners and Flood Relief during the 1920s," *Bulletin of the Institute of Modern History, Academia Sinica*, 54 (2006): 1–58.

22. See Wang Zhongxiu 王中秀, ed. and comp., *Wang Yiting nianpu changbian* 王一亭年譜長編 (Shanghai: Shanghai shuhua chubanshe, 2010); Shen Wenquan 沈文泉, *Haishang qiren Wang Yiting* 海上奇人王一亭 (Beijing: Zhongguo shehui kexue chubanshe, 2011); Chen Zuen 陳祖恩 and Li Huaxing 李華興, *Wang Yiting zhuan* 王一亭傳 (Shanghai: Shanghai cishu chubanshe, 2007); Siu Fun-kee (Xiao Fenqi 蕭芬琪), "The Case of Wang Yiting (1867–1938): A Unique Figure in Early Twentieth Century Chinese Art History" (M.Phil. thesis, University of Hong Kong, 2000); published in Chinese as Siu Fun-kee, *Wang Yiting* 王一亭 (Shijiazhuang: Hebei jiaoyu chubanshe, 2002); Shen Kuiyi, "Art in Shanghai Capitalist Networks: A Case Study of Wang Yiting," *Chungguksa yongu* 中國史研究, 35 (2005): 281–322; see also his revised version, "Wang Yiting in the Social Networks of 1910s–1930s Shanghai," pp. 45–64.

23. See, for example, the Buddhist periodicals described in chapter 2, as well as the Buddhist and Daoist temple gazetteers and Daoist genealogies discussed in the notes that follow. I am especially grateful to Wang Zhongxiu for sharing numerous important newspaper articles.

24. *Wang Yiting xiansheng guxi shouchen jinianqi* 王一亭先生古稀壽辰紀念啟. This work is preserved in the Shanghai Municipal Archives. I am deeply grateful to Professor Ma Jun 馬軍 as well as the Archives staff for their assistance during a visit there in October 2006.

25. This is not to deny that many people lost their fathers or grew up

in poverty, or both, during the chaotic years of the late nineteenth and early twentieth centuries. Moreover, I have yet to determine the extent of the personal hardship that these men faced, particularly whether it involved real poverty or a loss of wealth and status so common among declining gentry families. I am grateful to Peter Zarrow for raising these issues (personal communication, February 2, 2005).

26. For more on this point, see the biography of Wang in Yu Lingbo 于凌波, *Zhongguo jinxiandai Fojiao renwu zhi* 中國近現代佛教人物志 (Beijing: Zongjiao wenwu chubanshe, 1995), pp. 346–349.

27. For more on Ren, see Roberta May-hwa Wue, "Making the Artist: Ren Bonian (1840–1895) and Portraits of the Shanghai Art World" (Ph.D. diss., New York University, New York, 2001); Lai Yu-chih, "Remapping Borders: Ren Bonian's Frontier Paintings and Urban Life in 1880s Shanghai," *The Art Bulletin*, 86.3 (September 2004): 550–572.

28. Shen Wenquan, *Haishang qiren Wang Yiting*, pp. 83–110. A virtuoso in both literati painting and calligraphy, Li Weizhuang was not only a Qing loyalist, but also a lay Buddhist, and Wang may have acquired some of his skills in painting Buddhist deities from him.

29. Siu, "The Case of Wang Yiting," pp. 34–35. See also Knight Biggerstaff, *The Earliest Modern Government Schools in China* (Ithaca, NY: Cornell University Press, 1961).

30. "Wang Yiting xiansheng jiaxun" 王一亭先生家訓, *Xinghua* 興華, 28.48 (1931): 24.

31. For more on Wang's artistic career, see Tsao Hsing-yuan, "A Forgotten Celebrity: Wang Zhen (1867–1933), Businessman, Philanthropist, and Artist," in *Art at the Close of China's Empire: Phoebus Occasional Papers in Art History*, vol. 8, ed. Ju-hsi Chou (Tempe: Arizona State University Press, Ltd., 1998), pp. 94–109; Siu Fun-kee, *Wang Yiting*, pp. 29–31; Siu, "The Case of Wang Yiting," pp. 44–46.

32. Chen Zuen and Li Huaxing, *Bailong shanren*, pp. 65–66.

33. Christian Henriot, *Shanghai Ladies of the Night: Prostitution and Society in 19th and 20th Century Shanghai* (Cambridge: Cambridge University Press, 1997); Bryna Goodman, "What Is in a Network? Local, Per-

sonal, and Public Loyalties in the Context of Changing Conceptions of the State and Social Welfare," in Dillon and Oi, *At the Crossroads of Empires*, pp. 155–178.

34. Hu Danian, *China and Albert Einstein: The Reception of the Physicist and His Theory in China 1917–1979* (Cambridge: Harvard University Press, 2005), pp. 71–72. See also Chen Zuen and Li Huaxing, *Bailong shanren*, pp. 187–191.

35. Shen, "Wang Yiting in the Social Networks of 1910s-1930s Shanghai," p. 53.

36. See Katz, "'It Is Difficult to Be Indifferent to One's Roots'" and Tao Shuimu 陶水木, "Beiyang zhengfu shiqi lüHu Zheshang de cishan huodong" 北洋政府時期旅滬浙商的慈善活動, *Zhejiang shehui kexue* 浙江社會科學, 6 (2005): 177–183. See also He Kongjiao 何孔蛟, "Minguo Shanghai zui da de liuyanglei cishan jihou—Xin Puyutang" 民國上海最大的留養類慈善機構—新普育堂, *Wenshi yuekan* 文史月刊, 8 (2006): 52–56. Practicing philanthropy in Shanghai at times necessitated dealing with powerful yet shady figures such as Green Gang boss Du Yuesheng 杜月笙 (1888–1951); see Brian G. Martin, "Du Yuesheng, the French Concession, and Social Networks in Shanghai," in Dillon and Oi, *At the Crossroads of Empires*, pp. 65–86.

37. See the *Reports of Shanghai's Associations for Planning Rapid Relief for Those Provinces Stricken by Flood* (*Shanghai choumu gesheng shuizai jizhenhui gongzuo baogao* 上海籌募各省水災急賑會工作報告), preserved in the Library of the Institute of History, Shanghai Academy of Social Sciences. I am deeply grateful to Ma Jun 馬軍 and the library staff for their assistance during a visit there in October 2006.

38. Along with Shi Xingzhi 施省之 (1865–1945), these four renowned Buddhist laymen were known as "Three Zhi's and One Ting" (*sanzhi yiting* 三之一亭); see Shen Kuiyi, "Art in Shanghai Capitalist Networks," p. 299.

39. Joanna Handlin Smith, *The Art of Doing Good: Charity in Late Ming China* (Berkeley: University of California Press, 2009); Kathryn Edgerton-Tarpley, *Tears from Iron: Cultural Responses to Famine in Nineteenth-Century China* (Berkeley: University of California Press, 2008); Fuma

Susumu 夫馬進, *Chūgoku zenkai zendōshi kenkyū* 中國善會善堂史研究 (Tokyo: Dōbōsha shuppan, 1997); Angela Ki che Leung (Liang Qizi 梁其姿), *Shishan yu jiaohua: Ming-Qing de cishan zuzhi* 施善與教化：明清的慈善組織 (Taipei: Lien-ching Publishing Company, 1997).

40. This article is reproduced in Wang Zhongxiu, et. al., *Jinxiandai jinshi shuhuajia runli*, p. 41. See also Wang Zhongxiu, *Wang Yiting nianpu changbian*, pp. 12–13; Shen Wenquan, *Haishang qiren Wang Yiting*, pp. 83–110, esp. pp. 103–106.

41. Walter B. Davis, "For Fate, Faith, and Charity: Wang Yiting's Paintings of Street People" (paper presented at the symposium "The Challenge of Modernity: Chinese Painting in the Late Nineteenth and Early Twentieth Centuries," Guggenheim Museum, New York, May 22, 1998). I am profoundly grateful to Walter Davis for providing much-needed guidance and assistance and for generously sharing valuable source materials.

42. *Shibao* 時報 (Shanghai), 1920.8.28, 1920.8.30, 1921.5.7. For more on the importance of the concept of national essence (*guocui* 國粹) in modern Chinese discourse, see Wang Cheng-hua 王正華, "The Qing Imperial Collection Circa 1905–25: National Humiliation Heritage Preservation and Exhibition Culture," in Wu Hung, ed., *Reinventing the Past: Archaism and Antiquarianism in Chinese Art and Visual Culture* (Chicago: The Center for the Art of East Asia, University of Chicago, 2010), pp. 320–341.

43. *Taiji dawen* 太極答問 (Shanghai: Zhonghua shuju, 1929), p. 77. An outside instructor is someone formally recognized as a qualified teacher of Taiji boxing who also is allowed to teach these techniques and even take on disciples of his own. I am very grateful to Liu Xun for sharing this information with me.

44. *Taiji quanshu* 太極拳術 (Shanghai: Zhonghua shuju, 1925), p. 1.

45. *Taiji dawen*, pp. 39–40, 45–47.

46. Liu, *Daoist Modern*.

47. Chen Zuen and Li Huaxing, *Bailong shanren*, pp. 233–251. Wang was a native of Huzhou (Wuxing), which may help explain why he was an active member of this association.

48. Don Alvin Pittman, *Toward a Modern Chinese Buddhism: Taixu's Reforms* (Honolulu: University of Hawai'i Press, 2001); Francesca Tarocco, *The Cultural Practices of Modern Chinese Buddhism: Attuning the Dharma* (New York and London: Routledge, 2007); Chen Bing 陳兵 and Deng Zimei 鄧子美, *Ershi shiji Zhongguo Fojiao* 二十世紀中國佛教 (Taipei: Xinadai Chan chubanshe, 2003; originally published in China in 2000); Li Xiangping 李向平, *Jiushi yu jiuxin: Zhongguo jindai Fojiao fuxing sichao yanjiu* 救世與救心：中國近代佛教復興思潮研究 (Shanghai: Shanghai renmin chubanshe, 1993).

49. Chen Yongge 陳永革, *Fojiao honghua de xiandai zhuanxing: Minguo Zhejiang Fojiao yanjiu (1912–1949)* 佛教弘化的現代轉型: 民國浙江佛教研究 (1912–1949) (Beijing: Zongjiao wenhua chubanshe, 2003); Gao Zhennong 高振農, "Shanghai Fojiaoshi" 上海佛教史, in *Shanghai zongjiaoshi* 上海宗教史, eds. Ruan Renze 阮仁澤 and Gao Zhennong 高振農 (Shanghai: Shanghai renmin chubanshe, 1992), pp. 27–349, esp. pp. 170–188; You Youwei 游有維, *Shanghai jindai Fojiao jianshi* 上海近代佛教簡史 (Shanghai: Huadong shifan daxue chubanshe, 1988), pp. 80–84, 96–105; Ge Zhuang 葛壯, *Zongjiao yu jindai Shanghai shehui de bianqian* 宗教與近代上海社會的變遷 (Shanghai: Shanghai shudian chubanshe, 1999), p. 197.

50. Chen Zuen and Li Huaxing, *Bailong shanren*, pp. 143–167.

51. Zhong Qiongning 鍾瓊寧, "Minchu Shanghai jushi Fojiao de fazhan (1912–1937)" 民初上海居士佛教的發展 (1912–1937), *Yuanguang Foxue xuebao* 圓光佛學學報, 3 (1999): 155–190, esp. pp. 183–184. See also Jessup, "The Householder Elite"; Scott, "Classical Exegesis and the Dharma"; Tarocco, *Cultural Practices*, pp. 27–31. Tarocco makes the important point that Shanghai (and nearby Hangzhou) were home to many leading Buddhist (and Daoist) sacred sites and also lay along major pilgrimage routes.

52. Gao Zhennong, "Shanghai Fojiaoshi," pp. 188–206; You Youwei, *Shanghai jindai Fojiao jianshi*, pp. 87–94.

53. Gao Zhennong, "Minguo nianjian Shanghai Fojiaojie zhenzai huodong ziliao diandi" 民國年間上海佛教界賑災活動資料點滴, *Fayin* 法音, 10 (1998): 28–31.

54. Wu Ping, "Jindai Shanghai de Fojiao chuban jigou."

55. Chen Bing and Deng Zimei, *Ershi shiji Zhongguo Fojiao*, pp. 59–60, 197–200. Thanks also to Ma Jun 馬軍 for giving me a list of articles published in the *Zhongguo Fojiao huibao* 中國佛教會報 from 1931 to 1933, which document the work by Wang Yiting and Yuanying to protect Buddhist monastic properties (*huchi sichan* 護持寺產).

56. Qin Xitian 秦錫田 (1861–1940), "Wuxing Wang jun shilue" 吳興王君事略, in *Wang Yiting jushi shilue* 王一亭居士事略 (1938). This work is also preserved in the Shanghai Municipal Archives. This work was edited by Ye Erkai 葉爾愷, an artist, calligrapher, and former Qing education commissioner (*duxue* 督學) from Renhe 仁和 County (Hangzhou 杭州, Zhejiang), who was also a prominent lay Buddhist. See also Wang Zhongxiu, *Wang Yiting nianpu changbian*, p. 660.

57. Mark Elvin, "The Gentry Democracy in Shanghai" (Ph.D. diss., Cambridge University, 1969), 230–256.

58. For more on these events, see Taixu 太虛's necrology for Wang published in *Haichaoyin* 海潮音, 19.11 (1938): 3–4. Wang's obituary may also be found on p. 57 of the same issue. See also Yu Lingbo, *Zhongguo jinxiandai Fojiao renwuzhi*, p. 346; Chen Zuen and Li Huaxing, *Bailong shanren*, pp. 143–167. The cult of Guanyin as well as her sacred site at Mount Putuo are expertly treated in Yü Chün-fang 于君方, *Kuan-yin: The Chinese Transformation of Avalokiteśvara* (New York: Columbia University Press, 2001).

59. The Three Refuges are the Buddha (*fo* 佛), the *dharma* (*fa* 法), and the *sangha* (*seng* 僧).

60. You Youwei, *Shanghai jindai Fojiao jianshi*, pp. 85–87; Chen Bing and Deng Zimei, *Ershi shiji Zhongguo Fojiao*, pp. 63, 155–156.

61. *Shibao* 時報 (Shanghai), 1917.9.6, 1918.4.23.

62. Chiara Betta, "Silas Aaron Hardoon (1851–1931): Marginality and Adaptation in Shanghai" (Ph.D. thesis, University of London, 1997). See also Tarocco, *Cultural Practices*, pp. 30, 33–34; You Youwei, *Shanghai jindai Fojiao jianshi*, pp. 84–85.

63. Siu Fun-kee, *Wang Yiting*, pp. 135–140, 164, 166. See also Bailong shanren 白龍山人 (Wang Yiting), *Bailong shanren huace* 白龍山人畫冊

(Taipei: Taiwan Zhonghua shuju, 1968); Wang Zhen 王震 (Wang Yiting) and Wu Changshuo 吳昌碩, *Foxiang tishi* 佛像題詩. The latter work is located in the Fu Sinian Library of the Institute of History and Philology, Academia Sinica.

64. Yü Chün-fang, *The Renewal of Buddhism in China: Chu-hung and the Late Ming Synthesis* (New York: Columbia University Press, 1981).

65. Feng's life and artistic career are described in Geremie R. Barmé, *An Artistic Exile: A Life of Feng Zikai (1898–1978)* (Berkeley and London: University of California Press, 2002), see esp. pp. 32–37, 63–64, 157–161, 181–184.

66. Apart from the Birnbaum articles described above, see Chen Xing 陳星, *Li Shutong shenbian de wenhua mingren* 李叔同身邊的文化名人 (Beijing: Zhonghua shujum, 2005), pp. 204–206; see also Tarocco, *Cultural Practices*, pp. 16–20, 71–75, 99–105.

67. Wang's participation in and leadership of the World Buddhist Householder Association are clearly documented in the *Reports of the Achievements of the World Buddhist Householder Association* (*Shijie Fojiao jushilin chengji baogaoshu* 世界佛教居士林成績報告書, 1933), which contains records of his writings and also his photograph. The drawback of such fame can be seen in a notice published by Wang in the January 16, 1931 issue of the *Foxue banyuekan* 佛學半月刊, which warns fellow Buddhists to beware of fraudulent individuals who had been impersonating him and using his name card (*mingpian* 名片).

68. Taixu's views on the strengths and weaknesses of Chinese and Japanese Buddhist specialists are discussed in Tarocco, *Cultural Practices*, p. 37.

69. For more on these events, see Holmes Welch, *The Buddhist Revival in China* (Cambridge: Harvard University Press, 1968), pp. 40–45, 166–167; Pittman, *Toward a Modern Chinese Buddhism*, pp. 109–110, 130–133; Chen Bing and Deng Zimei, *Ershi shiji Zhongguo Fojiao*, pp. 59–69.

70. Zhong Qiongning, "Minchu Shanghai jushi Fojiao de fazhan."

71. According to Walter Davis (personal communication, December 2012), this photo may have been staged, but that in itself says something about the self-image Wang wished to project at that time.

72. Wang's pursuit of meditation also may have resulted from the business failures he and his sons suffered. See Liu Wenxing 劉文星, *Li Yujie xiansheng nianpu changbian* 李玉階先生年譜長編 (Nantou: Tiandijiao chubanshe, 2001), pp. 85–88.

73. Wang Zhongxiu, *Wang Yiting nianpu changbian*, pp. 714–715; Shen Wenquan, *Haishang qiren Wang Yiting*, p. 119.

74. *Shanxi Fojiao zazhi* 山西佛教雜誌, 10 (October 15, 1934): 515–516; *Hongfakan* 弘法刊, 27 (1935): 351–352; *Hushengbao* 護生報, 76 (July 1, 1935): 213.

75. I am very grateful to Lo Shih-chieh 羅士傑 for sharing this information with me.

76. For more on vegetarianism in Shanghai's urban life, see Tarocco, *Cultural Practices*, pp. 31–39.

77. This is clearly documented in Siu, "The Case of Wang Yiting," pp. 68–82. See also Walter B. Davis, "Wang Yiting and the Art of Sino-Japanese Exchange" (paper presented at the Japan Foundation Fellows' Seminar, session 6, July 25, 2006). Other important studies include Julia Andrews, "The Shanghai Art Academy and the Japanese Model of Art Education"; Walter B. Davis, "Wang Yiting and Japanese Visitors to Shanghai"; Hong Zaixin, "Modernizing the Tradition of Art Collecting in China and the Impact of the Japanese Market, 1900–1930." These three papers were presented at the conference on "The Role of Japan in the Institutional Development of Modern Chinese Art," Institute of Modern History, Academia Sinica, Taipei, Taiwan, October 19–20, 2007. Walter Davis recently has completed a book manuscript on Wang Yiting's links to Japan entitled, "Between Friends: The Sino-Japanese Art of Wang Yiting."

78. Wang Zhongxiu, *Wang Yiting nianpu changbian*, pp. 289–300; Shen Wenquan, *Haishang qiren Wang Yiting*, pp. 219–234; Chen Zuen and Li Huaxing, *Bailong shanren*, pp. 211–229. Moving accounts of these events may also be found in blog posts by Wang Yiting's grandson, Wang Xiaofang 王孝方: http://big5.news365.com.cn:82/gate/big5/blog.news365.com.cn/sp1/wangxiaofang/1304321371.shtml.

79. *Kantō daishinsai* 関東大震災 (Tokyo: Zaidan hōjin Tōkyōto ireidō kyōkai, 2005), pp. 9–13.

80. Shibusawa Eiichi, *Shibusawa Eiichi denki shiryō* 澀澤榮一傳記資料, vol. 40 (Tokyo: Shibusawa Eiichi Memorial Museum, 1955–1971), p. 101. For more information on this sixty-eight-volume resource, see the Shibusawa Eiichi Memorial Museum website http://www.shibusawa.or.jp/english/index.html.

81. Chen Zuen and Li Huaxing, *Bailong shanren*, pp. 235–242.

82. See especially Gregory Adam Scott, "The Buddhist Nationalism of Dai Jitao 戴季陶," *Journal of Chinese Religions*, 39 (2011): 55–81.

83. Shi Yinshun 釋印順 (1906–2005), *Taixu dashi nianpu* 太虛大師年譜 (Taipei: Zhengwen chubanshe, 1988), pp. 257–265, esp. p. 265; "Jiang zongsiling dui Wang Yiting de tanhua" 蔣總司令對王一亭居士的談話, *Haichaoyin*, 10 (1928): 1; Shen Wenquan, *Haishang qiren Wang Yiting*, p. 126.

84. Wang Zhongxiu, *Wang Yiting nianpu changbian*, p. 418.

85. Wang Yiting, Chen Tsung-hsi, and Wang An-tsiang, *General Chiang Kai-shek: The Builder of New China* (Shanghai: The Commercial Press, Ltd., 1929). I was able to locate a copy of this book at the Oriental Library (Tōyō bunkō 東洋文庫), thanks to the kind assistance of Professor Matushige Mitsuhiro 松重充浩 and Tatara Kei 多々良圭介. Thanks also to Professor Shiba Yoshinobu 斯波義信 and the library staff for their help, as well as Huang Tzu-chin 黃自進 for making the arrangements.

86. Chen Tiejian 陳鐵健, *Jiang Jieshi yu Zhongguo wenhua* 蔣介石與中國文化 (Hong Kong: Zhonghua shuju, 1992).

87. See Taylor, *The Generalissimo*, p. 12; Tong, *Chiang Kai-shek*, pp. 5–6, 435–438, 596–597.

88. Hou Kunhong 侯坤宏, "1930 niandai de Fojiao yu zhengzhi: Taixu fashi he Jiang Jieshi" 1930 年代的佛教與政治：太虛法師和蔣介石, *Sichuan shifan daxue xuebao (Shehui kexue ban)* 四川師範大學學報(社會科學版), 33.5 (2006): 126–132; Chen Weihua 陳衛華, "Chushi yu rushi: Renjian Fojiao de fenji—Yi Taixu he Jiang Jieshi guanxi de ge'an yanjiu wei li" 出世與入世: 人間佛教的分際－以太虛和蔣介石關系的個案研究為例, *Henan shifan daxue xuebao (Zhexue shehui kexue ban)* 河南師范大學學報(哲學社會科學版), 4 (2009): 18–21.

89. Chiang Kai-shek's 1927 visit to the Hole in the Snow Monastery is

described in Taylor, *The Generalissimo*, pp. 72–73. Mao Fumei also was a devout Buddhist, who apparently found comfort in this religion after having been divorced by Chiang that same year.

90. Liu Bingrong 劉秉榮, *Minguo guanchang mixin shilu* 民國官場迷信實錄 (Beijing: Dangdai Zhongguo chubanshe, 2007). See also Gao Feng 高峰, "Jiang Jieshi qing Taixu zhanglao xuan mudi" 蔣介石請太虛長老選墓地, *Dang'an shiguang* 檔案時光, 11 (2008): 37–38.

91. For more on this work, see Jeffrey L. Broughton, *The Bodhidharma Anthology: The Earliest Records of Zen* (Berkeley: University of California Press, 2009).

92. Wang Sihan 汪思涵, "1934–1937 nianjian Xinshenghuo yundong yu Jidujiao—Yi Jiaowu zazhi wei zhongxin" 1934–1937年間的新生活運動與基督教—以《教務雜誌》為中心, *Zhongguo shehui jingjishi yanjiu* 中國社會經濟史研究, 4 (2007): 65–82. See also Tong, *Chiang Kai-shek*, p. 550.

93. Prasenjit Duara, "Religion and Citizenship in China and the Diaspora," in Yang, *Chinese Religiosities: Afflictions of Modernity and State Formation*, pp. 43–64.

94. Bai Chun 白純, "Jiang Jieshi Ruhua Sanmin zhuyi zhi pingxi" 蔣介石儒化三民主義之評析, *Nanjing zhengzhi xueyuan xuebao* 南京政治學院學報, 1 (2003): 77–79. See also Wang Shou-nan, "Chiang Kai-shek and the Promotion of the Chinese Cultural Renaissance Movement," *Chinese Studies in History*, 21.2 (Winter 1987–1988): 66–90; Fukamachi Hideo, "Prairie Fire or the Gimo's New Clothes? Chiang Kai-shek's New Life Movement," *The Chinese Historical Review*, 17.1 (2010): 68–84; Taylor, *The Generalissimo*, pp. 13–14, 108–109; Tong, *Chiang Kai-shek*, pp. 546, 547, 550, 552.

95. See, for example, Cohen, *History in Three Keys*, pp. 146–172; DuBois, *The Sacred Village*, pp. 106–126, 129–138; Philip A. Kuhn, *Soulstealers: The Chinese Sorcery Scare of 1768* (Cambridge: Harvard University Press, 1991), pp. 39–48; Barend J. ter Haar, *Telling Stories: Witchcraft and Scapegoating in Chinese History* (Leiden: E. J. Brill, 2006), pp. 35, 329, 343–344; ter Haar, *The White Lotus Teachings*, pp. 173–195, 263–281.

96. David A. Palmer, "Chinese Redemptive Societies: Historical Phe-

nomenon or Sociological Category?" *Minsu quyi*, 172 (2011): 21–72, esp. p. 35.

97. Ownby, "Redemptive Societies in China's Long Twentieth Century."

98. DuBois, *The Sacred Village*, p. 120.

99. This was also the case for another prominent member of the Rescuing Life Association, Xu Qianlin 徐乾麟 (b. 1863), as data in the Shanghai Municipal Archives indicates that he also was involved in a wide range of religious organizations, including redemptive societies.

100. Another important leader was Li Yujie 李玉階 (1900–1994), also a Perfected Sovereign of the Tiandejiao 天德教, who later founded the Tiandijiao 天帝教 in 1979 in Taiwan. See Liu Wenxing, *Li Yujie xiansheng nianpu*.

101. Ibid., p. 85.

102. For more on this group's activities in Shanghai during the Second Sino-Japanese War, which expanded to include both Christians and Communists, see Nara Dillon, "The Politics of Philanthropy: The Balance Between Public and Private Refugee Relief in Shanghai, 1932–1949," in Dillon and Oi, *At the Crossroads of Empires*, pp. 179–205.

103. Duara, *Sovereignty and Authenticity*, p. 112; Sun Yusheng 孫語聖, "Shijie Hongwanzihui Zhonghua zonghui yu Minguo shiqi de shehui jiuji" 世界紅卍字會中華總會與民國時期的社會救濟, *Anda shixue* 安大史學, 2 (2004): 192–200, esp. p. 198. See also Wang Jianchuan 王見川, "Minguo shiqi Daoyuan Hongwanzihui zhenzai jilu" 民國時期道院紅卍字會賑災記錄, *Minjian zongjiao* 民間宗教, 1 (1995): 217–224.

104. Ownby, "Redemptive Societies in China's Long Twentieth Century." See also Thomas D. DuBois, "The Salvation of Religion? Public Charity and the New Religions of the Early Republic," *Minsu quyi*, 172 (2011): 73–126.

105. Originally she was known as the Goddess of the Privy (Cegu 厠姑), being worshipped by women who asked her about their prospects for marriage as well as other domestic and personal affairs.

106. See especially Jordan and Overmyer, *The Flying Phoenix*, as well as Shiga Ichiko 志賀市子, *Chūgoku no kokkurisan: furan shinkō to kajin*

shakai 中国のこっくりさん: 扶鸞信仰と華人社会 (Tokyo: Taishūkan shoten, 2003).

107. For an early Western eyewitness account of these rites, see Herbert A. Giles, "Mesmerism, Planchette, and Spiritualism in China," *Fraser's Magazine* (February 1879): 238–245.

108. Fan Chun-wu, "Feiluan, xiuzhen yu banshan."

109. Xu Dishan 許地山, *Fuji mixin di yanjiu* 扶箕迷信底研究 (Changsha: Shangwu yinshuguan, 1941).

110. *Shishi xinbao—Jianshang zhoukan* 時事新報・鑑賞週刊 (August 31, 1925); Wang Mengji 王夢吉 (fl. 1668), *Zuben Jigong quanzhuan* 足本濟公全傳 (Taipei: Shijie shuju, 1959). These two accounts, as well as other sources, are discussed in Hsu Wen-pi 許文筆, "Taiwan Jigong xinyang zhi jiushiguan" 台灣濟公信仰之救世觀 (master's thesis, Hsuan Chuang College of Humanities and Social Sciences, 1999).

111. Reports about such practices may be found in the following issues of *Shenbao*: 1932.07.20, 1926.05.25, 1926.06.10, 1926.07.22, 1926.10.02, 1928.09.06, 1929.01.04.

112. Yau Chi On, *Shan yu ren tong*, pp. 153–155.

113. Liang Qichao 梁啟超, *Qing xueshu gailun* 清學術概論 (Taipei: Taiwan shangsu yinshuguan, 1994), p. 166. Both Fan Chun-wu and Huang Ko-wu cite Liang in their articles.

114. For more on this phenomenon, see Fan Chun-wu 范純武, "Jinxiandai Zhongguo Fojiao yu fuji" 近現代中國佛教與扶乩, *Yuanguang Foxue xuebao* 圓光佛學學報, 3 (1999): 261–292.

115. Ibid., p. 290. See also Wang Jianchuan, "Jindai Zhongguo de fuji, cishan yu 'mixin'—Yi Yinguang wenchao wei kaocha xiansuo."

116. Tao Shuimu, "Beiyang zhengfu shiqi lüHu Zheshang de cishan huodong."

117. For more on the history of Jigong and his cult, see Shahar, *Crazy Ji*.

118. Wang Jianchuan, "Qingmo Minchu Zhongguo de Jigong xinyang yu fuji tuanti." See also Wang Jianchuan, "Jindai Zhongguo de fuji, cishan yu 'mixin.'" Additional data on Wang Yiting's involvement in the association may be found in Wang Zhongxiu, *Wang Yiting nianpu chang-*

bian, pp. 190, 198, 204; Fan Chun-wu, "Jinxiandai Zhongguo Fojiao yu mixin," p. 290; Yu Lingbo, *Zhongguo jinxiandai Fojiao renwuzhi*, pp. 347–348, 349; Yau Chi On, *Shan yu ren tong*, pp. 155–160.

119. Reports about such practices may be found in the following issues of *Shenbao*: 1917.10.02, 1917.10.27, 1918.05.17, 1918.12.07, 1919.01.22, 1919.06.22, 1919.09.06, 1919.12.18, 1920.02.03, 1920.07.26.

120. Hupao cuanzhichu 虎跑纂志處, ed., *Hupao Fozu zangdianzhi* 虎跑佛祖藏殿志 (1921), in *Zhongguo Fosizhi congkan* 中國佛寺志叢刊, ser. 1, vol. 72, eds. Bai Huawen 白化文, et. al. (Yangzhou: Jiangsu guji chubanshe, 1996), pp. 15–16, 81–84, 341–342; Shi Anren 釋安仁, *Huyin chanyuan jishi* 湖隱禪院記事 (1921), in *Zhongguo Fosizhi congkan xubian*, vol. 7, eds. Bai Huawen, et. al. (Yangzhou: Jiangsu guji chubanshe, 2001), pp. 5, 41–44. See also the following issues of *Shenbao*: 1917.09.29, 1922.10.20, 1923.06.01, 1934.05.23, 1934.05.28, 1934.06.12, 1929.01.04.

121. Wang Jianchuan, "Qingmo Minchu Zhongguo de Jigong xinyang yu fuji tuanti," pp. 155–159.

122. See DuBois, "The Salvation of Religion? Public Charity and the New Religions of the Early Republic"; Wang Jianchuan, "Minguo shiqi Daoyuan Hongwanzihui zhenzai jilu."

123. *Taiwan Nichi-nichi shimpō* 臺灣日日新報 (May 25, 1918).

124. Wang Jianchuan, "Qingmo Minchu Zhongguo de Jigong xinyang yu fuji tuanti," p. 159. The character "*jue*" 覺 in "Jueqi" derives from the Association's lineage poem.

125. Chen Boxi 陳伯熙, ed. and comp., *Shanghai yishi daguan* 上海軼事大觀 (1924; reprint, Shanghai: Shanghai shudian chubanshe, 2000), p. 371. See also *Hupao Fozu zangdianzhi*, pp. 318–319; Wang Jianchuan, "Qingmo Minchu Zhongguo de Jigong xinyang yu fuji tuanti," pp. 160–161.

126. Wang Jianchuan, "Jindai Zhongguo de fuji, cishan yu 'mixin.'"

127. Shanghai Jiyunxuan 上海集雲軒, ed., "Jishi tayuanzhi (1939)" 濟師塔院志 (1939), in *Zhongguo Fosizhi congkan xubian* 中國佛寺志叢刊續編, vol. 6, eds. Bai Huawen 白化文, et. al. (Yangzhou: Jiangsu guji chubanshe, 2001), pp. 9, 11–12, 15–18, 45–47.

128. *Huyin chanyuan jishi*, p. 71.

129. The text in question may be found in Xu Shanghu 許尚樞, *Tiantaishan Jigong huofo* 天台山濟公活佛 (Beijing: Guoji wenhua chuban gongsi, 1997). See also an electronic version of this text at http://www.360doc.com/content/11/0719/01/10830_134400917.shtml. Despite being destroyed during the Cultural Revolution, this temple was rebuilt during the late 1980s, with construction completed in 1990.

130. Meihua guanzhu 梅花館主 (Wang Yiting), "Xin Wutai paiyan Jigong huofo zhi qianyin houguo" 新舞台排演濟公活佛之前因後果, *Xiju yuekan* 戲劇月刊, 2.5 (1929): 4–5. I am deeply grateful to Vincent Durand-Dastès for telling me about both of the above sources in the course of personal communications from October 3 through October 6, 2011.

131. This painting may be found in the *Bailong shanren huace*.

132. Vincent Goossaert, *The Daoists of Peking, 1800–1949*, pp. 308–319. See also Mori Yuria 森由利亞, "Identity and Lineage: The *Taiyi jinhua zongzhi* 太一金華宗旨 and the Spirit-Writing Cult to Patriarch Lü in Qing China," in *Daoist Identity: History, Lineage, and Ritual*, eds. Livia Kohn and Harold D. Roth (Honolulu: University of Hawai'i Press, 2002), pp. 165–184.

133. Shiga Ichiko 志賀市子, "The Manifestations of Lüzu 呂祖 in Modern Guangdong and Hong Kong: The Rise of Spirit-Writing Cults," in Kohn and Roth, *Daoist Identity*, pp. 185–209; Lai Chi-tim 黎志添, "Hong Kong Daoism: A Study of Daoist Altars and Lü Dongbin Cults," *Social Compass*, 50.4 (2003): 459–470. See also Graeme Lang and Lars Ragvald, *The Rise of a Refugee God: Hong Kong's Wong Tai Sin* (Hong Kong: Oxford University Press, 1993).

134. Vincent Goossaert, "The Quanzhen Clergy, 1700–1950," in *Religion and Chinese Society: The Transformation of a Field*, ed. John Lagerwey (Paris: École Française d'Extrême Orient and Hong Kong: Chinese University of Hong Kong Press, 2004), pp. 699–771. See also Qing Xitai 卿希泰, *Zhongguo Daojiaoshi* 中國道教史 (Chengdu: Sichuan renmin chubanshe, 1995), vol. 4, pp. 298–304. The concurrent worship of Lü

Dongbin 呂洞賓 and Jigong 濟公 was also a feature of religious movements such as the Society of the Way (see the essays by Wang Jianchuan and Thomas DuBois cited previously).

135. Monica Esposito, "Daoism in the Qing," in *Daoism Handbook*, ed. Livia Kohn (Leiden: E. J. Brill, 2000), pp. 623–658, esp. pp. 645–650; Monica Esposito, "Longmen 龍門 Taoism in Qing China: Doctrinal Ideal and Local Reality," *Journal of Chinese Religions*, 29 (2001): 191–231; Monica Esposito, "The Discovery of Jiang Yuanting's *Daozang jiyao* in Jiangnan: A Presentation of the Daoist Canon of the Qing Dynasty," in *Kōnan dōkyō no kenkyū* 江南道教の研究, ed. Kunio Mugitani 麥谷邦夫 (Kyoto: Jinbun Kagaku Kenkyūjo, 2007), pp. 79–110; Cao Benye 曹本冶 and Xu Hongtu 徐宏圖, *Wenzhou Pingyang Dongyueguan Daojiao yinyue yanjiu* 溫州平陽東嶽觀道教音樂研究 (Taipei: Xinwenfeng, 2000), pp. 18–20, 31–34, 42; Chen Yaoting 陳耀庭, "Shanghai Daojiaoshi" 上海道教史, in *Shanghai zongjiaoshi* 上海宗教史, eds. Ruan Renze 阮仁澤 and Gao Zhennong 高振農 (Shanghai: Shanghai renmin chubanshe, 1992), pp. 353–438, esp. pp. 400, 413–428.

136. Gao Wansang 高萬桑 (Vincent Goossaert), "Jingaishan wangluo. Jinxiandai Jiangnan de Quanzhen jushi zuzhi" 金蓋山網絡：近現代江南的全真居士組織," in *Quanzhendao yanjiu* 全真道研究, vol. 1, ed. Zhao Weidong 趙衛東 (Jinan: Qilu shushe, 2011), pp. 319–339; Wang Zongyao 王宗耀, *Huzhou Jingai shan Gu Meihuaguan zhi* 湖州金蓋山古梅花觀志 (Huzhou: Huzhou Daojiao xilie neibu congshu, 2003); Wang Zongyu 王宗昱, "Wuxing Quanzhendao shiliao" 吳興全真道史料, in *Scriptures, Schools, and Forms of Practice in Daoism: A Berlin Symposium*, eds. Poul Andersen and Florian C. Reiter (Wiesbaden: Harrassowitz Verlag, 2005), pp. 215–232.

137. *Longmen zhengzong Jueyun benzhi daotong xinchuan* 龍門正宗覺雲本支道統薪傳, in *Zangwai Daoshu* 藏外道書 (Chengdu: Bashu shushe, 1994), vol. 31, pp. 438–445. See also Wu Yakui, *Jiangnan Quanzhen Daojiao*, pp. 256–258.

138. Yan Heyi 嚴合怡, ed., *Daotong yuanliuzhi* 道統源流志, vol. 2 (Wuxi: Zhonghua yinshuaju, 1929), p. 30.

139. Vincent Goossaert, personal communication, April 22, 2009.

140. Wang Lianyou 王蓮友, ed., *Chongjian Jinling Yuxu Guan jishi zhengxinlu* 重建金陵玉虛觀紀事徵信錄 (1936), in *Zhongguo Daoguanzhi congkan xubian* 中國道觀志叢刊續編, vol. 15 (Yangzhou: Guangling shushe, 2004), pp. 3–4, 17.

141. Yau Chi On, *Shan yu ren tong*, pp. 160–164, 332–333. The *Fushou baozang* is also described in Takai Sadao 酒井忠夫, "Jinxiandai Zhongguo de shanshu yu Xinshenghuo yundong" 近現代中國的善書與新生活運動, trans. Lai Hsu-chen 賴旭貞, *Minjian zongjiao*, 2 (1996): 101.

142. Chen Chuanxi 陳傳席, "Ping xiandai minjia yu dajia, xu—Wang Yiting" 評現代名家與大家・續一王一亭, *Guohuajia* 國畫家, 3 (2006): 7–9, esp. p. 9.

143. Tarocco, *Cultural Practices*, pp. 34–35.

144. Tsou Mingteh, "Christian Missionary as Confucian Intellectual: Gilbert Reid (1857–1927) and the Reform Movement in the Late Qing," in *Christianity in China: From the Eighteenth Century to the Present*, ed. Daniel H. Bays (Stanford: Stanford University Press, 1996), pp. 73–90; Hu Suping 胡素萍, "Li Jiabai yu Shangxian Tang—Qingmo Minchu zai Hua chuanjiaoshi huodong ge'an yanjiu" 李佳白與尚賢堂一清末民初在華傳教士活動個案研究, *Shixue yuekan* 史學月刊, 9 (2005): 57–63; Liu Xun and Mei Li, "Constructing Modern Daoism"; Palmer, "Chinese Redemptive Societies."

145. Sun Guangyong 孫廣勇, "Rongru yu chuanbo—Jianlun Li Jiabai ji qi Shangxian Tang de wenhua jiaoliu huodong" 融入與傳播一簡論李佳白及其尚賢堂的文化交流活動, *Shehui kexue zhanxian* 社會科學戰線, 6 (2005): 299–301; Yao Minquan 姚民權 and Zhang Letian 張樂天, "Shanghai Jidujiao shi" 上海基督教史, in *Shanghai zongjiaoshi*, eds. Ruan Renze and Gao Zhennong (Shanghai: Shanghai renmin chubanshe, 1992), pp. 787–1019, esp. pp. 847–850; Tarocco, *Cultural Practices*, p. 38.

146. This couplet is preserved in the Shanghai History Museum; see the essay by Hu Baofang 胡寶芳: http://www.historymuseum.sh.cn/content.php?ID=68&PHPSESSID=a4241752e730a0756ce55c364ab30aa1.

147. Cohen, *History in Three Keys*, pp. xii-xiii, 59–68.

148. For more on these issues, see Vincent Goossaert and David

Ownby, "Mapping Charisma in Chinese Religion: Introduction and Glossary," *Nova Religio: The Journal of Alternative and Emergent Religions*, 12.2 (2008): 3–11; Vincent Goossaert, "Mapping Charisma Among Chinese Religious Specialists," *Nova Religio*, 12.2 (2008): 12–28.

149. I am grateful to J. Brooks Jessup, Vincent Goossaert, and Peter Zarrow for their valuable insights on this issue.

150. See this book's introduction, as well as Szonyi, "Secularization Theories and the Study of Chinese Religions"; Weller, "Taiwan and Global Religious Trends."

151. Goossaert and Palmer, *Religious Question*, pp. 303–306; Weller, *Alternate Civilities*. Patrick Hanan has translated into English a fascinating early twentieth-century novel titled, *The Money Demon* (Honolulu: University of Hawai'i Press, 1999). Its author, Chen Diexian 陳蝶仙 (1879–1940; Chen Shousong 陳壽嵩), seems to have shared some traits with Wang Yiting, especially the quest to blend the traditional and modern forms of life. Hanan has also written an essay on Chen Diexian in his *Chinese Fiction of the Nineteenth and Early Twentieth Centuries* (New York: Columbia University Press, 2004), pp. 199–216. I am grateful to Meir Shahar for guiding me to these works.

CONCLUSION

1. Kuo, *Religion and Democracy in Taiwan*; Madsen, *Democracy's Dharma*. See also Robert P. Weller, "Worship, Teachings, and State Power in China and Taiwan," in *Realms of Freedom in Modern China*, ed. William C. Kirby (Stanford: Stanford University Press, 2004), pp. 285–314.

2. Adam Chau, "Expanding the Space of Popular Religion: Local Temple Activism and the Politics of Legitimation in Contemporary Rural China," in Ashiwa and Wank, *Making Religion, Making the State*, pp. 211–240; Kenneth Dean, "Further Partings of the Way: The Chinese State and Daoist Ritual Traditions in Contemporary China," in Ashiwa and Wank, *Making Religion, Making the State*, pp. 179–210.

3. Sébastien Billioud, "The Hidden Tradition: Confucianism and Its Metamorphoses in Modern and Contemporary China" (paper pre-

sented at the international conference on "Modern Chinese Religion: Value Systems in Transformation, Part 2: 1850-present," Chinese University of Hong Kong, December 12–15, 2012). See also Sébastien Billioud, "Confucian Revival and the Emergence of *Jiaohua* 教化 Organizations: A Case Study of the Yidan Xuetang 一耽學堂," *Modern China*, 37.3 (2011): 286–314; Anna Sun, "The Revival of Confucian Rites in Contemporary China," in *Confucianism and Spiritual Traditions in Modern China and Beyond*, eds. Yang Fenggang and Joseph Tamney (Leiden and Boston: Brill, 2012), pp. 309–328.

4. Ownby, "Redemptive Societies in China's Long Twentieth Century."

5. Richard Madsen and Fan Lizhu, "The Catholic Pilgrimage to Sheshan," in Ashiwa and Wank, *Making Religion, Making the State*, pp. 74–95; Carsten T. Vsala, "Pathways to the Pulpit: Leadership Training in 'Patriotic' and Unregistered Chinese Protestant Churches," in Ashiwa and Wank, *Making Religion, Making the State*, pp. 96–125. See also Cao Nanlai, *Constructing China's Jerusalem: Christians, Power, and Place in Contemporary China* (Stanford: Stanford University Press, 2011); Lian Xi, *Redeemed by Fire: The Rise of Popular Christianity in China* (New Haven and London: Yale University Press, 2010); David C. Schak, "Protestantism in China: A Dilemma for the Party-State," *Journal of Current Chinese Affairs*, 40.2 (2011): 71–106; Daniel Bays, "Protestantism and Modern China: Rejection, Reconciliation, and Rebirth" (paper presented at the international conference on "Modern Chinese Religion: Value Systems in Transformation, Part 2: 1850-present," Chinese University of Hong Kong, December 12–15, 2012).

6. Oakes and Sutton, *Faiths on Display*.

7. Goossaert and Palmer, *Religious Question*, p. 402.

8. Yuri Pines, *The Everlasting Empire: The Political Culture of Ancient China and Its Imperial Legacy* (Princeton: Princeton University Press, 2012). I am most grateful for his guidance in considering these issues.

9. Sun Yanfei, "Religions in Sociopolitical Context: The Reconfiguration of Religious Ecology in Post-Mao China" (Ph.D. diss., University of Chicago, 2010).

10. Xiaobing Wang-Riese, "Popular Religious Elements in the Modern Confucian Cult," in *Chinese and European Perspectives on the Study of Chinese Popular Religions*, ed. Philip Clart (Taipei: BoyYoung Publishing, 2012), pp. 329–369.

11. Gareth Fisher, "Morality Books and the Revival of Lay Buddhism in China," in *Religion in Contemporary China: Revitalization and Innovation*, ed. Adam Yuet Chau (London: Routledge, 2011), pp. 53–80; Stuart Chandler, *Establishing a Pure Land on Earth* (Honolulu: University of Hawai'i Press, 2004); Philip Clart, "Merit Beyond Measure: Notes on the Moral (and Real) Economy of Religious Publishing in Taiwan," in *The People and the Dao: New Studies of Chinese Religions in Honour of Prof. Daniel L. Overmyer*, eds. Philip Clart and Paul Crowe (Sankt Augustin: Institut Monumenta Serica, 2009), pp. 127–142. See also Clart, "Sacred Texts, Religious Publishing, and New Technologies in China & Taiwan."

12. Philip Clart, "Mediums and the New Media: The Impact of Electronic Publishing on Temple and Moral Economies in Taiwanese Popular Religion," *Journal of Sinological Studies*, 3 (2012): 127–141. See also Stephen D. O'Leary, "Utopian and Dystopian Possibilities of Networked Religion in the New Millennium," in *Religion and Cyberspace*, eds. Morten T. Højsgarard and Margit Warburg (London and New York: Routledge, 2009), pp. 38–49; Lorne L. Dawson, "The Mediation of Religious Experience in Cyberspace," in Højsgarard and Warburg, *Religion and Cyberspace*, pp. 15–37.

13. Chau, *Religion in Contemporary China*, pp. 19–20. See also Thomas Borchert, "Worry for the Dai Nation: Sipsongpannā, Chinese Modernity, and the Problems of Buddhist Modernism," *The Journal of Asian Studies*, 67.1 (2008): 107–142; Sara L. M. Davis, *Song and Silence: Ethnic Revival on China's Southwest Borders* (New York: Columbia University Press, 2005).

14. Chandler, *Establishing a Pure Land on Earth*; Clart, "Sacred Texts, Religious Publishing, and New Technologies in China & Taiwan."

15. Goossaert and Palmer, *Religious Question*, pp. 271–275. The huge gap in respondents claiming to have a religious affiliation as opposed to engaging in religious practice should call into question facile inter-

pretations about the secularization of Asian religious traditions, not only in China but also Japan. See, for example, Ian Reader, "Secularisation R.I.P? Nonsense!: The 'Rush Hour Away from the Gods' and the Decline of Religion in Contemporary Japan," *Journal of Religion in Japan*, 1.1 (2012): 7–36.

16. Goossaert and Palmer, *Religious Question*, pp. 275–286.

17. Kang Xiaofei, "The Changing Place of Women in Religion and Society in Twentieth-Century and Contemporary China." See also Kang, "Rural Women, Old Age, and Temple Work: A Case from Northwestern Sichuan," *China Perspectives*, 4 (2009): 42–53, as well as Ellen Cline, "Female Spirit Mediums and Religious Authority in Contemporary Southeastern China," *Modern China*, 36:5 (2010): 520–555; Maria Jaschok and Shui Jingjun, *Women, Religion, and Space in China: Islamic Mosques & Daoist Temples, Catholic Convents & Chinese Virgins* (New York: Routledge, 2011); Lee Anru, "Women of the Sisters' Hall: Religion and the Making of Women's Alternative Space in Taiwan's Economic Restructuring," *Gender, Place & Culture: A Journal of Feminist Geography*, 15:4 (2008): 373–393; Jessie G. Lutz, ed., *Pioneering Chinese Christian Women: Gender, Christianity and Social Mobility* (Bethlehem, PA: Lehigh University Press, 2010).

18. Katz, "Religion and the State in Postwar Taiwan."

19. Dean and Zheng, *Ritual Alliances of the Putian Plain*, vol. 1, pp. 3, 8–14, 210–218; Katz, "Festivals and the Recreation of Identity in South China."

20. Michael Szonyi, "Lineages and the Making of Contemporary China" (paper presented at the international conference on "Modern Chinese Religion: Value Systems in Transformation, Part 2: 1850-present," Chinese University of Hong Kong, December 12–15, 2012).

21. Kenneth Dean, "The Return Visits of Overseas Chinese to Ancestral Villages in Putian, Fujian," in Oakes and Sutton, *Faiths on Display*, pp. 235–263; see also Dean and Zheng, *Ritual Alliances of the Putian Plain*, vol. 1, pp. 10, 39, 230–253.

22. Robert Weller, "Chinese Cosmology and the Environment," in Palmer, Shive, and Wickeri, *Chinese Religious Life*, pp. 124–138.

23. Goossaert and Palmer, *Religious Question*, p. 403.

24. For example, it will be interesting to see how the ongoing globalization of Islam and Judaism influences the future development of Israel.

25. Shahar, *Crazy Ji*, pp. 221–225.

INDEX

THE MENAHEM STERN JERUSALEM LECTURES

Sponsored by the HISTORICAL SOCIETY OF ISRAEL
and published for BRANDEIS UNIVERSITY PRESS
by UNIVERSITY PRESS OF NEW ENGLAND

Paul R. Katz, *Religion in China and Its Modern Fate*

Richard J. Evans, *Altered Pasts: Counterfactuals in History*

Patrick J. Geary, *Language and Power in the Early Middle Ages*

G. W. Bowersock, *Empires in Collision in Late Antiquity*

Sanjay Subrahmanyam, *Three Ways to Be Alien: Travails and Encounters in the Early Modern World*

Jürgen Kocka, *Civil Society and Dictatorship in Modern German History*

Heinz Schilling, *Early Modern European Civilization and Its Political and Cultural Dynamism*

Brian Stock, *Ethics through Literature: Ascetic and Aesthetic Reading in Western Culture*

Fergus Millar, *The Roman Republic in Political Thought*

Peter Brown, *Poverty and Leadership in the Later Roman Empire*

Anthony D. Smith, *The Nation in History: Historiographical Debates about Ethnicity and Nationalism*

Carlo Ginzburg, *History Rhetoric, and Proof*